THE LAST ILLUSION

Letters from Dutch Immigrants
in the "Land of Opportunity,"
1924-1930

Translated, edited
and introduced
by
Herman Ganzevoort

University of Calgary Press

University of Calgary Press
2500 University Drive N.W.
Calgary, Alberta, Canada T2N 1N4

Canadian Cataloguing in Publication Data
Main entry under title:
  The last illusion

  Includes bibliographical references and index.
  ISBN 1-55238-013-0

  1. Dutch--Canada--Correspondence. 2. Dutch Canadians-- Correspondence.
3. Canadian immigration literature (Dutch)--1919-1945. 4. Canada--Emigration and immigration.
5. Netherlands--Emigration and immigration. I. Ganzevoort, H., 1942-

FC106.D9L37 1999   971'.0043931   C99-911206-6
F1035.D8L37 1999

Canada  We acknowledge the financial support of the Government of Canada through the Book Publishing Industry Development Program (BPIDP) for our publishing activities.

We also acknowledge the financial support of the Canadian Journal of Netherlandic Studies. This book is also volume XX (1999) of the Canadian Journal of Netherlandic Studies, and is being sent to all subscribers of that Journal.

The Alberta Foundation for the Arts
COMMITTED TO THE DEVELOPMENT OF CULTURE AND THE ARTS

COMMUNITY DEVELOPMENT

Publication and promotion of this book has been made possible by financial assistance from the Alberta Foundation for the Arts.

Printed and bound in Canada by Veilleux Impression à Demande Inc.

∞ This book is printed on acid-free paper.

Cover and book design by Glitch Graphics.

Series Preface

This volume is part of the Legacies Shared series. The aim of the series is to publish material that either has never been published or is out of print.

The mandate of Legacies Shared is broad, as we plan to make available parts of our "legacy" of historical memories that have been overlooked or have disappeared. Each volume contains an introduction appropriate to the subject, which might be a work of history, a memoir, collections of letters, photographs, art work, maps or recipes, works of fiction or poetry, or sets of archival documents. Oral history will also have a place in the series.

The geographical area covered by this series is the Canadian west and north, but also across the Canada/U.S. border.

Janice Dickin, Series Editor,
Professor, Faculty of General Studies,
University of Calgary, Alberta

Acknowledgements and Dedication

In the course of preparing this book for publication, I have come to owe a great many people an immense debt of gratitude, which cannot ever be repaid. Their faith in the work of the immigrant writers and their belief in this immigrant's ability to translate those writings bouyed me through many disappointments and rejections. There are also those who deserve special mention because without them this book would never have become a reality. I remember and thank the anonymous writers who left their work for me to discover; Walter Hildebrandt who not only believed that the book should be published, but did something about it; Gerrit Stallinga who did not live to see it in print but believed in it and me, and last but certainly not least, my loving wife Karen, who kept not only the dream alive, but in the end kept me alive and able to write these wholly inadequate words of thanks.

Herman Ganzevoort
Calgary, 1999

Table of Contents

Introduction

W hen the outbreak of war disrupted the summer peace of August 1914, Canada, as part of the British Empire, came without hesitation to the defense of Great Britain. Enthusiastic volunteer enlistees from across the country quickly swelled the minute army to an unmanageable size. Thousands of British immigrants rushed home to fight for King and Country as bewildered German and Austro-Hungarian immigrants, now considered enemy aliens, examined the stark options that were theirs by the accident of birth. A few would choose to flee to the, as yet neutral, United States or to Mexico, perhaps to eventually make their way to Germany. Some would find themselves incarcerated in internment camps and still others would reluctantly don the uniform of their new homeland. Most, however, would live an uncomfortable and tenuous existence, on the one hand avowing their undying love for Canada and on the other, defending their natural attachment to the cultural values of Deutschtum.

In the midst of the increasingly strident war propaganda, many immigrants from neutral European countries found themselves pressured by Canadians to take a stand against barbarism of the Hun. Dutch immigrants, who were scattered across the prairie provinces from Winnipeg to the foothills of the Rockies, found themselves in a unique and uncomfortable, position. The great majority had emigrated to Canada after 1895, coming either directly from the Netherlands or through the Dutch colonies in the United States. They had taken up homesteads, ripped farms out of the tough prairie sod, built homes, churches and schools, and had fit themselves into the Canadian mosaic, yet they held little affection for the English-language homeland of so many of their fellow citizens.

Tradition, culture and history attached the Dutch more closely to Germany, perhaps, than to England. Yet Canada, their new fatherland, although an English-speaking country, was not England. As often as not, the Dutch found themselves to be more welcome than the "effete English" who were often regarded by Canadians as poor immigrants and the "nadir of degeneration." England's imperialistic adventure in South Africa and the resulting Boer War, with its conquest of the Afrikaner homeland, had left a bitter taste in the mouths of some Dutch immigrants, but they could hardly fault the Laurier government's reluctant support of that campaign. The Dutch understood the ties of blood as well as the limits of Canada's newly acquired autonomous Dominion status and were willing to forgive, if not forget, its involvement in that tragic conflict.

The outbreak of war in Europe and the Netherlands' precarious neutrality did little to encourage enlistment in the Canadian army. Immigrants who had been part of the military reserve forces in the Netherlands returned home immediately in response to mobilization orders which clearly reflected their government's fear of an imminent invasion by Germany. While some young men would enlist in the Canadian Expeditionary Force, perhaps as a response to the tragic invasion of Belgium, the great majority watched the growing crisis with concern, but expended their energies in the ongoing struggle to wrest a living from the land.

Canada, as the "Land of Opportunity," had been a focus of interest for the Dutch since the 1880s. At that time, Amsterdam investment-houses and members of Holland's economic elite had become involved in the business opportunities presented by the construction of the Canadian Pacific Railway and the opening up of the new lands of the Northwest Territories. Some invested directly in the railway, while others were drawn into the acquisition of vast land grants for the purpose of speculation or ranching. These entrepreneurs were also at the leading edge of the technical and business revolution that was rationalizing and reorganizing the Dutch society in response to the devastating effects of the economic depression that had savaged the Netherlands since 1873. In the course of their efforts to set the Dutch economy upon a more secure footing, they came to believe that one of the solutions to their homeland's problems was the encouragement of emigration.

Significant Dutch emigration to the United States had begun in the 1840s as a response to growing sectarian and agricultural problems in the Netherlands. This emigration had focused on agricultural settlements in Michigan, Wisconsin and Iowa; by the 1880s, these had reached the limits of their arable development. To find new land, the Dutch Americans turned their eyes westward to Montana and Washington. Inevitably as these areas became settled and overcrowded they were forced to turn their attention to the newly opened land in the Canadian prairies. Their interest coincided with that of the Dutch entrepreneurs and the Canadian government, which regarded its western lands as the keystone to the development of the nation as a whole.

Starting in the 1890s, members of the Dutch economic elite began to play an active role in the formation of local emigration societies whose sole aim was the emigration of unemployed agricultural labourers to the Canadian West. They came to believe that Canada, as the world's last great agricultural frontier, could serve as a safety valve to drain off the surplus population of farm labour that had been made redundant by the changes which they themselves had helped to initiate in the Dutch economy. Depending upon modest provincial, municipal and private funds, they established a framework of organizations that was to be the base of the Dutch emigration system until the late forties. They were joined in this work by religiously oriented emigration societies, both Catholic and Protestant, which were concerned with the preservation of the immigrant's faith in the alien land. Regardless of orientation—God or Mammon—all agreed that emigration was a legitimate and useful tool with which to release the growing social, political and economic pressures of a burgeoning rural population that would increasingly find itself unable or unwilling to adjust or contribute to a steadily mechanizing, industrializing and urbanizing society.

The promise of Canada lay not simply in its ability to provide work for redundant agricultural labourers. The vast unsettled prairies offered the opportunity to acquire uncultivated land or even "ready-made farms" for very reasonable prices. This was particularly appealing to small and marginal farmers who were being pushed out of Dutch agriculture because of their inability to compete in a rapidly changing world. Many small holders and renters did not have the financial resources to try new techniques, crops or machinery, and no chance at all to enlarge their holdings. Inevitably they would have to give way to those who could. The promise of millions of acres of free or cheap land in Canada seemed to be a heaven-sent opportunity to relieve the critical problems of all those who were no longer able to contribute to the Dutch economy in a meaningful way.

Starting in 1890 and continuing until the outbreak of the war, Dutch emigration societies, the Canadian government, the CPR, the Salvation Army, transportation companies and other interested individuals all focused on the promise of the "Last Best West." To labourers, farmers and anyone else who would listen, they stressed the opportunities which awaited anyone who wanted to make something of himself; anyone who had the grit to endure the difficult but rewarding task of taking up a homestead and beginning a new life. Although no-one promised gold in the streets, the propaganda certainly intimated that opportunities sprang from the soil ready for harvesting. All one needed was a little initiative and work. Half-truths and deceptions were the stock-in-trade of many recruiters, and wilful blindness and the desire to believe in the possibility of a better future were the responses of the recruits. This suspension of disbelief was to cost some immigrants dearly, while others would reap rewards beyond their wildest dreams.

Slowly but surely, Dutch immigrants from both the Netherlands and the American settlements began to make their way to the Canadian West. Usually starting off as farm hands and railway navvies (unless they had capital) they acquired the experience and financial resources to take up homesteads, undeveloped land or ready-made farms. It soon became apparent to many that the possibility of acquiring instant wealth was as ephemeral as the "champagne air" which was said to invigorate and stimulate the new settlers of the West. Hard work, patience and single-mindedness were the order of the day, but certainly there was no guarantee of success. Some would fall by the wayside and retreat to the cities or even back to Holland looking for an easier life, but the majority would endure. The Dutch settlements in East Kildonan, Manitoba, Edam, Saskatchewan, Monarch and Strathmore, Alberta and the isolated homesteads and farms scattered across the far reaches of the rolling landscape became monuments to their unremitting labour. Many Dutch immigrants, however, would regretfully conclude that the success of the homestead was "built on the bones of the homesteader."

Success, it seemed, demanded a high price and was certainly not assured. Yet, to many, even to those who had failed on the land, emigration had given them something far more valuable than mere material. It was something indefinable, that could only be couched in such amorphous terms as independence or self-respect. On the Canadian prairies they were no longer held ransom to their past, their social class, their lack of education. They were truly free to fail or succeed without the predetermined strictures of the old world society holding them down. They could breathe in and out, assured that the stale air of their small cramped homeland lay far behind them. Even if the promises of the recruiters did not match the reality of their experiences, most had not expected heaven on earth, and as the old Dutch saying had it: "A bird in the hand is worth ten in the air."

By the eve of the Great War the Dutch had established a good reputation for themselves on the Canadian prairies. Almost indistinguishable from the preferred White Anglo Saxon immigrants, they were welcome both as employees and neighbours. No "racial" barriers stood between them and their fellow settlers, which led to an ease of relations that was, no doubt, the envy of their eastern and southern European counterparts. The Dutch farm hands were welcome at the dinner tables of their employers and were seldom directed to sleep in the barn with the farm animals.

Canadian farmers, however, were not philanthropists and demanded a full day's work or more for a day's wage. They were not reluctant to fire their inexperienced farm hands if they were dissatisfied, and did not hesitate to take full advantage of their prerogatives as employers, yet they recognized an equality with the Hollanders that was not necessarily extended to other immigrants. In the hierarchy of acceptable types, the Dutchman came to be seen as imbued with the virtues of hard work, cleanliness and sobriety. If he had any shortcomings they lay in his penchant for a Germanic stubbornness that could reach truly awesome proportions. All in all, however, most Canadians agreed that a Dutchman was the kind of man you could fully accept as a partner or even as a brother-in-law.

The fire storm that threatened to consume all of Europe after September of 1914 mercifully spared the Netherlands. As the armies of the belligerents swept all around them, the Dutch managed to maintain a shaky neutrality between their traditional friends and trading partners, England and Germany. Emigration to Canada, small at the best of times, shriveled to nothing because of shipping restrictions, military call-ups and unrestricted German submarine warfare against Allied shipping. The entry of the United States into the war in 1917 put an end, for the moment at least, to any movement to North America.

As the guns fell silent on the Western Front on November 11, 1918, a collective sigh of relief escaped the millions who had seen the continent ravaged by the spirit of irrationality for over four long years. That sigh, however, was premature. Belligerents and neutrals alike now faced the unenviable task of reassembling and reconstructing a Europe which, as yet unbeknownst to them, had forever disappeared on the shell-torn battlefields and in the blood-sodden trenches. Victors and vanquished alike did not yet comprehend that they would have to deal with far-reaching and often calamitous changes, changes that would alter the reality not only of their small worlds but would even extend to the vast and unsettled regions of Canada.

The brisk emigration movement that had characterized the prewar era in North America was not immediately reestablished at the end of the war. The United States, fearing Bolshevism and a massive inundation by hordes of unassimilable immigrants from Eastern and Southern Europe, began to assemble a body of immigration legislation that would put an end to the unrestricted flow of the past. Even the highly assimilable Dutch, always near the top of the acceptable list, would be limited to a quota of fewer than 2,000 immigrants per year. The growing fear of the importation of Bolshevism and other alien radical philosophies merely strengthened American determination to limit the entry of the clamoring masses of Europe.

In Canada, the swift arrival of an economic recession on the heels of the peace chilled the overheated economy. Unemployment, the fall of commodity prices and the loss of overseas markets combined with the social disruption caused by the reintegration of demobilized soldiers to create a period of unrest and dislocation. The Canadian government's decision to emphasize "quality, not quantity", although not as restrictive in emphasis as the newly developing American immigration policy, did little to encourage the movement of immigrants, Dutch or otherwise.

The Netherlands, as well, had to face an uncertain future in the immediate postwar period. The economies of its two major trading partners were severely disrupted, if not, as in Germany's case, destroyed. Emigration, once again, appeared to hold out the greatest hope as an answer to growing unemployment but with the United States moving toward increasing restriction, Canada seemed to be the only viable destination. Canada, however, was attempting to come to terms with its own economic problems and had little need for agricultural or industrial workers at this time. The intention to resettle demobilized soldiers on empty prairie lands, and the scarcity of homestead or cheap lands in readily accessible areas further discouraged those who hoped to take up farms in the Canadian West. Only a turnaround in the Canadian economy could release the pressure that was building for emigration.

This stream was loosed by the slow return of a vibrant and developing economy after the recession reached its nadir in 1923. Growing urbanization and industrialization, and increasing dependence for trade and investment on the United States stimulated the growth of industry and opened up thousands of new jobs in the urban areas. Demobilized soldiers and young men and women just entering the job market streamed into the cities, abandoning the farm to their elders. The lure of urban life could not be denied.

By 1925, responding to the growing demand for agricultural workers, the Canadian government and the Canadian National and Pacific railways began active recruitment campaigns in Europe to find replacements for Canadian workers who had abandoned farms, fields and gardens for easier and more remunerative employment in the cities. Their intention was clearly not to add to the growing populations of the cities but rather to direct suitable agriculturists to the areas of greatest need. The focus of immigrant interest now shifted from the prairie west to the farm lands of Ontario, where the demand was the greatest and the jobs most remunerative.

The Netherlands, with its large surplus of agricultural labour, was of immediate interest to the Canadians. Hollanders were not only of the preferred racial origin; they had a long-standing reputation for hard work. As a result, the Dutch countryside was soon inundated with a flood of officials, representatives, advisors, consultants and emigration sharks. Dutchmen and Canadians alike fed on and profited from the emigration interest which had been thwarted by the war and the recession. Canada became a hot topic in the daily and weekly press and in the journals and magazines published by such diverse groups as unions, churches and farm organizations. While some of the stories and assessments were well informed, many were based on fragmentary evidence and were therefore often misleading. Recruiters, in the game for their own financial benefit, disseminated clearly dangerous and misleading propaganda and recruited any and all, whether agriculturists or not. The interested public in Holland soon found it almost impossible to distinguish between truth and fiction.

Two semi-official Dutch organizations which had developed out of the prewar emigration societies attempted to combat the activities of the unscrupulous recruiters. The Netherlands Emigration League (NEL) sought to provide accurate information about conditions in Canada while the Central Emigration Foundation of Holland (CEFH) looked after the task of arranging travel subsidies, transportation, job placement and after-care in Canada. While these two organizations would end up handling only a small percentage of the emigrants who left the Netherlands in the twenties (the majority were recruited and handled by private agents) they did keep a watching brief on the emigration field.

One way of doing so was to monitor and collect any material appearing in newspapers, magazines, journals or pamphlets pertaining to emigration and settlement in Canada, or to other possible emigrant destinations such as the United States and Latin America. When misleading propaganda was discovered, the NEL quickly responded with corrective information. In cases of obvious false advertising that might lead to the failure or fleecing of the emigrant, the NEL sought to use the Dutch courts to curtail such practices even though the legal penalties were all but non-existent. One activity which the League targeted in particular was the selling, sight unseen, of Canadian land to would-be emigrants. Recruiters naturally disliked such restraints but, given the speed with which they carried out their confidence games, they were seldom seriously hindered in their nefarious practices. Perhaps harder to understand was the attitude of many emigrants who seemed to resent any interference with their God-given right to be gulled.

The activities of the CEFH also often ran counter to the desires of those agents representing transportation companies. The Central tried to provide cheap transportation for the emigrants while the agents busily touted the splendors and conveniences of their employers' ships, whether these were the CPR's Beaver Line or the Red or White Star lines of Antwerp. It also warned against one of the more common scams: the selling, in Holland, of overpriced Canadian train tickets from the place of the emigrants' disembarkation in Canada to their final destination. Canadian Pacific agents and independent operators also promised guaranteed employment and high wages upon arrival in Canada. Such promised jobs seldom materialized. While the Central's placement and after care system in Canada did not always function adequately, primarily because it depended upon volunteer help, it was one of the few organizations involved in the emigration movement that did not have a pecuniary interest.

Despite often unfair criticism from recruiters and emigrants alike, the NEL continued to extract useful information from the reams of emigration material that appeared in the press. Aside from blatantly propagandistic advertisements put out by those with financial interests, most common were letters from emigrants who occasionally wrote to their home-town newspapers to inform friends and neighbours about their lives in Canada. The tenor of the letters ranged across the whole continuum of human emotions. Some emigrants were elated by their experiences, others depressed, some optimistic, others ruing the day they had left the fatherland. Most agreed that Canada held great promise for the immigrant but they also warned that the cost of success was often extremely high.

The compilation of the letters permitted the semi-official emigration societies to build up a clearer and more informed picture of Canada as a potential emigrant destination. No longer were they solely dependent on Dutch consular or volunteer reports, or on the hyperbole of recruiters and Canadian government agents. The pros and cons of the emigration question were clearly delineated by the personal testimonies of the emigrants. Since the correspondents wrote from all parts of

Canada, the geographic specificity of their experiences, which had always hindered a general situational overview, disappeared under the weight of evidence. One experience could be tested against another and its veracity evaluated.

As valuable as such occasional correspondence was, more valuable yet were the extended series of letters that were written by people who were, or had been, immigrants in Canada. By following their week-to-week or month-to-month adventures in the newspapers, the societies, and more importantly friends, relatives and general public were able to gain some idea of the difficulties and successes of emigration. The truth of the statements was tested over time and was not simply dependent on an impression created by a single unhappy or fortuitous event. Furthermore, such correspondence gave insight not only into life and conditions in Canada, but also often into the innermost experience of the writers. Many of them clearly expressed the ambivalence that underlies so much of the whole immigration experience.

Little did the directors of the societies know, nor could they have imagined, how important a legacy they would leave by initiating the collection of this correspondence. The scrapbooks continued to grow as the emigrants wrote to the newspapers during the twenties and into the first few years of the thirties. The rapid decline of world markets and the virtual closure of Canada to immigration choked off any significant movement from Holland. The societies saw the disappearance of the recruiters and agents, of their financial subsidies and of the primary reason for the existence of these: the emigrants. The outbreak of World War II put a cap on their activities, not to be removed until 1947 when emigration once again came to be regarded as an important safety valve for the war-ravaged Dutch state. Revived and restructured, the emigration societies concluded that the material they had gathered in the pre-war period was now dated and irrelevant, and they consigned the volumes of newspaper clippings to their archives.

Researchers of Dutch emigration to Canada face serious problems when attempting to reconstruct the events and circumstances that surrounded the intimate lives of 1920s' emigrants. While Dutch and Canadian government sources are available to clarify the political and economic events that spurred the emigration movement, the emigrants themselves seem to have become lost in a blizzard of official paper. Unlike other ethnic groups, the Dutch of the twenties do not appear to have kept diaries nor, with one exception, did they write books about their experiences. Most, it appears, were avid letter writers but unfortunately, time, assimilation, economic depression and war slowed or even ended many correspondences. Despite attempts to collect such letters in the Netherlands in recent years, few appear to have survived. The newspapers that existed in the twenties also did not fare well. Many are now defunct, others did not maintain their archives and some lost their holdings to fire and destruction during the German occupation of World War II. Little evidence appears to remain of the Dutch immigrants who followed their dream to Canada in the second decade of this century.

In 1969, as I began my research into Dutch emigration to Canada at the Netherlands Emigration Service (NES) in the Hague, I was amazed to discover that while NES had vast holdings dealing with the post World War II emigration, nothing seemed to exist for the period 1890–1945. After many false starts, dead ends and disappointments, I found myself in an all-but-abandoned Roman Catholic girl's academy in the middle of the red-light district in the Hague. An official at the NES had discovered the pre-war archive in the basement of the NES building under an immense coal pile, and, fearing that time and rising damp would soon destroy the material, had sent it to the Netherlands Economic and Historical Archives (NEHA).

The NEHA, already overwhelmed by many metric tonnes of archival holdings, had in desperation lodged the NES archive in the unheated girl's academy where conditions were, to say the least, on the verge of disaster. Stacked ten feet high on wobbly shelves, nibbled by mice, covered in soot, and rotting from the rain which seeped down the flaking walls of the hallways and classrooms, the archive looked ready for the incinerator. Yet after a few minutes of careful but exhilarating scrutiny it came to resemble the golden treasure horde of a sunken Spanish galleon.

Due to the cold and the damp, it was impossible to work at the academy so the entire archive was sent back to the NES, but this time it had an office on the second floor all to itself. The archive was an unbelievable find, made up of government reports, correspondence, emigration society reports, pamphlets, photographs and other material relating to the emigration of the Dutch from 1890 to 1940. In the process of roughly indexing what I had unearthed, I stumbled across eight volumes of newspaper clippings from the twenties: clippings composed primarily of letters and articles written by immigrants in Canada to the newspapers in Holland. Buried as they were among the tens of thousands of pages of government and society records, I did not immediately recognize their importance. Only later did I realize that the letters and articles represented a unique opportunity to delve into lives previously hidden and forgotten.

Government reports, applications and statistics can only go so far in recreating the personalities of those who emigrate. Place of birth, occupation, state of health and work experience tell the researcher little about the motivations of those who decide to leave their homeland and begin anew elsewhere. For the first time, the emigrants could begin to assume identities and personalities. They would no longer remain mere numbers entered into the endless unread government record. I now had the flesh to fill out the bare bones left by the record keepers in the statistical wasteland.

The letters opened up for view the inner dimensions of the immigrants: people who wrote about the reasons for their emigration, their hopes, their fears and best of all, their experiences in Canada. As I read through the volumes, the letters began to give substance to the formerly amorphous characters. Shadowy individuals took on personalities as their backgrounds began to emerge. I was permitted to follow them from the polders to the prairies, from Friesland to Manitoba and beyond. They became familiar and distinct as they shared with me those events that would go to make up the very core of their being in the future. They commented on what they liked and disliked, they compared the old country to the new and in the process, perhaps unwittingly, revealed themselves and their innermost thoughts in a way that might have otherwise been impossible. Emigration, for good or ill, sometimes created an inner awareness and openness that might never have been achieved—and certainly never shared—in their small homeland where privacy was always at a premium.

While heartened by this informative and insightful revelation, I was still faced with the problem of determining the validity of the material. How true were the sentiments that were expressed in the letters? How accurate were the assessments, and could they be valuable in recreating the past and the individuals who were part of that past? The real test of any source lies in the balance that is achieved when one has examined all of it. If one reads and assesses all the letters, the good and the bad, the insightful and the naive, do they balance out the facts to some believable weight? Do they hold up to scrutiny when tested against known and accurate accounts from other writers, do they fit within the context of the times? Do they resonate with letters from writers of other ethnic groups or are the insights ultimately too different and unique to be believable? Fortunately, the letters met all the tests, both internally and externally, and they painted a fascinating and insightful picture of those who had made the choice to take a different turn in the road from the majority of their countrymen.

A close examination of the letters suggests that the correspondents reflected the general character of the immigrants who entered Canada in the twenties. The writers were predominantly working class single males, twenty-two to thirty-five years of age, with at least six years of elementary education. While many fulfilled the Canadian criterion of having some agricultural experience, a large minority had little or none. Most, however, like fellow immigrants from other countries, seemed to possess a strong sense of adventure and a willingness to adapt themselves to a new, and strange society.

While there was a strong representation of correspondents from the West in the volumes, these correspondents, like many others, were aware that the settlement-focus had shifted from the homestead to agricultural jobs in the East. In part, this was a response to the lack of cheap arable land, the dearth of single family housing and the growing demand for agricultural labour. As well, it signified a deep loss of faith among the emigrants in the great promise of the Canadian prairies. Soldier–settlement schemes and veteran preferment put the immigrant farther back in the line for land and jobs, but more importantly: the 160 acre homestead was no longer regarded as the cornerstone of future financial security.

The immigrants had read the negative reports about life on the prairie farm and they were familiar with the high cost demanded of body and spirit to succeed. Most preferred the less demanding work on the developed farms of Ontario. A period employed as a farm hand not only provided Canadian experience but helped improve the language skills which were necessary to move into the more remunerative jobs available in the cities. Those who wanted to farm on a permanent basis would have the opportunity to realistically examine the possibilities all across the country as they gained both farm experience and language facility. The immigrants who eventually wanted to emigrate to the United States knew that Canadian citizenship gave them a preferential place in a much larger quota, and their stay in Canada was simply seen as a necessary pause that would open up better possibilities in the future.

Although the demand for female domestic workers was high on Canadian farms and in the cities, Dutch single women did not respond

1. J.L. Aberson, *From the Prairies with Hope,* R.E. Vander Vennen, ed., (Regina:Canadian Plains Research Center, 1991)

in any significant fashion to this appeal. During the 1890–1914 period the percentage of unmarried female emigrants had never exceeded the single numbers, and even appeared to fall in the twenties. Most single women immigrants arrived in Canada to the welcoming arms of sponsoring fiancés, and were required by law to marry within a short time of their arrival so that they would not become "public charges" dependent on municipal or provincial welfare. While there is no indication that such marriages were undertaken only to bypass the immigration regulations, there is some evidence to suggest that the arriving female immigrants did not always end up marrying their designated sponsors. Apparently, absence did not always make the heart grow fonder!

Even a casual reading of the letters made it patently clear that female correspondents were few and far between. One was Jane Aberson-Uges who detailed her family's experiences on the Canadian prairies in an extended correspondence directed to a Groningen newspaper. While her correspondence did appear in the volumes of newspaper clippings, I did not include it in this manuscript because her letters have appeared in book form both in the Netherlands in Dutch and in English with a critical introduction in Canada.[1] The lack of a feminine perspective other than that of Aberson-Uges' places serious obstacles in the way of the researcher. As a result, the nature of the experiences of women immigrants in the twenties must remain largely speculative and almost totally dependent on inferences made by male correspondents. Despite a very careful perusal of all the letters, I failed to find any correspondence which I could definitively ascribe to a female writer. However, the series entitled "Toronto the Beautiful" which appeared in *De Nieuwe Rotterdamsche Courant* from 29 September, 1929 to 1 June, 1930 gave me considerable food for thought. Although there is no clear identification of the name or gender of the correspondent, internal evidence from the letters suggests that either a woman or a gay male immigrant was the author of these letters.

One must assume that there were gay immigrants among the thousands who came to Canada. Immigration regulations, public attitudes and the law of the land regarded homosexuality as a "perversion" and denied gays, immigrant and citizen alike, their full civil rights. The overt practice of the gay lifestyle was not only condemned, but was subject to the full punitive measure of the law. A gay immigrant, no doubt, remained in "the closet" not only to gain entry to Canada but also to avoid the excoriation of both his fellow immigrants and his new countrymen.

This series is distinctly different from all the others. Unlike the other correspondents, the author deals only with the urban environment. Yet there is no discussion about occupation or occupational goals. The writer is clearly interested in the more "domestic" aspects of Canadian life. Home decoration, furnishings, food, domestic servants and many other things having to do with the Canadian style of home life are discussed in detail. Forays into such subjects as capital punishment, religious movements, Canadian burial customs and real estate sales indicate an omnivorous interest and a well informed viewpoint. While such subjects do not eliminate the possibility of a male correspondent the general tenor of the letters bears no similarity to that of the identifiably male correspondents.

The adjustment to a life in a new country must have been doubly hard for such an immigrant and life as a farm hand, under the watchful eye of the farmer would have been virtually impossible. The relative anonymity that could be maintained in the city, and the broad diversity of peoples gathered there, would not only have held great attraction but would have provided a sense of security impossible elsewhere. Whatever the case, this author's views and opinions provide an insightful and rewarding perspective uniquely different from those of the other writers. Dutch newspapers, attempting to satisfy a growing interest in emigration, readily made room for the correspondence of the emigrants. Occasional letter writers seldom generalized beyond their own experiences and concerns and the volumes are littered with their all too predictable and often mundane assessments. Those correspondents who were willing to carry on beyond an initial few letters were encouraged to exercise their wit and insight, and to contribute as often as possible. No doubt the readers looked forward to the next instalment, thereby raising the circulation of the paper and keeping the editors happy.

It is in the extended correspondence that the reader begins to appreciate the depth of personal change that was demanded by the emigration experience. Not only do these letters discuss the reasons why some emigrants chose to leave Holland, but also how they attempted to restructure their lives in Canada and make it more familiar. In commenting on their experiences they reflected upon the nature of Canadian and North American society as only outsiders can. What is most important to today's reader, is that these opinions are contextual and of the moment. They were not reminiscences screened and filtered by a great passage of time or embroidered by nostalgia. There is an immediacy to their feelings of pain caused by separation and loss and a sense of shared joy and exhilaration when they reach their goals. Their reflections are personal, often poignant, angry, funny, and ironic. In other words, they run the whole gamut of human emotions. The Dutch are generally regarded as a blunt, plain-speaking people and the correspondents appear to be no exception.

However, in some ways they were exceptional, in that they were willing to share an introspective view that most emigrants usually kept to themselves. They shared feelings and showed an openness that was uncommon in their culture and time. One can only speculate that perhaps loneliness and separation brought down the carefully guarded barriers of self-protection and the need to be seen to be in control of all aspects of their lives all of the time. Their ability to admit to failure or the collapse of their well-laid plans distinguished them from those who set greater value on appearing successful. Subtle shading of the truth or outright prevarication in regards to one's success was an all too common practice for those who looked for validation in other's eyes. Unlike these correspondents, they dreaded discovery and often simply disappeared, never to be heard from again. It took a measure of bravery and self knowledge to tell the truth and accept another's judgement on the course of one's life.

Having read the letters numerous times, never tiring of them and wanting to share my discovery, I came to the conclusion that they should be made accessible to the general public so that it could also appreciate the struggles and victories of these forgotten immigrants. I thought that it would be fairly simple to extract what I might consider to be the best of the letters and put them together in manuscript form for a Dutch publication. I also hoped that I might eventually be able to translate them into English so that Canadians could get some idea as to the role which immigration had played in the formation of the country. To that end I chose those letters which I thought exhibited the greatest historical accuracy and at the same time bore undeniable literary value.

While choosing the best, I also wanted to make sure that while Dutch emigration had been primarily focused on the West in the pre-WWI period and on the East after 1918, letters were included from all regions of Canada and from both rural and urban areas. What was clearly needed was a judicious mix of extended and occasional correspondence that highlighted both the positive and negative views of the immigrant experience. I realized that immigration often presents a hard struggle for the immigrant and that success can be measured by many standards. To that end I wanted to create a manuscript composed of letters that blended together to form a realistic picture, being neither too enthusiastic nor too pessimistic. I committed myself to creating, to the best of my ability, what the Dutch would call a *nuchter* (sober) and balanced view.

My hopes for a Dutch publication were not to be fulfilled and, as a result, I decided to translate the letters for a possible Canadian edition. I was unfamiliar with the art of translation and not very skillful in a language that was not my mother tongue. I had learned Dutch without formal training by reading the Dutch Bible and speaking a northern home dialect long corrupted by the addition of Friesian and English words. I had painfully struggled through the government documents and now realized that formal Dutch, in many ways bore little resemblance to the colloquial language of the letters. Not knowing any better, or perhaps stubbornly refusing to be defeated, I began.

The first drafts were crude but miraculously did not destroy the powerful and heartfelt sense of the original writers. My Dutch-English dictionary grew ragged as the months went by, but my Dutch friends and relatives patiently aided and abetted what I at times believed could only end in an embarrassment. I learned that translating is not simply substituting one word, sentence or paragraph for another. The sense, the real meaning of the thing must be captured and given life. As well, I discovered that every language and every writer has a rhythm: a music. A translator who ignores it does so at his own peril. The hardest task was to grasp the music of the language of the letters and make it sing in English as it had in Dutch. Sometimes a phrase or sentence took a day, sometimes a week, but slowly and surely the pages added up and every writer, I hope, got his due.

Translation is a labour of love. No-one can ever pay the translator what it costs in time and effort and personal commitment to make that literary music, so the reward lies in the doing. It lies in the joy of capturing the perfect word or phrase which will express not only the author's meaning but also the emotions and feelings which he has poured into his work. In a sense, the translator must become a re-creator by taking the spirit of the old work and melding it together with a new language body. Sometimes the new creation looked and sounded like Dr. Frankenstein's monster and had to be consigned to a literary grave. However, somehow, slowly, there appeared out of this language melange, a spirited symphony of words. The voice of the immigrants was heard again, but this time in English.

This book includes the letters of a number of occasional correspondents and six who wrote extended series of letters. The identities of only a few are known and even then these may well be *noms de plume*.

Anonymity permitted some writers a freedom not accorded to the others and so they chose to conceal their identities. Despite attempts to trace the correspondents in both Canada and in the Netherlands, their identities and fates have remained a mystery. The writer of "On Canada's Devil's Island", seemingly a traveler and adventurer, wrote anonymously from Brazil. The author of "Prairie Pedagogue or Lost Among the Ruthenians" disappeared along with his schoolhouse in the Vermilion Valley of northeastern Alberta. No trace was found of the northern adventurer who wrote "An American Scene" or Jaap van der Meulen who opined that "Canada is a Funny Country." The author of "Toronto the Beautiful", like all the others has vanished. Frans van Waeterstadt, the prolific and insightful author of "The Last Illusion", was lost in the dark whirlpool of the Great Depression. Did they go back to Holland or did they end up struggling to survive in Canada or elsewhere? Up to now no-one has come forward with the answers.

It has always been my hope that if this manuscript were ever published, someone would recognize a name, an event, a peculiar turn of phrase or a family story and connect it with the letters in this manuscript. I have advertised in Canadian newspapers, and friends have undertaken genealogical research in the Netherlands hoping to find even the smallest trace of those who have unwittingly contributed to this work. Those searches have been fruitless. It is possible, though highly unlikely, that one or more of the correspondents is still alive. I only hope that they would approve of what has been re-created here.

Even if the true identities and histories of these immigrant correspondents remain forever untraceable, they have left an open door through which the reader is permitted a glimpse of a distant time and place. In the foreground are people not yet shorn by time of their humanity and their emotions, in the background a country struggling to define itself in a new century. The immigrants brought to their correspondence and observations all their European views and prejudices and they did not hesitate to evaluate, criticize and appreciate the society of which they now found themselves part.

In great measure they approved of what they found. They had already somewhat distanced themselves, in body and spirit, from the land of their birth, and now were given the chance to re-create themselves. Perhaps some were disappointed that Canada was not the golden land of the United States, yet it did in great measure offer the hope and opportunity that no longer existed for them in the Netherlands. As outsiders, they had perhaps a clearer perspective on Canada and its people, and for most it was to remain the land of the second chance. Canada was a country in which the dreamer could still dream with the realistic hope that hard work and struggle would reward him in the end.

Frans van Waeterstadt, perhaps the most insightful of the immigrant correspondents, expressed the universality and depth of those dreams. He envisioned a new homeland where he would find the opportunity to work and a chance to make something of himself. Yet his hopes and dreams were tempered by brutal reality. He had remarked in his first letter to his hometown newspaper on 4 April, 1927:

> *I have, in my short life, cherished a considerable number of illusions. More than I can now possibly remember. Most had a brief existence and died out by themselves, only to be quickly replaced by new ones. Others took possession of years of my life. Again and again, they formed the themes of my deepest thoughts and were the cause of many dreams. But slowly and surely I got older, I came to understand the reality of life... and that reality shattered my most beautiful illusions into shards.*

In his last letter, written on 11 April, 1929, a mere six months before the Wall Street Crash, his tone was tempered but optimistic:

> *... I'll take a chance. Not on a grand scale, however. I've rented a small farm, seven acres is small, especially in Canada. But it's enough for a poor bachelor such as myself. And if the weather isn't too miserable this coming summer I should be able to get enough potatoes, carrots and beets, etc. off it to pay the rent and save a few pennies. Nothing ventured, nothing gained! About the rent — 30 dollars a year is not too much for seven acres of good land, a house (very simple and small) and a barn. This will be my third summer on this side of the ocean. I wish myself a lot of luck...*

Frans van Waeterstadt, like so many other immigrants, hoped that Canada was the answer to a dream of freedom and success and not simply another illusion. One can only hope that his dream and those of all the others would eventually be fulfilled and that new ones would take their place in this land of opportunity.[2]

Herman Ganzevoort
Calgary, 1999

---

2. For a history of Dutch immigration to Canada see: Herman Ganzevoort, *A Bittersweet Land: The Dutch Experience in Canada, 1890-1980.*

De Vrije Socialist, 2 July, 1924
(THE FREE SOCIALIST)

How things are for the Unemployed who were exported to Canada.
The new fatherland, which the old one gives us as a gift.

WAGES FALL!

Driven by the impossibility of earning a crust of bread in the "fatherland," or in the hope of having a little more, quite a few people go to America and (because the United States only permits the entry of a small number) especially to Canada. It's about the latter that I want to say some things that might be of some use, especially to those who go to Canada under the aegis of the Holland Emigration Central, Anna Powlonastraat, The Hague.

When they arrive in Canada, they'll be met and taken to the train by someone who doesn't understand a word of Dutch.

When you arrive at your destination, e.g. Toronto: again the same, and you'll be put up in a Salvation Army hotel which is crawling with vermin.

The following workday, the emigrants go to a bureau, a sort of employment office, where they will be helped to get work. At best, a farmer will come and ask: "what kind of work can you do and how high does the wage have to be?" (Everything in the English language). In that office, there's no one who understands anything but English and French.

The foreigner doesn't know what the standard wage is and no one tells him, so he simply asks something. The farmer always finds this to be too much and the director of the office (government) helps the farmer to haggle and convince the emigrant. This almost always succeeds, as the Emigration Central, before the people's departure, has assured them that those government agents are trustworthy. In the other more common cases, you get an address, usually one or more day's train travel away; you arrive, the farmer's at the station and an agreement is reached there.

The emigrant usually has little money when he arrives; besides that he has to pay for the trip(s), he's been softened up a bit; the farmer can again take advantage of the circumstances. Something which he does abundantly.

A few facts:

Two people are sent a day's train journey away by the government agent. The man doesn't know the wage, but it'll be alright.

They were met and taken advantage of because of their needy circumstances. They agreed to a wage of 20 and 10 dollars a month with room and board. The first was a first class workman, the second was not.

They had to work from five thirty in the morning to eight thirty at night, relieved only by mealtimes. Break time is unknown, it's: eat up, work. They left on the second day and the farmer made them walk the one and a half hours to the station with their heavy suitcases.

There are hundreds of cases like these.

A great number of people walk away and come to the city after working for one or two months.

I don't have to say much about this, only that over 7,000 from Toronto alone have gone to the United States to work because there was nothing to do for them here. An emigrant is permitted to enter the United States and can starve.

As a result of a snowstorm, the municipality had 6,000 men shoveling snow, 1,500 so-called war invalids were sent home as unsuitable. One can imagine how great the misery must be if 1,500 invalids report for such work, when the snow is a metre high and it's storming terribly. There are Hollanders walking around who have been unemployed for five or more months without a chance of things improving.

Those who are working earn 16 to 30 dollars a week, but most earn around 20; 30 only for very good craftsmen who have fortuitously been able to enter their craft.

One of my acquaintances went to the Dutch consul to straighten up some private affairs but... the Dutch consul only spoke English and my friend only spoke Dutch: the interpreter had disappeared and the result was that the consul said: "What are you doing here if you can't speak English?" He went back again later, but took an interpreter with him. One can imagine what kind of help such a person gives to people who come to him for advice.

Even so, the Emigration Central says: "If you get into distress go to the consul."

I just happened to read a letter of reference from the Emigration Central to the government agent here. In it, among other things, it said: "this is one of the 175 *capable* farmhands, about whom I telegraphed" on such and such a date. The good man had never even seen a plough, much less ever done any farm work. And of the thirty, there were probably fifteen or twenty like that.

The Netherlands government knows, or should know, that there's great unemployment here, and that thousands of new ones are added, and yet, it still permits the Emigration Central to go ahead and make new victims. Continually more unemployed, always lower wages (a dollar has the same purchasing power as a guilder) and slowly but surely a large number of emigrants go to the dogs.

There are cities which financially support the Emigration Central, The Hague, Amsterdam, and Utrecht. They get rid of some of the unemployed that way. They croak here, there's no work and so no food for them.

But the goal is reached, the shipping barons profit from the crossing, the Canadian government supplies cheap beasts of burden, the Canadian capitalist laughs because he earns a profit and the Netherlands government delivers the victims.

It will probably have to be the revolutionary movement again, that shows the people the truth; that warns them of the lies about Canada, that says: "be on your guard against a government which will surrender you to the Canadian Exploiters without compassion and then will get rid of you for a penny."

But the Canadian government is playing with fire and that's dangerous.

The downtrodden from other countries will have to form the revolutionary nucleus here!

De Arnhemsche Courant, *17 January, 1925*

East West, Home's Best

Lately, a name keeps running through our minds, the name is Canada. We know the country from Curwood's romantic stories, but that's not the real Canada, that's a fantasy land, with fantasy people. We know Canada from all kinds of travel writings, but that's merely veneer; they teach us almost as much about actual life in Canada as we could come to learn about the joys and sorrows of the inhabitants of a house by the examination of the facade.

In the end, we can come to learn about Canada, and this time the real Canada, from the letters of countrymen who, because of the struggle for existence in our overpopulated little country, emigrated to the land of immeasurable prairies, the land where there's still room for many millions. Within the last few weeks, different letters from such emigrants have come to our attention and all of them sound the same tone: disillusionment, disappointment, sometimes mixed with a dose of indignation about the false visions which were used to lure them to that foreign land.

Two young fellow citizens, Frans and Cor Niermeier, who are now working as farm hands in Argusville, Manitoba, write the following:

"Since, as we understand it, the Holland Emigration Central has a plan to encourage the emigration of a great number of Hollanders to Canada this year, we want to share some of our experiences with those who are entertaining this idea, mindful of the fact that he is a happy man who takes warning from another man's mistakes.

"In short: Hollanders here and in the neighbourhood have discovered that they, the emigrants, are being fleeced by the farmers. In the spring and the summer, hard and heavy work has to be carried out on the land for very little money (16 dollars per month). The farmer treats his employees well during that time. As soon as winter arrives, however, and the land is unsuitable for cultivation, the hired man is informed that he's become redundant. These sentiments are primarily demonstrated in the announcement that the employee can leave, and in the worsening of the food. However, it often happens that the employee is permitted to stay during the winter but he has to promise to work for the first three months without a wage. This action should not elicit surprise, as the farmer knows that new and cheap labourers are continually being brought in from other countries by agents of the emigration offices.

"The Canadian farmer, as well as others, understands the manner by which benefits accrue to him from the concept of supply and demand. As long as that interaction continues, the worker–immigrant will have a worrisome existence. A logical result of this is that a great number of the foreigners will go back to their homelands again, impoverished and discouraged.

"If the employee points out to the farmer the unreasonableness and unfairness of his actions, and that they clash with the contents of brochures and news reports that are given out by some emigration offices in Holland, the latter throws the blame on the Canadian government who, he says, doesn't hesitate to deliberately influence the big Dutch newspapers by presenting the life of the immigrant in a much better light than it really is and thus violates the truth. Naturally, we'll leave the onus of that assertion on the farmers. However, we don't believe that the major newspapers accommodate themselves to producing intentionally misleading publications.

"We, who were also set on the prairie in that manner, cannot and will not be content with a skeptical shrugging: 'Après nous le déluge.' At present, we strongly recommend that those who are weighing emigration to Canada not take that step. Think before you jump! Un homme averti....

"Those who are interested, and want to know more details about our experience in Canada, are urged to read our forthcoming article, dealing with the emigration question, in the *Avondpost* of 13, 14, and 15 January. Other Dutch dailies are probably also prepared to publish the above: as a warning. Our 'supposition' does not exclude individuals from requesting various editors to do that."

At the very moment that we are issuing this warning in our paper, the mail has brought us the following letter:

"It has come to the attention of the Director of the Netherlands Emigration Foundation, that once again an attempt is being made to convince Netherlanders, who are considering settlement in Canada, to buy land (on instalment) on incredibly rosy terms.

"The Director, in the general interest, strongly advises everyone not to get involved in the offer. One should first go to the Netherlands Emigration Foundation, Bezuidenhoutscheweg 97, The Hague, for further particulars, if they, at least, place some value on being spared serious disappointments and financial loss.

"Along with the gentlemen, Frans and Cor, who are two stalwart, sound, young Dutchmen, prepared to get their hands dirty, we also say, but then in pure Dutch: 'Think before you jump. Into the world. All the best! But then with Dutch caution, have a good look first'."

De Avondpost, *13 January 1925*

Emigration to Canada
By a Canadian Immigrant

During 1924, articles appeared in a number of the big Dutch newspapers which, other than travel accounts, reflect views and impressions about transatlantic emigration that are also of interest in light of Holland's serious emigration question. Because this journalistic effort might be of value to those who are interested in this question, either because of their professions, or because they have a particular interest in the New World or the manner in which the facts were assembled for these articles it is, in our opinion, only just that interested people be given a correct and trustworthy portrait of the circumstances in Canada. In that light, some articles appeared, among others, which were assembled based on data provided by others. This is dangerous, because the writer expands on what others and not he himself has experienced. Fantasy then has to come into play and that's absolutely disastrous for a subject like this where others might take action based on it.

One's own observation and one's own experience is required here and that's what this writer wants to give, because he's been living here for a while as an ordinary hired man.

Israel Querido didn't go to someone from the Jordaan to ask for information, instead he went to live in the Jordaan for a while, so that he could relate his impressions after his own observations.

Up to now, in a relative sense, no insider has had anything to say about this very important subject and so it might be useful to give the immigrant himself the word, so that one thing or another might be conducive to supplementing and elucidating.

This writer, a Hollander, having gone to Canada (Manitoba) a while ago, desires to do some good by describing his experiences and impressions as a farm labourer, so that they might serve to inform and warn those who also wish to emigrate.

The premise that Canada needs good workmen, and farm workers especially, is accepted. This land offers a good living to healthy energetic people and they can look forward to a decent future. The Dutch farm worker who's used to working in his own country and therefore isn't lazy in Canada succeeds, unless he has bad luck. Even for those who have never done farm labour there's plenty of opportunity, if they want to work, to become good farmers.

However, the emigrant will do himself a real favor if he doesn't form any wonderful illusions about this lovely and fruitful land; it's advisable to set oneself on the firm ground of the truth, with both feet.

In most cases, the emigrants have felt disappointed in the beginning. Unfamiliarity, insufficient knowledge of the language and information, the local—different than Dutch—habits and customs, seem strange and unwelcome to many. The emigrant then cannot be encouraged enough to become familiar with the English language, especially before his departure. The chance of becoming homesick is much less then.

In our opinion, Canada is the land for strong young men. It's a pre-eminently suited outlet for the excess labour force of Holland; not only for manual labourers but also for civil servants—this writer was formerly a junior public servant—who can always find lots of jobs as farm workers. The majority of immigrants have never been involved in farming and yet these inexperienced farm hands find jobs.

About the country itself and country life, more later. In my opinion, the Dutch government in her future expansion policy would do well to engage herself with the English Dominion of Canada. That policy will bring us closer to the solution of the emigration question and will also need to be directed at the elimination of unemployment, which is the result of the disproportionate relationship between population and means of support.

Because it's obvious that most of the emigrants are those who have the least control of capital, emigration is greatly hindered by the lack of money. Neither the government nor the municipalities offer help in this question. If they get serious about the emigration problem, the Netherlands government will have to expand emigration law in such a way that the municipalities will be required, in the first place, to loan money to cover the transportation costs of the unemployed who benefit from municipal treasury support.

Unemployment, which reigns everywhere, and the related expenses at relief offices and public assistance committees, which are mostly bounties for the encouragement of laziness, demand a different policy than that which has been followed up to now.

A part of the millions which have been given out for that purpose, turned into a subsidy for, let's say, the Holland Emigration Central of Amsterdam, would, in my opinion, make possible a considerably more moral and practical use of those monies. Although the Canadian government strongly promotes immigration by facilitating easy admittance—the possession of a certain sum of money is not required—that promotion has not yet found expression in the offer of financial support, and the farmers also have no interest in lending the immigrant an advance to cover the cost of the crossing. This circumstance is certainly one of the main reasons that the total number of Dutch emigrants going to the New World barely exceeds a few hundred per year.

Unemployment is not as widespread here in Canada, and then only primarily among the working class. A peculiar situation: there's a shortage of labour everywhere in the countryside and people have to come from foreign lands, and in the big cities there's unemployment. They simply refuse to do the hard farm labour and would rather draw from the unemployment funds, although they aren't as liberal here as in Holland. Whatever, all foreigners who want to work are welcome here. It just teems with all kinds of nationalities here: Poles, Irish, Austrians and lately even the number of Dutch is growing.

Of the few hundred Hollanders who are here, about 45 have been placed in the area around Silverton as inexperienced farmhands. Because of the great distances, they seldom meet each other. A fortuitous circumstance sometimes brings a number together and then the heated discussions follow. In general, the bitter feelings towards their country are great. A brochure, given out by the *Bemiddelingsbureau voor Transatlantische Emigratie* of The Hague, states, "in a foreign place, never revile the country which you have left," but no one pays any attention to it.

Now, first something about the trip and life in Canada.

The trip has been rather well described in several papers. Suffice it to say that the trip to middle Canada from Rotterdam lasts about 12 days. The aforementioned Bemiddelingsbureau Veenstra, Laan van N.O.l. 196, The Hague, takes care of the passage to and placement in, Canada.

You depart on the *Batavier* from Rotterdam for Gravesend, where you are inspected (those who are not fluent in the English language should under no circumstances take along any combustible materials or firearms; they cause nothing but bother). From there, you go by train, to Victoria Station, London. Here, the Hollanders, who are unfamiliar with everything and who, awestruck, observe the incredible activity, catch the attention of a representative who has been specially appointed to take them to Euston Station by bus.

From there, the trip is on to Liverpool, where the night is passed in filthy accommodations. The following day you have your medical exam and you step on board one of the Canadian Pacific Railway Co.

ships. After 8 days you land in Quebec, are once again inspected and after a three-day wonderfully beautiful train trip, you arrive in Winnipeg. Here you're taken to the Immigration Hall by a representative and the following day (Monday - Wednesday - Friday) you leave Union Station for the interior. Having arrived at the appropriate station (Silverton) you are met by someone who will take you to your final destination. The whole trip costs about 400 guilders.

The best time to emigrate is from April to June. The chance of finding permanent work is greatest then.

The farmers are usually Canadian, English immigrants, Poles and Austrians (Galicians). The majority are fairly well off and delight in an extended family circle. Practically all have telephones, because the great distances between the houses and the villages. Besides that, many families have an organ or a piano. Even though the jazz band is most popular here, Chopin and Liszt are also prized.

14 January, 1925

The average Canadian farmer is incredibly different from the Dutch farmer. He is—as farmer—very educated and has a great knowledge of machines and equipment. He likes nothing better than to take a machine (like a tractor) apart and no matter how difficult, he'll put it back together. This knowledge is very useful to him at threshing time when he has to know the tractor and the threshing machine or the separator thoroughly.

Besides that, almost all of them own an automobile and they're unequalled in their ability to drive on these rough and almost impassable roads. They are, with few exceptions, good natured and friendly, but very pessimistic, concise in business and very miserly. If something gets in a farmer's way that gives him trouble and no financial gain, he leaves it like it is: "Time is money" is his motto and hell go right through a swamp or crop with his machine and horses, if it shortens his way.

The housewife is less appreciated by the Hollander. Her cleanliness leaves something to be desired—a Hollander is superior in this matter—she is also generally more dour and less cordial than her husband.

The children are unbearable; they are ill-mannered and impudent, and they lord it over the hired man. They grow up faster than Dutch children; at twelve they drive cars, go hunting and ride unsaddled horses. Compared to Dutch farm children, they're very developed. Every village of any importance—that is a village with 100 or more inhabitants—has a school, which we can best compare with a ULO school. They learn mathematics, French and Latin. School attendance is required to age 12. After that age, the children decide whether they want to go to school or not! The parents have absolutely no control over them, as the children know that they're extremely valuable on the farm because each of them saves the cost of a hired man. Lately, however, many farmers' sons and daughters have gone to Winnipeg or Portage to be trained as teachers. This is a circumstance that again increases the shortage of labourers.

In the beginning, the emigrant has to endure quite a lot from these children and only ignoring it stops you from being too greatly annoyed.

The farmer treats his hired hand as an equal, in fact in many respects better. The food, in general, is outstanding; Dutch cooking is, nevertheless, heartier. As you are a boarder, you're completely accepted as a member of the family; usually you have your own room, although in some cases you have to sleep in a barn or a stall.

It's characteristic that, although Canada isn't dry, practically everyone abstains from strong drink. An intoxicated person is a rarity here and then as a rule he's a Galician.

The Canadians regularly attend church out of religious need. The majority are Protestant, that is Presbyterian and Methodist; all fall under the jurisdiction of the Union Church. The total number of Catholics is quite small.

The Reformed church service is quite different from that in Holland. Among other things, the service begins with the congregation reciting the "Our Father." After that, the congregation sings before the sermon. The verses of the hymns are beautiful and they're sung a lot faster than in our Dutch Reformed churches. Then comes the sermon, followed by a song from a little choir and ending with congregational singing. The relationship between the minister and the congregation is quite typical. The Reverend shakes every churchgoer's hand at the exit.

As mentioned, the Canadian farmer is quite educated. This is a situation which the immigrant will have to take into account because the Canadian doesn't judge someone on the basis of his well groomed appearance, nor on the immaculate condition of the jacket, nor on the beautifully polished shoes or the assumption of a certain "air", but he asks if the person, who stands in front of him as an employee or a servant, has a pair of able hands on his body, possesses a broad education and last but not least, is a gentleman. Those kinds of personalities are in great demand in this country and they know how to appreciate them. This appreciation for first class men is expressed in all levels of the society. Such a person will be given help, so that he will reach the place where he ought to be by virtue of his ability, daring and personality. Nepotism and wheelbarrow politics is rarely or never noticeable, particularly in the countryside. Those, who occupy important positions are then, without a doubt, self-made men.

It's hard to understand that so few enterprising young people, who have healthy bodies, diplomas from the Mulo, HBS or Gymnasium and who are not afraid of barn or field labour, would trade Holland, where even pleading for a job doesn't help, for this truly beautiful land.

Canada is beautiful, especially for people who choose the healthy country life over that of the often musty and turbulent city. Immense woods are to be found in the province of Quebec and in more northwesterly districts. The middle provinces (Alberta, Saskatchewan and Manitoba) are hilly and low. The fertility of the soil is so great that you never have to fertilize it. Every 2 or 3 years, however, you leave a part of the land uncropped, the so-called summer fallow. The land which you want to crop, you simply plough and sometimes you go over it later with a disk to kill the weeds. Cultivation is the same in most of the provinces; in the East and in the West (Ontario and British Columbia) a lot of fruit is grown, in Alberta, Saskatchewan and Manitoba it's only grain: wheat, oats and barley. In the first two provinces you also find cattle ranching. That doesn't mean that the grain provinces don't have cattle; on the contrary, every farmer has his cows and pigs, but only enough so that he has his own milk, butter and meat. Keeping cattle is very cheap. Hearing that a hired man has some cattle is certainly no sign of prosperity.

The first farmers settled here about 30 years ago when everything was still prairie. They began to bring the best parts under cultivation and after that they chopped the brushwood but the trees and high bushes are still standing. The cattle range under them and find their food. Besides that, after the harvest they're chased into the stubble where there's plenty to eat. They're usually outside, even in the winter.

The time that you could buy a piece of land for a song has passed. You always buy by the section (640 acres) or by the half or quarter section. For that matter a great amount of land has now been developed; the effort that it costs to clear 1 acre of land is much greater than the benefit you later derive from it.

Therefore, you have to be very careful of the offers of the Canadian government or the Canadian Pacific Railway Co. You can buy a whole patch of land for a song (1.20 guilders per acre) but then it's bush, swamp or thicket. After decades of slaving and toiling you might succeed in owning a sort of farm, but the bottom line is that you haven't worked for your own good but for the Canadian government which has seen its land brought into cultivation in a cheap manner.

If you really want to operate a good farm, then there are three ways of doing it: 1) Buy. 2) Rent. 3) Run the farm as a tenant farmer. The cost of a farm is, on average, 30 dollars an acre and in order to live you need at least 60 acres. Besides that, you need house furnishings, cattle and equipment, so a small farm comes to about 2,500 dollars.

If you rent one, you pay a third of the yield of the harvest as rent. The owner is, however, required to pay the taxes of the renter. As a tenant farmer you get a good wage as a rule and sometimes a certain percentage of the harvest.

In any case, if you want to begin farming in one manner or another, you have to have some capital. Taking out a chattel mortgage is dangerous because you'll almost never pay it off. Even if the profits of a harvest are great, so are the expenses. If you have a farm, say a half section, then the proceeds of the harvest, if it turns out well (50 to 60 bushels per acre), are about $2,000. If you begin for yourself, you usually can't buy a threshing machine ($2,000–4,000). If you have someone thresh for you, it costs $12 an hour. If you go on like that, there's certainly not much left and you always have to figure on a bad year and having money at your disposal. The harvest can fail because of hail rain or frost (and that chance is very great) or drought. You can insure yourself against this but the premiums are very high and the payments low.

The taxes are high for the individual farmer. If he falls behind in the payments, someone else can do that for him and then *he* owns the farm, unless the original owner can pay up his taxes within one year. The mortgage companies are also very strict: not a week goes by without a mortgage sale.

From this short overview, it's obvious that farming is a risky business.

15 January, 1925

Not much is necessary for subsistence; only clothes are very expensive. They grow their own vegetables; they bake their own bread and cake. 500 kg of flour ($20) is enough for one good sized family for

6 months; 100 kg of sugar ($10) for one month. Besides that, all kinds of fruits grow wild here, such as cherries, raspberries, strawberries etc. and you can shoot ducks, partridges and prairie chickens. These are, however, only a few of the fascinating and distinguishing features of this country, although they can't compensate for all that had to be left behind in Holland. Then there's the silence which lies spread over the immense fields of grain, a silence which is pleasant after work and encourages meditation. The pleasant faces of the inhabitants seem to mirror their souls and are in complete harmony with the surroundings.

The loss of the blessings (?) of the eight-hour day doesn't seem to have any effect on their good humor.

But the thought that Canada is a kind of paradise should be given up immediately. You really have to put your shoulder to the wheel here. Usually, you get up at 5 o'clock on the farm and don't finish before 8 in the evening. So you're on your feet for 15 hours and you can be assured that you'll work incredibly hard; what's done in Holland in 8 hours is done here in 3 hours, and much better. There is, however, less work in the winter when you begin at 7:00 a.m. and finish at 6:00 p.m. On Sunday you don't work as hard; in the afternoon you even have a few free hours.

The division of labour over the whole year, from the beginning until after the harvest, is as follows: As soon as the fields are cleared, you begin to plough until the snow and the cold make this impossible. The ploughing, like most of the other work, is done with 4 or more horses or a tractor. You use a 2, 3 or 4-shared plough. In the winter, the chief work is keeping the barns clean and feeding the animals. Besides that, you have to haul hay from the field (where you've built a haystack for safekeeping) and straw from the stack thrown up by the threshing machine, and also chop wood. In the spring there are ploughing, sowing and harrowing.

After that comes a calmer time; after that the chief work is haying. Because of the many animals that have to be fed during the winter, they need an incredible amount of hay, on average 50 loads, which is partly put up in the hay fields and partly behind or in the barn. During unloading, you sometimes throw a number of ropes around the load and two horses pull it up with a pulley, so that the wagon is unloaded in a minute. Besides haying—which takes a lot of time—the thistles in the grain are cut or plucked out, depending on whether they are Canadian or Scotch thistles. Generally, harvest time begins in the middle of August.

A binder, with a 9 horse span and a 6, 7, or 8-foot blade, moves the grain and binds the sheaves. This work, however, is for the farmer or his son; the Hollander, or whatever hired man, has to continually set 8 sheaves against each other to form one shook, a hard job. This goes on for a number of weeks and then you begin to thresh. Usually each man gets a team, that is a hay wagon with two horses. He has to build his own load and throw it into the feeder of the separator, which is run by a tractor or a steam engine. This is the busiest time of all; you work right through, even if the moon and the stars are in the sky.

Sometimes, however, you don't have a team but you're a pitcher whose only job is throwing the sheaves on the wagon while another builds the load. The pitcher's job is the most awful of all and is, as a rule, the job for the inexperienced Hollander who isn't trusted with his own team.

Then one begins again at the beginning with ploughing and so forth.

The wage for this heavy labour, done by the inexperienced Hollanders sent out by the *Bemiddelingsbureau-Veenstra*, is scandalously low, that is 16 dollars a month plus room and board. Being "inexperienced" means nothing; once you've done something you know it for life; it's precisely that tremendously hard work in harvest time which requires no experience and making stooks is easily learned, especially if you make thousands and thousands in a week. Loading up sheaves doesn't demand much experience either.

What's the reason that we Hollanders earn 50 cents a day, while every other hired man gets $4 a day for exactly the same work? A hired Englishman declared that "inexperienced" is merely a cunning expression. Experienced work is: driving the binder, the separator or the tractor, being able to determine if the grain is ripe or doctoring the cattle: all jobs which a hired man never gets. So it's incomprehensible how the representative of the *Bemiddelingsbureau*, who's been here for years, could have established this starvation wage. It's true, you're permanent here for 6 months and work is very scarce in the winter but it doesn't balance the services which the farmer gets from a Hollander, especially since room-and-board is so inexpensive. You have to buy your own clothes out of that $16 and they wear out very quickly, and your winter outfit. So what's actually left of that wage? A bagatelle, if you live very frugally. Besides that, you work three months only for room and board, and you don't earn anything at all then. The Austrians regard the Hollanders with sorrow because they depress the wages.

No matter how unjust the circumstances may be here, it's still better than in Holland when you earn absolutely nothing. It's also very healthy here and you've a greater feeling of freedom of movement. You certainly don't have to have any intention of becoming or staying a farmer; most stay here so that they can look for a new position while working, only a very few are interested in becoming farmers.

In closing, please note that those who wish to emigrate would do well to bring along a small sum of money, about 100 guilders, because it's customary here to pay the worker his first wage only after 6 months, if the farmer has any money. One should also take into account that the farmer is not required to pay any wages if the worker leaves before the end of that time, unless he fires him.

The emigration offices and bureaus in Holland would do a lot of good if they informed the emigrants correctly so that disappointment would be prevented on their arrival in Canada.

It needs to be said here that the emigrant worker is virtually without rights during the first 6 months, and in great measure dependant on the morality of the farmer.

Besides the many who are looking for other jobs, many also leave because of homesickness and disappointment. For many, the work is absolutely too heavy and a great amount of will power is necessary to endure. Only those whose motto is: nil *volentibus arduum* will succeed. As proof of how many are capable of doing this, the following: in July there were 12 Hollanders around Argusville; 4 have already returned to Holland, 6 will go as soon as their 6 months are over and only the writer and his brother remain and they'll leave if they see a good opportunity but not in any case to Holland. Not that things are really bad for us but the wage disparity is too great.

Besides that, what's often the case? In harvest time you're useful, very useful: and cheap. After that, however, you're superfluous and only the contract forces the farmer to keep the employee. How? It's happened more than once, that the farmer becomes so difficult and harasses his Hollander so much, that he has to leave. And what does the farmer always say? Well, let them leave for this winter, next summer enough will come and then we'll hire them again. That's not an expression of their bad character; only their miserliness drives them to that.

In one of the newspapers, not too long ago, it said that there was a plan to send 200 Dutch young men to Canada next year, under the same conditions as exist now. There would also be an English course attached to it. In the same paper there was an article by Dr. Brandes, chairman of the German Council of Agriculture and Prof. Dr. Sering, which says among other things:

"The big farmers in export countries like Canada, the United States and Argentina have to struggle with the same difficulties as German agriculture. These problems result because the difference between the prices of the agricultural products and industrial goods is too great and to the detriment of agriculture, and at the same time Central Europe is not able to take delivery of huge stockpiles. The result is that ten thousand Canadian farms are being threatened with economic disaster.

"What's actually the reason that they want to import 200 others? The emigration offices make a business of it and live from the percentage they get from the steamship companies and from the money the immigrant has to deposit, in order to be so lucky as to earn 50 cents a day. After arriving in Canada the emigrant pays another $4 to the representative. An emigration office which is not well informed is nothing more than a clip joint for down-and-out young men. These offices profit from sending out as many young men as possible, and an end has to be put to that. The total number of failures is great and they come back poorer and unluckier than when they went away. May the plan to organize 200 young men remain a plan and never be realized, if not, then at least may it not happen as long as the inequitable conditions hold sway in Canada. Besides that, the sending out of new emigrants does not improve the conditions of the Dutch emigrant already here, who has a hard enough job to keep his head above water in the winter. As long as the emigration offices take advantage of the adventurousness of emigration at the same time, it's just no good. The only solution that exists for sending out young men without exaggerating the future is to organize an emigration office that works completely altruistically and is supported by the government.

"In summation, we come to the following conclusions: those who want to go to Canada with the aim to become well off as quickly as possible should remain at home. Those, however, who can't take it anymore in Holland, who don't want to play the gentleman without work and at the cost of their parents or others, should go if they're not afraid of hard work."

May this essay—however pessimistic it may be, it is true—result in giving some insight into the conditions in which the Dutch emigrant finds himself.

Frans Niermeier,
Argusville, Manitoba,
November 1924.

Clinton, 26 November, 1925

Mr. Editor!

As you have received news from Jansen, formerly living at Kerkenveld and later in America, you know that he came to me on October 11 and took French leave [absconded] on November 20. We have heard nothing more of him.

We gave him six weeks of free room and board, a separate room and bed and I went around helping him look for work for 6 or 7 days. At the same time, I went to the station with him 5 or 6 times for his trunk. But no thanks for this. When he got work, he had no work clothes. I gave him work clothes, but I didn't get them back. Then he wanted me to rent a house for him. I did that, it cost $15 a month. The landlord wanted a month's rent in advance but our Jansen didn't have $15. Then he asked me, "Will you advance it? When I get the money from the factory, I'll repay you." I did that.

Subsequently, he asked me if I had an old bed to sell him, because his wife was going to come over. Then my wife said, "We have a bed but it isn't old, we bought it two years ago for $20. But as our family is steadily getting smaller, we don't use it anymore. You can have it for $8. It's just like new.

"Oh", he said, "that's cheap and it's still a fine bed, I can use that." Then I sold him a stove for $5. I gave him a table and chair. So he had a good start, because he was always telling us that his wife would be coming over soon.

But when it came to the day that he was going to be paid by the factory, he told my wife in the morning: "I'm sick, I'm going to the factory to tell them I'm sick and then I'll hurry back." Indeed, he went to the factory for his money and then he was gone.

So much for doing good. And you know how good we were to him because he published a piece in the Hoogeveensche Courant describing how well we treated him. But now it turns out to be totally different. So that's the thanks we get for all the good that we've done. If he had said, "I want to go to another place, can I keep that little bit of money and pay you back later?" Sure, that would have been alright with us. He would have been free with just some thanks. We'll get along without those few pennies. But I had expected something different.

The costs were as follows: rent $15, bed $8, stove $5, plus 6 weeks room and board. Sir, will you be so kind as to publish the preceding in the newspaper so that he will be well known. And because he didn't thank me, I want to thank him. And if there are any more of those Jansens in Kerkenveld, then let them stay there. I won't take in any more Hollanders.

Frans Bruggewirth and Family,
North America.

WARNING

Because of the bad experience with Hendrikus Jansen, formerly living at Kerkenveld,

NO HOLLANDERS WILL BE PERMITTED ENTRY

to my farm, unless they are of good family and provide good references.

Frans Bruggewirth   North America

De Nieuwe Tilburgsche Courant,
29 December, 1925

Dear Editor:

In April of this year we emigrated to Graham Island in Canada due to the insistence of Mr. and Mrs. Rutten, both Tilburgers. The above-mentioned had distributed a circular in which the primary contents came down to the following: 1) The government has contracted the construction of roads here which provides regular work at $3.75 a day. 2) You can catch fish here and sell them to a cannery in Tow Hill. 3) The government grants free land which when developed can be sold for $25 an acre. 4) In order to get here everyone must have 426 Guilders passage money and at least $25 (62.5 guilders) landing money. Thus far their circular. Now the truth. The fellows (nearly all Tilburgers) came here about the middle of May after a long trip which had taken almost four weeks. First to Massett from where they were sent to Tow Hill supposedly to dig clams. It was said that you could earn $7 to $8 a day at it. They moved on about 30 km further and lived there on the beach in a very big house in which there was nothing. The fellows, for the first time, suffered hunger there. Lacking a pot or pan they ate raw potatoes. They even ate an eagle, a black crow and a sea gull (this only serves to prove that they were truly hungry). How were the earnings? The first days they weren't able to do better than 50 cents a day, that's all together, 7 people. But of course this was a period of training, even though when they knew how to do it, and there are truly good diggers among them, they were never able to earn more than $1 or $1.50 a day per person. So that was the first lie.

Mrs. Rutten told us then that it would get better and that everything was fine, as a result the fellows regularly wrote good letters home.

Finally, after three months, we began on the much-promised road work. We moved again, about 16 km further on and worked there not quite 2 months when the work was stopped because, according to the engineer, the road was useless because no people lived there. Most of the fellows, before they began work on the road, had contracted some debts because they could not earn a living.

Just as the work stopped, three new boys arrived, misled by the Ruttens' alluring circular and reassured (so the fellows later found out) by the fine letters which they had written home at the urging of Mrs. Rutten.

After being bored in Tow Hill for 14 days and making only debts, because there are no people and no work, we began other road work, however this was 100 km further on. The road to the place, which had to be traveled primarily on foot, was for us a true "via dolorosa." We each carried about 60 pounds of freight on our backs and traveled on an almost impassable road. As a result we arrived at our destination more dead than alive and were allowed to rest on plank beds. We were there for three weeks, then the boss stopped the work because he saw that it just wouldn't work any longer. For that matter 3 of the boys had already become sick because of the sleeping accommodations. Our beds regularly got soaking wet from the damp that came out of the ground.

Then back to Massett; but during the three weeks, the road that we needed to go back on had flooded and so we crossed a lake on a raft of tree trunks. It still surprises me that nobody drowned because it was an extremely dangerous trip, even though it ended well. Then we had to walk a distance of 12 km and following that we were taken to Massett in a boat. When we arrived there it was 8 o'clock in the evening and we had left home at 7:30 a.m., so we had been underway for about 12 hours. We arrived in Massett dead tired and hungry and passed the night, without food and bed, in a house about 20 steps from that of Mrs. Rutten. When we told Mrs. Rutten where we were and asked her for a lamp, because it was dark, her husband replied that he wasn't going to pay any attention to us.

Now the fellows had had enough and they decided to leave the island. As three of them didn't have a cent, one of the boys asked the aforementioned lady if she would lend them some money against security, but she refused. When she heard that all the fellows were prepared to help the three empty handed ones, she loaned us enough money to get to the next place but at security of three times the value.

We are now off the island and we recommend that anyone who wants to emigrate to Graham Island on the importuning of Mrs. Rutten first seeks some good information about the place.

Now something about the place:

Every fellow got 160 acres of land in his name. We went to see it once, but two of the boys almost drowned in it. It's completely under water and we heard from everyone here that the land is completely worthless. We also have a real farmer with us and he says the same thing. For that matter if the soil was good and you could grow enough on it, then you still couldn't sell the produce because there aren't any people here to buy it. At Tow Hill, which is 20 km from the land, there are 40 people in the summer (mostly Indians) and not one in the winter. In Massett, that's another 30 km further on, there are perhaps 40 whites and 400 Indians, although the latter buy little or nothing, so that you can freely say that there are no people in those places.

In closing, Mrs. Rutten says that she earned her money (and she has a lot) on the island. This is absolutely untrue as she earned all her money in Prince Rupert, thus not on the island. What her purpose is in luring Tilburgers to the island I have no idea.

But let everyone be warned by this letter. There's nothing there now and it will never become anything. The connections are nothing either; there's not one good road, there are no people and the land is good for nothing.

We thank you dear editor for the space and we remain with the highest regards, A. Smulders, B. Laurijssen, J. Bisschop, H. Kemps, J. Couwenberg, A. Kemps. Old Colonists of the Golden Gate

De Nieuwe Tilburgsche Courant,
16 March, 1926

Dear Editor,
Vancouver, 23-2-26

In our previous letter we forgot to note that two Tilburgers had stayed behind on Graham Island when we left there. The one could not leave because he was waiting for his girl, who has since arrived; he has now been off the island for three months and lives in Prince Rupert. The other is still on the island but totally against his will, because when we left he said to us, "Boys I can't go with you and I can't say why not, there's something going on I can't tell you about." Those are his own words.

Now it seems that his family in Tilburg is saying that the island is good and that he (the staybehind) is regularly sending money home. But sending money home is no proof if you figure that the first time that he sent money home to Holland about 10 months ago "he had not yet earned a penny" and he was still in debt. He also borrowed the money from Mrs. Rutten. We would have said nothing about this but everyone of us has family in Tilburg and they hear from us that you can't make a living on Graham Island, while another writes to Holland that "it's good there." Appearances seem to be against us, thus this piece. The truth is that no one can make a living on Graham Island, no one can work year round, maybe 2 or 3 months in the summer, but that's all. All the under-signed are in agreement as to the truth of this writing.

Thanking you again dear editor, we remain,
Old Colonists of the Golden Gate

De Nieuwe Tilburgsche Courant,
25 March, 1926

He who digs a hole for another will fall into it himself

Dear Editor:

It is important for the interested as well as the family members of the emigrants to learn what their exact situation is.

Thanks to the willingness of the editor, the full truth will now finally come out. Therefore we won't deal with all of the lies. Those who are interested will be able to see through this tissue of lies and for the readers it follows that, "From this one, learn about the many." We support the truth of our writing with official documents from both secular and spiritual authorities, and perhaps the editor of this paper will be so good as to inform you as to the authenticity of these things, which is for all the greatest guarantee that everything rests upon truth.

So to the issue:

1. The road construction engineer declares, "that all proper care was taken for the colonists, they were provided with good food, had access to washing and repair of clothes. He believed that they were city folk and 'not willing' and for these reasons he temporarily stopped the work."

2. The Inspector of Immigration in Massett declares: "The treatment of the immigrants was outstanding. It appears that a mistake was made in supporting these people in their emigration to Canada."

3. A spiritual authority (RC?) declares that he "visited these people in the camp, housing and treatment were outstanding, they were really not suitable people for pioneer work."

4. A member of the British Columbia government declares: "D., a Hollander (a civil servant), translated the letter with the concluding remark that the signers had expected to find a land of milk and honey. I believe that they could have created something like that with a little hard work. It's certain that these people had full-time work here and

that the road construction was undertaken solely for their benefit."

5. The Minister of Agriculture declares that, "Mr. and Mrs. Rutten have been residents of that place for 12 years and are sufficiently familiar with the circumstances."

6. Mr. Meerman who arrived here on 29 November 1925 writes, "The winter is mild here and I've been able to work the whole winter through; we can become something more here than in Holland."

From these declarations it follows:

a. that all had work, paying a wage of $ 3.75 for an 8-hour day, and that their treatment was outstanding and left nothing to be desired.

b. that the reason the engineer stopped the work was their own fault because they were unwilling to work.

c. that all their claims about their misadventures on Graham Island are based on untruths.

From letters of Messrs. Beurden and Meerman it is abundantly clear that they were not without work on Graham Island, for even one day during the whole winter, and that the men who quit their work did this exclusively for reasons of a different nature, which we will now see.

In the previous letters you have been able to read how trustworthy the colonists are in the peoples' estimation. Now we will let them speak for themselves.

After their departure from Graham Island for the big city of Vancouver, B. Laurijssen wrote to us (how is it possible that this man after being so badly treated and after he signed a letter with such contents still writes to me?) that none of the unsuccessful immigrants had been able to find work in Vancouver. He regretted that he had not stayed on Graham Island and completed his full year. He is planning to return to Graham Island and would certainly not have left if he had known that Mr. Meerman and his family had settled there.

He doesn't know what will become of the others, in any case they would have done better to stay on Graham Island. The remaining five members of that fine troop are living together in Vancouver. They tell what happened to them in a 29 December letter to one of the members of our colony and try to get him to come over to them and join them.

One writes for all of them:

"I'll write the truth. None of us have work. Up to now things haven't gone well for us, but it'll get better. Boy you have to join us quickly, because every day you stay on Graham Island you're a thief of your own life."

The rest of the contents are, alas, not fit for publication. In great detail, he paints a complete portrait of the seductiveness and the temptation of the sinful pleasures of city life, and entices those who have stayed behind to that hotbed of animal passions.

Dear readers, this is alas the only reason why the colonists have left Graham Island. They go looking in a city for what, luckily, is not to be found here. Two of them had been here from the beginning and we had no reason to complain. Out of sympathy with their circumstances we brought over three others from Prince Rupert and supplied them with abundant work. However, in great part, they made misuse of our goodness and after having worked here for three weeks they asked for an advance on their monthly wage in order to then also take the others along on an adventure to the big city. (They called this making debts).

Dear readers, there are well paying job opportunities here for thousands, but wilfully they run away from them. They'd rather be in the city, perhaps living on welfare, than be here putting their hands out for a good salary. Without doubt, it is the money that was earned here that is dissipated in the city and in Holland mothers and parents wait in vain for remittances from husband or son.

This is, alas, the ignoble end of these adventurers. Their complete failure and their behaviour must be justified. Thus an article in the paper hammered out of slander and lies, in order to manipulate family and public opinion and to horrify potential emigrants for Graham Island: to make sure that no other Tilburger ever goes there and discovers their slanderous campaign....

Mrs. A. Rutten.
Mr. D. Rutten
Golden Gate Colony
Tow Hill, B.C.
Graham Island
Canada

De Nieuwe Tilburgsche Courant, *26 May, 1926*

Dear Editor:
We departed for Canada on 16 April 1925. We were in Alberta for two and a half months where together we worked on a farm for $50 a

month. But when we heard that there wouldn't be any work there during the winter and that the winters were very severe, we decided together to write to Mrs. A. Rutten with whom we had conversations in Tilburg about Graham Island. But we were advised against it at that time and so did not dare to go along. Mrs. Rutten answered us right away and wrote that we should come there directly. We decided right away and arrived on Graham Island on the 22 July 1925, went to work on 25 July and have worked all the time since then, first with Mrs. Rutten building roads and after a small period of layoff we started working at a sawmill in the neighbourhood and are still at the same job and haven't been laid off the entire winter for even one day. The climate is outstanding here, we haven't had winter yet this year. There are several other places close by, in Tow Hill there's a fish factory were many people can work and the same company is building a new factory in Massett. A little further on there are two more fish factories. As well, there are several more sawmills on the island in which hundreds of people are working. The fishery promises a rich living with salmon and halibut.

We have decided to stay on Graham Island and to begin farming on our own. We do not know yet if we are going to take up a free place or buy one that has just been cleared. Everything suits us very well here and there is more than enough room for hundreds of families, workers who are familiar with all sorts of difficult jobs, such people as farmers and labourers who also very much want to begin farming for themselves. The government gives 160 acres of land free, land which still has to be cleared. There are a lot of people here who take a piece of free land and work on it in the winter until they have it completed, and take advantage of the high daily wages in the summer. The situation here is outstanding for families, the reason being that boys and girls, on reaching the age of 18 years, can also claim a piece of land of 160 acres for themselves and in that way enlarge their farms. In order to prove to you that Graham Island is good for working people, I dare to tell you that we have been able to save $600 on Graham Island above all costs and have eaten and drunk what our hearts desired.

Kind thanks Mr. Editor for the space, signed by the two of us, Mr. & Mrs. Wesel

Haagsche Post, *24 April, 1926*

The Canadian in a Higher Vocation

Mr. Editor:

A number of days ago, I received the February 6 issue of the *Haagsche Post*. It's an outstanding weekly with a great deal of news of all varieties, clear political views and nice short sketches. On page 222, I found an article "Surprises, a conversation with the Canadian." It's witty and pleasantly written, but it contains a number of statements which are far from the truth. I also cannot understand why a well travelled and cultured Hollander with a university degree, as the writer appears to be, displayed so little understanding of humanity that he didn't surmise that this Dutch Canadian was a very stupid and immature person even before he left Holland.

I left the little city of Doetinchem in 1883 and have, almost continuously, lived in English speaking countries in South and North America since that time. Married to a Canadian and with a grown up Canadian family, it speaks for itself that I never spoke Dutch anymore or heard it. So that's about 43 years: but I'll never forget my own language. The Dutch Canadian masqueraded as a man who had forgotten his mother tongue in 21 years: Humbug! Every once in a while, I meet one of these types on my travels through Canada. They introduce themselves to me in broken English, swear to have forgotten their language in 10 or 12 years, revile Holland etc., but it's silly affectation.

It's too bad that the writer of this knowledgeable article takes it for granted that our forgetful Dutch Canadian is a "sample" of a real Canadian. But we shouldn't judge such bunglers too severely: and the phrase "pitiable idiot", which the writer uses, is, I think, a little too harsh. Thousands of Hollanders have left their country because they only knew poverty and want there. They earned good money in Canada and the United States, and very quickly had their own houses with modern conveniences; their children became ladies and gentlemen etc. Is it any wonder that they remember their fatherland with bitterness. Culture! Yes, they're not familiar with any but they can do without it. In the land of their birth, where according to the writer, culture flowers so luxuriously, they suffered hunger, in their new land they have plenty.

The writer goes on: "Then I describe to him (the Dutch Canadian) the wonderful riches, the immeasurable worth of that reviled

Europe... and I'm struck dumb with surprise, when our poor Dutch Canadian replies with marked disdain: 'You're getting sentimental!'" It's too bad that the writer has never been in Canada and doesn't know about the life of the cultured Canadian.

Everything that comprises the art of music, the best of Europe, is fully appreciated here in Canada. Our great music hall here in Toronto (Massey Hall), with a seating capacity of 5,000, is filled four days a week during the winter months. The list of artists that we hear consists of such names as Caruso, Paderewsky, Melba, Kreisler, etc.; we don't pay 50 cents as our Dutch Canadian asserted, but the tickets were $2, $3 or $4 a piece. The writer contends that our literature is imported and then the worst. How can he judge that? The best that Europe produces is in our public and private libraries. He accuses us Canadians of having no history. It's true—but our schoolchildren benefit from that—and therefore it's a blessing. He maintains that we or don't have any scholars or thinkers, and is angry because our people are "after the dollar." I find that to be a healthy sign. Seventy-five years ago, this city was a wilderness with wolves and bears roaming about; now it's an up-to-date city of over 600,000 inhabitants. What were Rotterdam, The Hague and Amsterdam when they were 75 years old?

I admire Holland. I miss that warm cozy Dutch life, I miss the Dutch cuisine, but I deny that we, in Canada, are behind in music, art, architecture and scholarship in all kinds of fields. I contend that Canada and the United States are, at this moment, the most fortunate and rich countries of the world for the workman as well as the businessman.

Toronto, 28 February.
G.B.C. Van Der Feen

Arnhemsche Courant, *4 February, 1928*

Chatham, 6 January, 1928

A WORD OF WARNING
FOR ALL THOSE WHO ARE THINKING ABOUT
EMIGRATING TO CANADA

Dear Mr. Editor,

Considering that the conditions in Canada are not as rosy as are being represented by the various paid agents of the steamship lines and Canadian railways, we want to inform our fellow countrymen of the following:

Due to the great flow of immigrants to Canada in 1927, unemployment is so great that the majority of the new arrivals are walking around without work and if there is work the Canadians and English get preference. Even the Dutchmen who have been here a long time and know the language well can't get any work. Occasionally an individual is lucky enough to get work, but then the wages are also so low that it isn't worth the effort to leave the homeland for that. Great big sturdy guys work for $10 or $12 a week in a factory and many can't even get a job on a farm for just room and board. Many, who have earned a little in the summer have to collect the money with the help of a lawyer. As a result, in Chatham alone—a city with 17,000 inhabitants with many big factories, in which there is nothing to do—there are so many unemployed that the streets are black with them and they are forced to eat up the pennies that they managed to save up from the summer, if they have them, or else live on poor relief. Three weeks ago, a half starved Hollander without a decent place to sleep was found in the fields. He wasn't placed in the poor house but thrown into jail instead and will now be sent back to Holland. Three months ago a Hollander committed suicide due to despondency and poverty and there'll be more. A lot of people suffer from poverty here, not only just among our people, but also among the Canadians who, after all, are citizens here. There's always a lot of boasting here about the tobacco harvest. But there are a lot of people walking around with worried minds because they can't even sell it. A great number of people, who had a few pennies, grew tobacco for half shares of the profits. They ate up the money they had and are now waiting for the profits from the crop that they can't even sell. The farmer tries to steal your half from you with all kinds of mean tricks. They don't leave one stone unturned. A couple of examples: 3 men from Friesland had ten acres of tobacco on half shares and 3 acres of potatoes. The potatoes have been sold and the farmer won't give them their half share: 60 times 90 lbs. are still on the land and he won't give up their share of that. And now he's trying to steal their half share of the tobacco. All three together worked about 50 days for that farmer and now that they ask for their money, he won't pay. Another example: One person had a whole farm on half shares. The boss was quite accommodating in the beginning and advanced him some money. When the harvest was ready, he suddenly asked for the payment of the advance. The man couldn't pay immediately and he put it up for a sheriff's sale which was to take place at two o'clock in the afternoon. The boss and a notary public arrived at 9 o'clock in the morning when there were no other buyers. An immediate sale was concluded and the boss bought everything for a third of the price. Naturally this was all done in a premeditated fashion. So this man and his family worked hard the whole summer and are now put out on the street. He was also falsely accused and shoved into jail. There are more like that here. There's also another here who works in a factory as an ordinary labourer for $10 a week. Here, $10 is not like 25 guilders there but more like 10. Such people don't want their stay-at-home relatives to know that they are so very poor here. It's difficult for married people to save the money for a return passage in order to go back home. There are a lot here who would very much like to return to Holland. It's a little different for single young men, but we wouldn't recommend anyone to emigrate to Canada. We're talking about the province of Ontario, which is the best of the bunch, as many who were in the West jumped on the buffers of the trains in order to get here to the East. This is not exaggeration, but the pure truth about the past year and this year will certainly not be any better considering the cheap passages that are being offered. We ought to be able to get such cheap tickets for the return passage, then hundreds, yes thousands would go back to the old country. We think that our countrymen are thus well informed and we advise them to think things out well before they begin to think about going to Canada. This is to safeguard our fellow countrymen from the disappointment which we ourselves have experienced.

A number of Hollanders:
  H. Denkers,
  J. Oostema,
  J. Terpstra,
  W. Molewijk,
  P. Verplakke,
  P. Carmejoole,
  C. v. Loef,
  H. C. Leenders,
  J. De Zeeuw,
  J. W. v. Raay.

ON CANADA'S DEVIL'S ISLAND

10 March, 1929

Cheney's Island (Devil's Island), is one of the smallest of the Grand Manan Islands and is located in the Bay of Fundy some seventeen miles from the coastline of Canada. This island, as far as it is known, was discovered by Captain William Cheney in the beginning of the 19th century. History tells us that Captain Cheney fled to the East Coast of Canada and buried himself on this small island, far from civilization, after having shot down two members of his ship's crew. He was married and although we did not find his or his wife's grave, the graves of their son and his wife (died in 1884 and 1876) indicate that the Cheneys lived on the island until shortly before the coming of the 20th century.

It was in the fall of 1925 that the current owner asked us to occupy the island and make it productive. This had been attempted a number of times before but up to then it had been impossible to find permanent inhabitants. The residents of the neighbouring islands, simple, sturdy fishermen, didn't like Devil's Island and at first tried to discourage our plans because, they claimed, the island brought bad luck to its inhabitants.

Nevertheless we accepted the offer and our small group (composed of husband and wife, three children and myself) arrived on the island after it had, in some measure, been brought up to an inhabitable state. The trip from St. John, New Brunswick took four days and was made in part by boat, wagon, canoe and on foot. As soon as our animals (a small number) arrived and the most necessary repairs had been finished on the farm buildings, the specially hired labourers returned to their islands and our truly isolated life began.

Because we had been supplied with plenty of wood and food it was not necessary to go to work immediately and so we had some time to initiate a more careful exploration of our estate. Our first scouting trip, in the farm buildings themselves, in fact, was crowned with success. We found traces of earlier habitation such as a copy of a 1898 *Montreal Star* addressed to Mr. Warren Cheney. According to the information we had previously received, Warren Cheney had sold the island to our employer in 1899. After the house had been examined from top to bottom and the lady and the children had been settled in a relatively satisfactory manner (even though it was primitive), Jan, the farmer, and I decided to begin our own scouting trip.

We set out at dawn accompanied by Brown the dog, and after having left the hilly area we began to cut a path through the dense bush which covers a significant part of the island. We soon realized we couldn't accomplish anything without a knife (machete?) and axe. Now the real pioneer work began. The trees were so crowded and the brush so thick, that cutting a path could only be done very slowly and with great difficulty. If we had only wanted to get through it would have been easier to start at another spot but this trip of ours had another goal, which was the blazing of a shortcut from the farm, through the bush, to the sea. The road had to be wide enough to be traveled by ox and wagon.

We worked from dawn to dusk and although we moved ahead extremely slowly we were absolutely determined to build the road. From now on, we took the saws along and used our two oxen to clear up troublesome stumps. On the fourth day we found the previously mentioned graves, right in the middle of our path. They were rough, weathered stones and while there were traces of an inscription we were not able to decipher them clearly. The entire following day we dedicated ourselves to cutting back the brush and cleaning the gravestones. There were three graves, those of the man and his wife and the grave of a daughter who was buried in 1864 at the age of 23.

Meanwhile it had become necessary to take short breaks from our work in order to look after our animals. We had two horses, two oxen, four cows, five pigs, one hundred sheep and some thirty chickens. Among our rusted tools and used equipment we found some bells which we tied on the ram, the oxen and two of the cows. We then let them run free and were at all times able to locate them. Slowly the effect of our reconstruction became more apparent. We built two new wooden bridges, cleared and ploughed land, something we had originally thought impossible because the soil was so full of big stones that even the tremendous strength of our two oxen, Back and Dym, was barely enough to haul them out. We even found two neglected boats in a small collapsed boathouse. After a day's difficult work we were able to repair them to the extent that we could float around in them without being in mortal danger.

Because I'm not a farmer by vocation, this rough life seemed somewhat difficult. The loneliness, in particular, was quite pressing as was being absolutely cut off from the outside world. Often, while I was working, my thoughts would wander back to the far distant Netherlands and I would think about my former occupation which had been so totally different. Evenings, after work, we three would sit around the big open fireplace; not much was said but a lot of thinking was going on. I sat there in my rocking chair, sleepy and dead tired, staring into the flames which took on all kinds of fantastic forms and filled the room with whimsical shadows and lit the faces of Jan and his wife with a red glow. If we spoke, it was about our plans or about the Netherlands, so far away. Jan and his wife would then speak about their little village in the Betuwe and I talked about The Hague, which they had once visited. It seemed so impossible, there in our wilderness, that cities, trains and electric street lights really existed. But there were problems, of course, which appeared from time to time in our Robinson Crusoe life. For example, bread had to be baked. Jan's wife, although unfamiliar with the task, approached the job with some enthusiasm. When it was ready we ate it with manly courage even though we had to bear down on the knife with considerable energy when cutting it. A number of hours after eating we all had violent stomach cramps and came to the conclusion that the intention had been better than the result. However, after a number of weeks the bread got better and we began to direct our attention to churning and cheese making, a job the lady was completely familiar with. The supply of pork was almost gone and so we decided to slaughter a sheep.

I discovered that wild cows are not the most agreeable company. While I was milking a particularly sensitive one, I slid off my stool and totally against my will, directed a terrific kick into the stomach of the unsuspecting animal with my heavy rubber boots. She acquitted herself well—the best proof of that was the condition of the stall when she had said her piece. The last thing I saw was Jan who, as he was working himself out of a big puddle of milk, was trying to reach the door on his hands and feet. This cow later went mad and had to be shot.

And so, the days went by, far from the cities and their bustle, with numerous seals in the bay and the Northern Lights in all their beauty in the heavens in the evening. The road through the bush was finished, the barns and stalls were repaired, the land was ploughed and we hoped that when we ploughed again in early spring everything would be ready for cultivation.

As we moved steadily into fall, and winter was almost upon us, we decided to supplement our wood supply. Long days were spent in the bush and after we felled and transported the logs we had more than a week of sawing and stacking. Now we had a supply which we hoped would see us through the severe freeze-up. Meanwhile November had arrived and the days were getting shorter. The evenings, which were getting longer, were spent in the house but even then there was more than enough work to do, such as sharpening axes, saws and so forth.

Before the severe frost came we still had a lot to do, among other things we had to get new provisions. The trip would take days and then we would see the outside world again. We were already rejoicing at the expectation of fresh cigarettes and a visit to the local barber who, we hoped, would be able to rectify the havoc created by our own clipping efforts.

17 March, 1929

While the original intention had been to make the journey together, we had to give up this plan. After mature deliberation we decided that I would go alone. My route would carry me over Ross Island which was within reach of our island in a number of ways. Because the Bay of Fundy has an ebb and a flood, just like the North Sea, we decided I would leave the following Saturday morning at slack tide and try to reach the other side with a horse and wagon. Although the trip would not be totally without danger, we had been told that it could be done. It looked better than going with a boat at high water, as I would be able to use the horse and wagon on my further journey.

Friday afternoon and evening were spent making up a list of necessities although when this was finished, we concluded that, considering the amount of supplies, it would be much better to have a moving van than a small two wheel buggy. As a result, one or another necessity was reduced.

The moment arrived the following morning at eight o'clock as Jan and I rode away from the farm. Jan would turn back at the shore but he wanted to assure himself that I was leaving it at the right spot. If you use the shallow parts it's possible to reach the surrounding islands at low water. When we arrived at the shore Jan got out and after having once again warned me to be careful, he urged me to reach the other side as quickly as possible because, according to his calculations, a crossing between the two tides was just possible with very little play

Darling, my horse, familiar with water, obeyed immediately and we were soon on our way. I turned around once more, called a word of goodbye to Jan and then focused all my attention on the water ahead of me. Some places were treacherously slippery and others deep, so great care and dexterity were necessary. Although it was my intention to cross over as straight as possible, I soon discovered that I had to drive in a zig-zag pattern because of the deep spots. As a result, I progressed very slowly. A number of times, the places were so deep that I was forced to stand on the wagon box as Darling swam, more than walked. After a number of hours I neared the other side, just in time because the water had come back up and during the crossing of the last deep spot it flooded my riding boots. The horse had to swim a number of metres and I felt how the powerful current almost dragged us along.

On Ross Island I was met by Wesley, my employer. The little man with lively blue eyes smiled at me and said, "You're just in time Sonny!" and he was right, I had completed the journey in the nick of time. After lunch I went on to the other shore of the island. Wesley accompanied me mat far. The plan was to leave the horse and wagon behind and to take a boat from Ross Island to Woodward's Cove. On arrival, we put the buggy and Darling in a stall on one of Wesley's farms and went on our way to the waterfront, readied our boat and set out from shore. Wesley had offered to accompany me to Woodward's Cove and would return the following morning. Meanwhile, evening had come and dead quiet lay on the whole area, broken only by the occasional splashing of a seal or the rush of a flock of ducks passing over, our heads.

Just as the sun disappeared the sky lit up with a fiery glow as if Woodward's Cove was engulfed in fire and flame. Wesley and I took turns rowing. We spoke little and smoked our pipes. Since I wasn't going to go on until the following day we didn't have any particular haste. One by one the lights began to appear on the islands, at the same time as the darkness fell quickly and the islands themselves became less distinct. It was so quiet that I almost didn't want to break the silence with words. Involuntarily my thoughts drifted back to my friends and relatives so far away from me. I was so immersed in my thoughts that I was suddenly surprised by Wesley's friendly voice, "What's wrong Sonny? Let's hear one of those old Dutch songs."

At about eight o'clock we ran up the beach at Woodward's Cove and set out for Bill Russel's farm. A visit in these back districts is so unusual that it's practically a celebration. Soon after our arrival we were sitting at a heavily laden table. After supper came the big attraction, the gramophone, and hidden away in a big chair by the fire I listened to the music. They were old English songs such as "Sing me to Sleep" and "Home Sweet Home." Perhaps that's where I learned to appreciate the humble coal oil lamp whose soft yellow light has compassion and hides us from the glances of others with its soft shadows.

These simple people like to go to sleep on time and by ten o'clock everything was in deep rest. After having helped with the milking the following morning, we went on; that is Wesley went back while Bill accompanied me. We went on foot and in order to combine the pleasant with the useful Bill shot two ducks which he left temporarily with a farmer, intending to pick them up on the way back. My destination, North Head, the principal town in the Grand Manan Islands group, is separated from Woodward's Cove by a so-called passage which can be waded at low water. Bill was going to accompany me to the store to see if there was any mail for him and to stock up on cigars and tobacco. Because they wear high rubber boots secured by a belt at the waist on the islands, wading across such a passage is an everyday event. It was a real thrill for me and when we arrived at the water and began our trip, I once again thought of the tremendous contrast with The Hague.

Some places were so shallow that the water was no higher than my ankles but sometimes the water reached the very top edge of my rubber boots and every move had to be made thoughtfully and carefully. Towards noon we arrived at North Head after I had acquired soaking wet feet because I had slipped on the slick seaweed covered bottom. The water which had run into my boots made walking very difficult.

In North Head we were driven to the General Store and Post Office by a friendly farmer in a Ford and when I was comfortably seated in that little Ford I almost felt like an explorer back in the inhabited world. That afternoon I did my chores in the little town, ordered and paid for my supplies and then was free until the following morning.

At the barber's I let them cut my hair short and even though it wasn't on my list, I bought hair clippers with the intention of immediately repairing the havoc on Jan's head on my safe return. Meanwhile, the whole village had invited me to stay the night but because Wesley had given me the address of a friend I went to his house. Jack Wetmore's house was one of the most convivial places in the world that you could imagine, a real "Home." That evening there were more visits to Jack's than had occurred in months and he poked me in the side, laughingly saying that the female section of the visitors appreciated the "Handsome Dutchman."

The following day we brought the provisions and the rest of the purchases to Jack Wetmore's homestead and I made my preparations for the return trip which would begin the following morning. That evening Jack and I went to the Store; the gathering place for the masculine part of the population. One sits there on benches around a large open stove and hears the news of the day in those remote regions. That evening I got a good look into the hearts of those simple fishermen and hunters and the story which I wrote a number of years later in America was therefore entitled: "Hearts of Gold."

My return journey, which I began the following morning at dawn, was made (with a few small differences) in almost the reverse order of the trip to North Head. Only now there were some very serious problems because I had with me some four hundred pounds of foodstuffs and other goods as well. Even though I had all kinds of help from my new friends, the transfer of goods from wagon to boat and boat to wagon took up a lot of time. Three days later I was greeted on Ross Island by Wesley and Jan.

Darling and the wagon had, in my absence, been brought back to Cheney's Island by Wesley and because it seemed to make more sense to make the last stage by boat the two had crossed over to Ross Island, each in a boat. It was now exactly a week since I had set out. After breakfast we went to the shore and loaded the packages in the two boats, distributing the weight as much as possible and keeping in mind that Jan weighed eighty-five pounds more than I did.

We were almost in the middle when I discovered that my boat was leaking and taking on water in a most disquieting manner. I rowed with all my might and at the same time transferred as much of my freight to Jan as possible. I reached the shore at the same moment as my boat filled up and sank and Jan reached over with a powerful swoop and brought the one hundred pound barrel of flour to safety. We got off pretty lucky and after we had piled our goods on the shore we went to the farm to get Darling and the wagon. On returning to the shore we loaded everything on the little wagon, emptied our boats, which we dragged high up on the beach and set off.

That was an unlucky morning for us because, suddenly, one of the two wheels of the little wagon broke and almost all of the baggage was thrown to the ground. The already somewhat-damaged, barrel of flour landed on its side with a violent crack and only by a handy manoeuvre were we able to save most of the contents. Jan, violently angry, sat gathering coffee beans in his cap, while I was busy sorting out our belongings. When we had things organized again, Jan went and got the flat wagon and Dym and Back from the farm and this monster, calculated at thousands of kilos, brought us safely home.

I don't have to say that we drank and ate things that night, that are not often eaten or drunk by islanders. As a worthy conclusion to a well-spent week I cut Jan's hair with the clippers. Having finished, totally tired out, we silently sat in front of the fireplace, the lady with a great big slab of chocolate and the men enjoying dime cigars.

The flames played with the great big chunks of pine, shadows danced their fantastic dance, thoughts wandered far, far away. Jan's voice seemed to become softer and softer. When Jan finally woke me up I was in Holland telling my friends and relatives about Canada, as I have just told you.

14 April, 1929

Meanwhile winter had made its entry and it was already beginning to get biting cold. Because we had lost sixteen sheep in one night (they had wandered out into the bay at low water and presumably had not been able to find their way back) we decided to take turns and make the rounds of the island every night. It was on one of these rounds that the wind blew out my lamp. I had neglected to bring along matches and had to go on without a light. It was a dark night and the wind howled through the trees in a most unpleasant manner. All of it made a very ghostly impression.

Slowly I made my rounds, choosing my way through the brush with care until I suddenly heard a sound that made my blood run cold. It was clearly audible over the howling of the wind. It sounded like the moaning of a human being and seemed to come from nearby. My first instinct was to throw away my lamp and run but I couldn't because my legs refused to move. It was as if I was nailed to the ground. Again I heard that awful moan and I shuddered with unexpected fear. I don't remember how long it lasted, it seemed like hours, then I suddenly heard a familiar sound. I realized that one of our sheep was stuck in a ditch nearby and this was the moaning that I heard. After several futile efforts I was lucky enough to free the animal. Because it probably couldn't walk, I took it under my arm and set out on the return trip to the farm. Even though the mystery of that grisly moaning was now solved, I was extremely happy when I once again sat safely in the warm farmhouse.

The surprises, however, were not yet at an end. It was probably about nine o'clock, the three of us were sitting around the fire when suddenly there was knocking on the door. Brown, the dog, barked fiercely. We were so astounded that nobody said anything. Jan was the first to stand and at the same time he took his rifle from above the fireplace mantle. The knocking was repeated and we heard voices outside. Meanwhile, I also grabbed my rifle and we carefully stepped towards the door. Jan slowly opened it but immediately took a step back because outside stood four or five black shadows. It didn't look very auspicious. One of the shadows moved into the light and said: "Put away those guns boys; we're friends." He then told us that they were fishermen and had been driven to our island by the storm. He said they came from the American coast and were lobstering. Would we be so hospitable as to give them shelter until the storm passed?

Jan looked at me and asked: "What do you think?" I answered that I didn't believe that the men had come with bad intentions. "Let's ask them in then," said Jan and going to the spokesman, he said, "Step inside." One after another five men came inside, two of them carried heavy bags on their backs. They were all young men about our age. Four nights and days they stayed with us and even now I think about Dave, Bill, John, Jack and Will with pleasant thoughts. By the time the storm had quieted and they were on their way again we had become good friends. When they left they promised to visit us again at the first opportunity.

After the departure of our five friends our everyday jobs started up again. Because it was cold we spent a lot of time working in the house or the stalls. I had now spent a number of months on Cheney's Island and while Jan and his wife were good to me, my attraction to the civilized world became stronger day to day. One evening after work I told them I wanted to go back to the mainland. Good souls, even though it was hard for them to part from me, they agreed with me and we concluded that I would bid farewell to Cheney's Island when our five friends made their first return visit.

About five weeks later "Dave and the Boys" made their second visit. When I told Dave that I wanted to go back to St. John, he offered to take me to White Head (one of the islands). A small schooner, *The Snowmaiden,* voyaging from Nova Scotia to St. John, was expected there sometime during the week and he assured me that the captain would be pleased to take me along. Because "Dave and the Boys" wanted to leave early in the morning I began to pack my suitcases in the afternoon. When I was finished with this, I made my last rounds with Jan and Brown. We took our guns along because we wanted to shoot a few ducks but even though lots flew into range we didn't shoot. We said little, parting was difficult for both of us although neither wanted the other to know it.

I still remember that last evening, although it was several years ago. Eight of us were sitting around the fire and the boys were talking about the various opportunities to earn money in Canada. We talked about the "Timberwoods" in New Brunswick and northern Quebec. Dave, who had been in Montreal many times, talked about the wonder of this metropolis with buildings thirteen to sixteen stories high (at the present time there's the Royal Bank Building which has 24 stories). The Boys also talked a lot about the "Canadian West" and they advised me to take the "Harvest Train" at harvest time (around August 15 each year) to Winnipeg, as the trip cost about a quarter of the normal price on this special train. Later on in the evening, the discussion began to slow down but Jan and I continued talking. We talked about Holland and also about the great country of Canada because even though we now lived in Canada there was still an enormous amount which we had not yet seen. The evening became rather late before we went to sleep.

Around eight o'clock we had finished breakfast and everything was ready for our departure. I felt so strange, the lady of the house, the children and especially Jan had become so dear to me in the few months that parting from them was extremely difficult for me. This was the second great leave-taking in my life and saying goodbye, like a lot of other things, has to be learned. Even today, I can see the five waving a last farewell on the rocky shore of our island.

After a number of hours our boat ran up the beach in White Head and we were met there by Arnold Russel. Immediately he heartily invited me to stay with him while I awaited the arrival of *The Snowmaiden*. On arriving at his home I was introduced to Mrs. Russel and her two children, Emmy and Edgar. I stayed there two full weeks because *The Snowmaiden* was often delayed by heavy snowstorms. When she finally came and the hour of parting arrived I had once again acquired a pair of trusty friends. That morning Mrs. Russel went around the house very quietly and I sensed that she was avoiding me. At the very last moment however, she arrived with a great big wicker basket which turned out to be full of edibles and other things. She spoke about the pleasant days we had passed, how I went fishing with Arnold, how we had built lobster traps together, how I had assisted in the building of his new boat and among other things had painted the name on it, but more than anything else, how I had helped her with the wash—but suddenly it was all too much for the good lady and the tears came. From time to time, I still keep the Russel family informed about my wanderings and it wasn't all that long ago that I sent them a letter from Buenos Aires.

Bill and John, the captain and his brother, made up the crew of

The Snowmaiden but when we left White Head that morning there were seven of us. In those remote districts it's the usual custom to take along passengers on those boats without a word being said about payment. As compensation one helps the captain with work on board and loading and unloading, which is more than sufficient. My fellow passengers were three hardy Canadians and one wife who got terribly seasick as soon as we were out in the Bay. We dropped the lady and her husband in North Head which we reached towards the evening of the same day and where we spent the night on land. I took advantage of this opportunity to look up a number of my old friends.

When I woke up the following morning I saw that a snowstorm had blown through during the night, something which didn't promise much good. After the ship was cleaned up in the morning and one thing or another was unloaded and loaded, we went on our way in the afternoon. There were five of us now and during the course of the day I wondered a couple of times: where are all of us going to sleep? The riddle was solved that same evening. We anchored, we all helped to make supper, ate, smoked our pipes and very pleasantly sat together in the little forecabin until about ten o'clock. Then we talked it over and agreed that two would sleep in the berths, two on the benches and one on the deck in between. The forecabin, in the bow of ship, ran to a point resulting in two slanting sides, on each was a berth and under each berth an attached bench. During meal times a large leaf was pushed between the two walls and our table was ready.

Before I tell the rest of the story, I have to honestly admit that there was no room, but even if we had had room I doubt that my new friends would have undressed to go to bed. The captain seemed to think it was a very simple business; he took off his shoes, his jacket and that was all—and so did the rest and so did I—because there was no room anyway. Five men lived, ate and slept in that little cubicle (at most about 6.2 m) for ten long days. A large part of our living space was taken up by a great big kitchen stove and keeping it in the desired state and looking after the firewood were a couple of my tasks.

Meanwhile the weather had become very rough. We had already run into a few light snowstorms but on the third day we sailed into a regular blizzard. It was "all hands on deck" and if I hadn't been so busy I probably would have (agonizingly) remembered all my sins because it looked pretty nasty and as if we might end up staying in it. Suddenly we heard a violent crack, then a ripping sound followed by a dull smack. The little ship seemed to stand on its head for a moment, then it dropped very, very deep. We were now extremely grateful that our ship had sails and an engine because it appeared that the top of our main mast had broken off and the sail had ripped. The captain was truly a wonder, he seemed to be everywhere at once, that is with his eyes, as he never left the wheel. After a hard struggle we ran into Deadman's Harbor. Anyone who has ever been there and who knows the history of that sheer, bald, black rock, knows that we had narrowly escaped great danger, thanks only to incredible seamanship.

After having temporarily repaired our damage in Deadman's Harbor, we went on. The following days were clear and bright but the temperature was very low and ranged from −15°C to −25°C which on a large body of water like the Bay of Fundy, makes things pretty uncomfortable. After 10 days we ran into St. John, where we were met with great joy because they had become slightly worried as we were days overdue.

There I was, back in St. John, New Brunswick, a place I had left a number of months before. My first task was to find a room and so I set out for the Y.M.C.A., an institution that has a very high reputation and which I heartily recommend to everyone. The Snowmaiden had to be unloaded now and I valiantly assisted even though the longshoreman's job looks a lot easier than it really is. Although I worked and ate on board The Snowmaiden, I slept at the Y.M.C.A. It was really a blessing that I could now take a bath every evening and have a comfortable bed to sleep in.

After a number of days the unloading was finished and the loading of The Snowmaiden was begun. It was hard work but interesting and healthy. However, everything must come to an end; The Snowmaiden had completed her task and was going back to the distant island world. I said my goodbyes to Bill and John and promised to look them up as soon as they came back to St. John, likely in about two months. The Snowmaiden set sail at high tide and took along a lot of greetings to my friends. I went back to my room and reality took over because I wanted to go and look for work the following day.

19 May, 1929

The Snowmaiden departed and I began to look around for work in St. John. It was the very heart of winter and bitterly cold. Even though the cold in eastern Canada is not as severe as in the West, one feels it a lot more because of New Brunswick's proximity to the sea and the humidity. My room in the Y.M.C.A., for which I paid $4 a day, was very comfortable. About 100 young men lived there and all of them did their best to make me feel at home. And, thanks primarily to their good efforts I finally found work. Finding work in the middle of winter in eastern Canada is not easy and I strongly advise anyone who does not have a large reserve of energy and stamina not to leave for Canada in the winter. I think the most suitable time is in the spring, April or May.

After I had lived at the Y.M.C.A. for about a week, I met a young Englishman, a teacher, Bert Woodard. Bert had come to Canada in the hope of getting a position as a teacher, but he hadn't taken into account that an English diploma was worthless unless one first took a certain course. Besides that, every province in Canada establishes its own requirements, for example, in the province of Quebec, where about 70 per cent are French Canadian, the requirement is that you must be able to teach in French.

Bert and I decided to take a room together because it would be more pleasant, and cheaper. While we both did our utmost best to find work we had little success. It was particularly difficult for Bert, who wasn't physically strong. We went from one office to the other and tried everything. One time, in a bar on the outskirts, where we had been sent to apply for the lumber woods, luck almost shone on us. But sad to say, Bert was not hired because of his lack of physical strength, and I turned the job down because we did not want to desert each other. It was now shortly before Christmas and quite a bit of snow had fallen. Very early on the 23rd of December one of the fellows knocked on our door to tell us that snow shovelers were being hired at City Hall for $2.50 per day. Though neither of us had any experience shoveling snow we cheerfully set out for City Hall and—we were hired. We were each given a big shovel and with six other snow shovelers a horse and wagon, and under the leadership of a foreman we went to work.

In most cities in Canada, in fact I believe in *every* city, they leave the snow on the streets as all the traffic in the winter is made up of sleighs. Naturally the snow has to be cleared up here and there, such as on the sidewalks, tram rails and so forth, but along the sidewalks on each side of the street they leave a sufficient reserve of snow to be able to make future repairs such as patching spots that have been worn away. We shoveled snow for two days and together earned $10.

Bert had received an invitation to dine out at Christmas and although he was committed to "out together: home together," and wouldn't go at first, I managed to get him to leave me at home. The invitation came from the minister of the Presbyterian church in which Bert, who had a good voice, sang with the choir. On the 24th of December, after having first freshened up with a bath as usual, we went out to eat. A terrific snowstorm was blowing outside and we were only able to move ahead with great difficulty. On the street corners stood the large well-known iron kettles of the Salvation Army and their silent guardians. I don't believe there's a wanderer in the world who could pass by without doing his—well, doing his duty! A young lady thanked us for our gift and we started talking. So far from home on alien ground, you sometimes get feelings which would otherwise never appear. I believe it was these feelings which made me suddenly ask the young lady if she wouldn't send me one of her "refugees" on Christmas morning so that we could spend a pleasant day together.

We went to bed early that evening because we were tired from that unaccustomed heavy work but it didn't do me much good because my sleep was disturbed by strange dreams. I dreamt that I was sitting next to a great big Christmas tree in my room on Christmas morning and every minute or so there would be a knock at the door and in would come a visitor who would say that he had been sent by the Salvation Army.

We got up the following morning at eight o'clock, wished each other a "Merry Christmas" and prepared our breakfast, which we ate in our room. After breakfast Bert went to the church where he was to sing with the choir and after the service he was going home with the minister. After Bert had gone, I picked up around the room and prepared myself to receive my guest who was to arrive at nine o'clock. I tried to imagine how he would look, where he would be from, what nationality he could be, etc., and I was just deep in these musings when someone knocked on my door. On my, "come in," in stepped a young robust fellow, dressed in overalls, cap in hand. I immediately recognized him as my guest and asked him to sit down. My new friend was called Humphrey, and was an English seaman who had been stranded in Canada and couldn't get another ship. He turned out to be an agreeable person with whom I passed a pleasant day. When I later left St. John he still owed me a small debt and as a point of interest I would like to note that after two years he sent me the last three dollars when I was already living in the United States. Many times during my years of travelling and trekking I have found, by experience, that under the humble duds of the wanderer beats a heart of gold. When Bert came back that evening and we shared our experiences of the day, it seemed that both of us had put a well-spent day behind us.

We had gotten in the habit of singing together in the evenings and that evening we sang the old familiar Christmas carols. We had just finished "The Holy City" when we heard an unassuming little knock on our door. Because it was already late in the evening we were at first afraid that the knocking signified nothing good, but our fear was unfounded because it was our neighbour, a missionary, who came to ask us if we would sing "The Holy City" at the St. John Hospital the following day. I must honestly admit that I found it difficult not to burst into laughter because (in my mind) I could already see us standing there. We argued that our voices were not good enough, that we had never done it before, etc., but the old gentleman was unrelenting. He said, quite nicely, that he thanked us for our acquiescence and that he would come and get us the following morning at ten o'clock and before we could think up anything else in our defence, he disappeared.

For just a moment we looked at each other helplessly and then we both broke into laughter. If the worthy reader has perhaps sometimes heard it said that an Englishman never laughs heartily, he would have been convinced of the opposite had he been able to see Bert, who, with his knees pulled up, lay shaking on my bed absolutely convulsed by laughter. When I finally fell asleep that night I dreamed of multitudes of Holy Cities and whole armies of the sick. On awakening, a blurred memory of something unpleasant came to me and I slowly realized that it was the second day of Christmas. I didn't regard this as unpleasant in itself but Bert was also awake and said suddenly, "Hello Holy City!" and then a light went on. I have always heard it said that pleasant hours pass quickly, though I can't guarantee that, but that a morning it was ten o'clock before we knew it. At exactly ten o'clock our friendly neighbour came to get us and when we were sitting in the streetcar on our way to the hospital we felt like lambs being led to slaughter. When I saw the feared hospital as we stopped, I felt like running. But oh poor fellow, it was too late. We were inside before we knew it. It was like a nightmare!

We were led into a big room where we were met by a friendly old doctor who thanked us in advance for our kindness. Anyway, when we realized that we had lost, we resigned ourselves to the inevitable. Beds were rolled in, nurses came, the pianist who had the courage to accompany us appeared (I believe that I secretly hoped for a miracle which would prevent the performance) and the moment had arrived.

We sang as if our lives depended on it, only I still don't know if the deadly silence which reigned was a sign of emotion or dismay. Everything went pretty well as desired until I suddenly noticed that besides the patients and nurses and others there was a fairly large group in the adjoining room composed mainly of young ladies. Surreptitiously I poked Bert, who hadn't seen them yet, in his side, and manoeuvred around so that he came to stand in my place. Bert had a very shy nature and blushed up to his ears and looked like he was on the point of abandoning everything and running away.

Luckily it didn't get that far and when the song finally ended we caught our breath and were looking forward to the sight of the familiar streets. But we had rejoiced a little early because the friendly old doctor insisted that I sing "Silent Night" in Dutch. While I was singing Bert was sitting comfortably in a corner and winking at me with a smug smile. I admit, that all during the song I was thinking how I could get even with him for his actions, once we were safely home. Anyway, everything comes to an end and finally, after being overwhelmed with thanks, we were outside again. We also felt very thankful, especially when we were sitting in the streetcar again.

After Christmas we went looking for work again. Bert generally had less success than I did. A couple of times I helped to unload ships in the harbor and received two dollars and a meal. On one of our trips through the docks looking for work and food I saw our tricolour waving for the first time since my departure from the Netherlands. I must admit that the sight of it touched me deeply, an emotion which was naturally not shared by my good friend Bert.

When we got closer we could read the name of the ship and I saw that it came from Rotterdam. In those days I was still very inexperienced, an example being that on seeing the Dutch ship I was convinced that we would get help and work. I learned from the crew that the ship was on its way to Australia, whereupon we inquired if there was a chance of being taken along. They then told us that was the captain's decision and that he was a hard master. I admit that the boys were right because he really was not an easy master. Curtly and to the point he told us that there was absolutely no chance of us working on his ship. The cook, however, had a bigger heart and gave us a beautiful meal and secretly supplied us with enough food for at least two days.

The following day we applied for a job at the Atlantic Sugar Refinery and I was hired. Even though I was sorry for Bert, we were both glad that at least one of us had work. I was assigned to the night shift which worked from seven in the evening to seven in the morning with an hour break at midnight. On the evening of the 31st of December I began my first night. I had brought a lunch pail and a thermos bottle and with both of them well filled, and in a good mood, I went to the factory accompanied by Bert, who wanted to see me off.

I worked in the Atlantic Sugar Refinery for six weeks, twelve hours every night. The work was heavy and consisted of piling up of bags of sugar, loading trains, ships and so forth. Rough characters worked there, many Negroes and the language certainly wasn't suitable for the salon. The halls where we worked were open and cold and even the "laziest" among us worked hard in order to stay warm. The air smelled revolting and while it wasn't paradise "it had to be done."

I'm convinced that first night will always stay in my memory. The unaccustomed work tired me out and the time seemed incredibly long. Finally the factory whistle went. It was five minutes to twelve. Most of the workers went to celebrate New Year's by drinking in the nearby bars but I preferred to quietly eat my sandwich. I had been told that I should go to the place where they cooked out the bags as it was the warmest place in the whole factory. It was true, it was warm, even though it was almost impossible to tolerate the sickly sweet air. Just as I had found a spot on a couple of bags and had a sandwich in one hand and a cup of tea in the other, the whistle went for the second time. It was twelve o'clock— midnight—1925 was gone: a new year, 1926, had arrived. Right there and then, sitting on those sacks, I yelled out, "To the New Year", drank my tea, ate my sandwich and wearily, fell asleep until I was awakened at one o'clock with the suggestion that I get back to work.

The following morning I heard that two of our fellow workers, Negroes who had drunk too much, had murdered a policeman in a quarrel that same night.

3 January, 1930

I've noticed, in the years that I've spent in foreign parts, that people cross the Atlantic Ocean every day, without having the least idea about the country they're going to. Most quickly sell their possessions, buy a boat ticket and collect all kinds of useful and useless things which are not only too expensive but usually impractical as well. Most usually have too little money when they arrive in their new fatherland but they do have all kinds of myths in their heads about "how much there is to earn and how easy it is to earn it."

This is the case with Canada. The government here warns the people never to go to Canada in the winter. The Canadian winter is extremely hard and very long and work is very scarce. However, many young people in the Netherlands have heard. talk about the "Canadian Lumber woods" without really knowing what this means exactly. They imagine that they, young and strong, can easily get a job in the bush. Numerous times I have seen how such young men, from all possible nationalities, risk coming to Canada in the winter. After having found fairly expensive lodging they went looking for Lumber Companies to offer their services to. But no matter how robust, strong and perfectly healthy, they were practically never sent to the bush.

Anybody who knows the Canadian Lumberjack will not be surprised because he's a rough, burly character used to hard physical labour, discomfort and hardship. Furthermore, the young European doesn't know the work methods. Even though he's probably waved an axe around or used a saw at home, he's never ever worked eight to ten hours everyday in the thick bush in deep snow and in intense cold with skilled workers who aren't pleased to be burdened in their work by clumsy colleagues. As well, there are thousands of young Canadians who have handled saws and axes since they were children at home and have always done things on their own. Early on, they helped with felling trees on the farm, building barns, in short they use the axe and saw like a Dutchman uses his bike. I would almost say that for these young men this work is recreation. They're at home in their own forests and used to their cold climate while the young Dutchman has to exert himself to the utmost degree not to fall far behind the others. Eating and sleeping conditions are also primitive and many can't tolerate the crude surroundings and the absence of spiritual contact. One will also notice that the Europeans he does meet are mostly Russians, Swedes, Norwegians and others; people who have lived in more or less similar circumstances at home.

Now, this young European who comes to Canada in the winter to earn money, preferably lots of money, and doesn't succeed in the bush begins to look around in the city for work. That's very difficult, however. He's a stranger; in the past he probably worked in an office or maybe he had technical training. Even though technology and administration, in principle at least, have the same rudiments all over the world, he will discover that what's possible in Europe is not necessarily so in Canada, or vice versa. Then there's the matter of language, or rather languages, because French is almost as desirable as English. And there's something else. Montreal harbor is frozen shut from December to May and during these months shipping is carried on at other places in the East. Naturally, if the shipping of a maritime city is shut down for five months every year, the commerce of the whole city suffers. So there's very little work in Montreal in the winter. Besides that, the little that is available is taken up by local workers. The young Canadians who have worked in "the harvest" for the whole season lose their jobs near the end. Many go to the bush, but many others also come to the cities, preferably Montreal, and look for something. The result is that the few jobs which the young foreigner would otherwise have been able to find can now presumably be better done by hundreds of ready and willing Canadians. I know that this all sounds very somber and not very optimistic but it's the truth and not exaggerated.

One should not and cannot expect support or help, therefore all too much poverty is endured in Montreal in the winter. The Salvation Army and other philanthropic organizations are often powerless to help the many unfortunate cases. The consul is also naturally not responsible for a decision to come out in the winter and is not able to do much more than you can yourself. They'll probably ask you there, in a very peevish manner, "Why didn't you stay home?", which, because of your touchy circumstances, will not make you any happier. I have heard people complain bitterly in such cases and even curse Canada. This is really unfair! It is absurd to expect that if you go to a foreign land you will better yourself financially. One is born in the Netherlands, grows up there, knows the customs and habits, speaks the language, in short, one is at home. Everything helps to the end that one has to and can make a living there. In any case the chance to develop one's talents is the greatest in one's own district. It would therefore be quite illogical if one would suddenly begin to earn lots of money in Canada where you first have to accustom yourself. It's quite apparent that you should consider yourself satisfied if you earn your daily bread in the beginning. Later, when you have accommodated yourself and truly have something to offer your new fatherland you'll probably be able to earn more money if the economic circumstances are better than in our homeland.

Adaptability is also a very desirable factor. How often does one hear young people abroad say "Oh yes, but at home they do this and that—at home that's better—at home... " etc. Imagine if a Canadian in the Netherlands criticized everything with: "in Canada this and that." I believe we'd soon think and perhaps even ask, "why didn't you stay there?" If you want to earn your bread in a foreign country, one of the first requirements is that you adapt yourself, make an effort to understand the people and appreciate and realize that what works at home might not necessarily be applicable elsewhere and that not everything that appears to be foolish and wrong is foolish or wrong in reality.

If you still have it in your head to go to Canada in the winter, then take special care to have a healthy amount of money with you because the possibility of finding work before April is very remote. Living in Canada is not all that expensive if you know where to live and eat. A room costs $3 to $5 a week. If you eat outside the home, something which is often done, you have to figure on about a dollar a day for meals. Full room and board costs $8 to $12 a week in Montreal. One can, naturally, by taking a small room and cooking for oneself, save a considerable amount. If you stretch it you only need $6 a month. It should be noted that you should have $50 with you for every month during the winter. In Canada you usually figure that about $300 are necessary to get through the winter without employment. Things are a little cheaper in the countryside or in the towns but the difference isn't great.

The Canadian is fairly domestic and during the long winter evenings he usually stays home. If he does go out in Canada's winter evenings its usually to practice one or another ice sport. Canadians are great lovers of skiing, snowshoeing, sledding, skating and hockey. There aren't as many public houses here as one finds in Europe. There are a few places where you can drink a glass of beer, there are ice cream parlors and the remainder are restaurants where you can eat. As a result, the newcomer will feel fairly lonely at first, but as soon as he's been introduced to Canadian families, he'll find ample compensation for all the public houses in Europe in their homes. Young and old putter around in the evenings. Hobbies are at a high level. Canadians like to sing and have a very pleasant, interesting song heritage. As well, there are few families without a radio. Nobody has to be bored on days off because Mount Royal, right in the middle of the city, is so beautiful that it's always a pleasure to climb.

I know of a few cases where a European was able to get work with a farmer during the winter, without wages, only for room and board. That's usually dismissed with, "does that guy think I work for nothing?," but you shouldn't do that. That is a completely wrong attitude. Bear in mind that there isn't much to do in the winter and so no money is earned. If you take a job on a farm, you save your own money and in addition learn something about Canadian farming so that in the spring you aren't a greenhorn any more and can go right to work under favorable conditions.

The Canadian farmer is generally an agreeable person. I've heard complaints once in a while, but I've also noticed a number of times that the farmers in question were Europeans who tried to pull the wool over their countrymen's eyes. The best way to look at it is as a training college where you receive free practical lessons and board besides. If one is a farmer by upbringing, he can, in this manner of studying during the winter, acquire a knowledge of Canada and conditions on the land that with coming of spring is equal to the knowledge of the average Canadian. The winter work on a farm is composed of: caring for the cattle in the stalls; supplementing winter supplies, repairs to harness, tools, machines and so forth. So when spring arrives, everything is ready because spring is short and there's plenty of work to do.

At that point the farmer will probably be prepared to pay a wage in addition to room and board, especially if the winter jobs were completed to his satisfaction. If in the spring the outdoors doesn't appeal, you can always go to the city to look for 'work. The chance of success is, in any case, great then.

Nieuwe Rotterdamsche Courant,
29 October, 1927 to 13 November, 1927

LOST AMONG THE RUTHENIANS

29 October, 1927

Almost four days and nights of rapid travel, through three provinces and halfway into a fourth, brought me into a different climate and to the goal of my journey: the hamlet of Innisfree in northern Alberta. It seems a great distance to come just to teach school but the lure of the West had been too great for a routine-sick Eastern teacher. Living the easy life with the Westerners just had to be fine. Tales of adventures among the Ruthenians of Alberta had found their way across the Dominion. In a humdrum existence, coloured by exaggerated expectation, they worked like a driving force.

I was in the midst of a delicious flight of fancy when the train arrived in Innisfree. There's nothing as depressing as a little hamlet in the West in the calm of an early morning. The magnificent "Trans-Continental Flyer" stopped to unload travellers and baggage. Looking around at the few scattered buildings, unpainted and wrapped in deadly silence, I soon felt that I had been thoroughly taken in.

Innisfree is a typical Western hamlet—most of them are the same—a railway runs through the centre with the station on one side and grain elevators on the other. The village is made up of two different sections, an English-speaking population to the south of the railway and immigrant Ruthenians in the northern part. The whole place can be seen in one glance. There are a couple of grocery stores, a hardware, garage, barn, post office bank branch, hotel, society building and farther on a public house mixed in with a number of separate houses. The other side is laid out in much the same manner, only the houses are newer and not kept up as well as those of the English-speaking population.

With rather general instructions for a journey of some thirty miles in a northerly direction, I looked for a way to get there. Through the gracious assistance of the little postmaster an opportunity was at last found whereby I could leave for the north in the late afternoon. I was to meet the people on the other side of the track near Pylpiuk's warehouse. Meanwhile I made the acquaintance of the local people. This is quite easy to do in the West. By the time the afternoon was half gone I knew just about everyone in that village. A number of us gathered around a big table in the public house and drank huge glasses of healthy full-flavoured beer at ten cents a glass.

Gloomy Tales

If I had taken any notice of gloomy tales I would never have set out on the journey to my school. My new friends painted dark scenes of poverty, adversity, difficulties and hardships. In the middle of one of these stories about the northern districts, the little postmaster arrived to tell me that my travelling companions were prepared to leave.

Right in front of Pylpiuk's big store stood an old and pathetic looking team of horses, hitched to an old worn-out wagon. Up front sat an old black witch of a woman with a grey kerchief over her head wearing a dark dress which hung down to her dusty high boots. Her face was weathered like the wrinkled skin of a frozen apple. Out of her otherwise toothless mouth appeared two yellow fangs which stuck out over her bottom lip. She looked at me. Hmm?

"Excuse me," I said, "Are you the people who are going to take the teacher to S...?"

She growled.

"Excuse me," I said, this time a little louder, "Are you going north to S...?"

She growled again and then pointed with her hand to the store, as she bared her teeth in a grisly, sickening smile.

Turning my head I saw the very attractive figure of a young girl coming out of the door of the store. She had pretty blue eyes and a very delicate face with a high blush. She placed her purchases in the wagon and turned to me, saying, "Are you the teacher, yes? My mother doesn't understand you. She doesn't speak English as well as I do."

I stared at her, wondering how it was possible that such a beauty could be the daughter of this ugly old crone. Perhaps noticing my puzzlement she went on, "Maybe you are ready now? We go far, night come queek, run in da dark no *dobra*, no goot." She sat down next to her mother and I rode along behind them in the bed of the wagon. My first look at the woman had made me think that the men in the bar had been correct, but the presence of such an enchanting daughter drove such thoughts away again. I was convinced that I could keep myself well amused in the winter.

Two long hours passed in this fashion. It was extremely uncomfortable back in the wagon box to be suddenly shaken among my baggage and to be bounced hither and yon against boxes of groceries and protruding nailheads. Besides that I had imbibed a little more beer than absolutely necessary and this greatly added to my discomfort.

After a little while we stopped to give the old horses a rest and to have a small snack composed of sardines, soda biscuits and lukewarm water. To my great satisfaction the mother spread a large blanket in the wagon box to sleep upon and in this fashion made it possible for me to take the place next to her daughter. The miles, which at first had been long and aggravatingly slow in passing, were now all too short and the ride seemed a pleasure. In this manner we slowly rode into the dark North. She told me, in her peculiarly precious accent, about the life of her people and listened, with amazed eyes, to the stories of the modern East.

The End of the Journey

We bumped along like this for about five hours. The land became rougher and wilder with every mile and by the end of the journey it was mountainous. The rocky road lay between and over mountains and hills and we passed many beautiful little lakes dimly lit by the moon. My little nymph, weary from the long journey, gave up the reins and leaned heavily against my willing shoulder. We were on top of a mountain when I spied a thatch-roofed house in the bush, standing in the bend of a small swift-flowing creek. Instead of passing it, the horses turned into the gate by themselves and went straight to the barn. The girl awakened from her dream and jumped from the wagon. Turning to the house she put her hands to her mouth and called out in a soft full voice "Hola!... Pietro!... Dmytro!... Hodda Sedda!... Veekya Hyto... pro-faasar pazjka!"

Two big sturdy boys appeared in the doorway and came walking towards us. The girl turned to me and said "Come on... we're home, I've called my brothers to unload your baggage and to put the horses in the stall. Come we'll go inside."

The old woman was busy in the kitchen of the hut fixing a light supper, while in the other room the daughter was busying herself with making up a bed for me. A little later the two sons came inside and shortly thereafter we were at the table. The supper was composed of the strangest food I had ever tasted: a soup made of beets and other vegetables, another dish was made out of an earth-coloured cheese and mashed potatoes rolled in dough and cooked in stock. After that a dish of wild berries and full glasses of whole milk. The boys were very shy and left the talking to their mother and sister. The mother was far from being a conversationalist. My bed was in the other room, for this occasion reserved only for me. They with their mother and sister slept in the kitchen on straw beds. Objections from my side against it were not accepted, it had to be that way and no other.

Sunday morning I woke up quite early because of the bustling in the kitchen, so at six o'clock I breathed in the fresh morning air. Mrs. Matzerchek, the witch of the previous day, was already busy putting the kitchen in order, the sons did a number of light morning chores, while Zanovia, the daughter was already in the fields after the cow. Workday, feastday or Sunday, the daily farm chores had to be done. Many people tend to ignore this. Besides the ordinary work on the land and bringing in the harvest it's necessary to look after the machinery, to prepare for the winter and to feed all kinds of cattle.

Around nine o'clock we sat down for breakfast and discussed the plans for the day. We would go to church, about three miles further on, where I would also find my school and be able to arrange the details of my contract with the settlers of the district. The chairman would accompany me to the school, show me this and that and tell me about the pedagogical work I was to do there.

The table was hurriedly cleared and the horses were harnessed, while the mother and daughter quickly dressed. Around ten o'clock we were on the road.

The Church Service

The road led us through low underbrush and over a great expanse of newly broken land before we came out on the highway. We passed many people on foot and in buggies. It was a lively hubbub.

The women and girls were dressed with kerchiefs of all kinds of sharp bright colours. They all turned around to look curiously at their new teacher and my blond Zanovia was proud of her companion. Her brothers were very reserved, if indeed they weren't completely silent.

Very quickly we were at the church, if the shack which served as a church could be permitted such an elevated name. It was a hut built of clay, on the top of a little hill, unpainted and with a sagging roof, giving the impression more of an old worn-out barn than a church. Wagons and buggies were scattered around the yard. The horses which were hitched to them picked at the hay and straw which had been thrown down in front of them. Men, women and children sauntered about, laughing and talking in their peculiar strange language. The crowd suggested a multicoloured painting; someone who had been there recently could easily have imagined that he was at a feast day in Middle Siberia.

The little church was filled with people, all standing. When we came in they were singing an old "Moody and Sankey hymn," translated into Ruthenian. A bench was set down for us. The song was followed by a prayer, the longest I have ever heard. Not only the minister but different members of the congregation also prayed and as one person quit praying another would immediately go on until he was finished, only to pass the prayer on to another. There was one whose prayer lasted seventy minutes. During his prayer the people wandered in and out without causing the least disturbance. I would have also dearly liked to do that because the air in that little place was almost unbearable. The only ventilation came through the opening and closing of the door. The Black Hole of Calcutta was an airy drawing room compared to this shed.

Zanovia's Fiancé Appears

The service ended and I had a terrible longing for some fresh air. A man in a boiler suit was waiting for me. He was not a very handsome character. He had a bristling beard which appeared not to have been shaved for at least three weeks.

He said, "My name is Pietro Boyda. I am chairman. We have meeting now, wait!" He left at once to round up the rest of the school committee. A little later he came back followed by three other men, whom he introduced.

"This is," he said, "Wasyl Taschuk, this one is Onesim Drabink and this is Ivan Sakusta." He asked me to wait a moment while they held their meeting a small distance away leaning against an old wagon. While they were discussing things with great gesticulations in Czechoslovakian I patiently stood waiting against the church wall. My girlfriend, the beautiful Zanovia Matzerchek, circulated among the people who were standing at a distance staring at me and brought them over to me one by one. Every woman made a small curtsey and every man took his hat off, each passing by to make room for the others who followed. This took about a half an hour.

This one she said is Wasyl Bohaichuk, this Anastasia Bohaichuck, this is Hryn Hryniw, this Pietro Topolinsky and this is Stephania Schertianka and so forth until I had met all of them, that is, all except one; and this was her fiancé. He stepped forward: he was a rough-looking fellow with a brutish face and very short hair, which stood up on his head just like nails.

"Dees," said Zanovia, "ees the man what I love and what love I'm. Hees name are Michael Taschuk."

I was immediately disappointed in the man. I found it difficult to believe that such a lovely girl could find even one attractive thing in this big brute. I would probably have put those thoughts into words if the meeting hadn't ended at that moment and I was called over to the school committee. They had decided to hire me at a salary of $1,200 on the condition that I would fulfil my obligations as is required of a good country school teacher. The contract was agreed to and the secretary led me to the school. I had to wait again at the school for the chairman, who would come a little later with the keys.

I had already attempted to imagine what the school would look like and came to a realization of the difficulties of teaching in such a sparsely settled district. When we arrived at the building, which stood alone in the middle of a great plain, I felt even more disappointed. It was about 20 feet long and 15 feet wide, unpainted and the few windows which were in it were cracked or broken. We came up to the old door by a poorly fastened set of stairs. The foundation had fallen out in one corner and as a result the whole monster leaned to starboard. But... I didn't see any teacherage! So I asked Zakusta if there was one. "Oh, yes, sure," he said, "we'll find it when we get to the other side of the school."

First a Look in the House

And indeed we found one. There stood the little house in all its insignificance as if it was itself aware of its shortcomings. An awful little hut, perhaps large enough for a big butcher's dog to live in. The doors and windows were closed so I couldn't do anything but wait patiently until the chairman arrived with the keys. While I waited, my attention was attracted to some rising wisps of smoke above the willows which stood on the opposite bank of a little stream. I went over there and saw that the smoke was coming from a clay house about as big as mine but built more solidly and comfortably. I knocked and a rough voice told me to come in. The single room was furnished with a bed, a table, a bench and a clay oven, everything was homemade and very tidy. The father, who had answered my knock, lay on the bed enjoying his pipe. The mother was busy feeding a year-old baby and meanwhile tried to prevent the other nine from bothering the father.

The man introduced himself with, for me, an unpronounceable name. A word which appears to me most similar to the name was "Loophole." In any case, Loophole was the name which I gave to him from that time on. Unfortunately enough he couldn't speak or understand a word of English, but he seemed to be a friendly fellow. A conversation with him in his own language must have been entertaining. With our mutual language ignorance, we couldn't do anything but sit and soberly gape at each other. The children gathered around the mother, and the whole family, the youngest baby included, stared curiously at me.

Having Decided to Return

Pietro Boyda had brought along the wrong keys so we had to force the door with an axe. A rusty old stove was hauled out of the school, along with a number of stovepipe lengths, and swiftly set down. The chairman seemed to be in a hurry to go home for supper.

When he was gone I made a fire in the stove, put this and that on to cook, unpacked my bed clothes and other necessities and began to put my furniture in order. There was an old bed, a stove, a chair and a few small shelves with a half dozen pots and pans, unpainted wall and floor, a battered door and two windows without panes in a sidewall: this was all that belonged to my cosily appointed house.

I began to feel very disappointed and dejected. After all the business of the day the silence was disconcerting. With the swiftly falling darkness the chilly landscape became chillier and chillier and the old school building, opposite my windows, appeared terribly spooky. This also became worse with the coming of darkness. The prospect of spending a winter in such a shack was too depressing to think about.

Waiting and blowing on the fire, my disappointment grew to anger. Meanwhile I began to make up my bed, and when I turned the straw mattress over I felt disgusted. There were innumerable bedbugs in it. Shuddering, I threw it back down. My anger now became rage. I turned back to the stove to stir up the fire a little. But I must have poked it up a little too hard as all the stovepipes fell down, covering everything with soot. The room filled up with thick smoke like that from green wood. I threw some water on the fire and ran away to get help from Loophole. After several hours we managed to clean the mess up somewhat.

After a half-cooked supper I lit up my pipe and tried to go to sleep. Because of the bugs my bed was completely unusable. So I took my blankets and for good or ill made up a bed on the floor of the school. It was uncomfortable, cold and very hard. For a long time, at least it seemed like hours, I turned and twisted to ease the pain which I felt in different parts of my body. Many mice gnawed on the floor and sometimes galloped right across my body. l had just drifted off to sleep when something gave a penetrating scream, not twenty metres from my door. In an instant I was sitting up in bed. The scream was followed by a choir of barking and howling which made me shiver. I quickly came to the conclusion that it must be prairie wolves. I turned myself over and went to sleep.

I had gone to the West for adventure and a change of work. Up to now I hadn't found any adventure, but surely change, which I had not longed for in the East and I thought to myself, "If only I had stayed at home where I belonged."

13 November, 1927

The Transformation of Young Russians into Canadians

The time quickly passed, the harvest was brought in. The frost and the cold north wind gave the land a bare appearance. One night a frigid snowstorm began which lasted for days. The fine snow drifted across the ground like winter ghosts howling out of the North. When the storm stopped the land was covered with a spotless snow carpet which came up to the knees. The winter had come to stay for eight months. For a number of weeks I was a captive in my house and school. Every day was an echo of the previous one and an exact duplicate of the next one.

I would wake up about seven o'clock in the morning, stick my head out from under the blankets (where I had tried to keep it warm) and peer at the stove, trying to get up enough willpower to get up and start a fire. After a little while I would jump out of bed and run to the stove, pile some paper and other flammable things in it and quickly start them on fire. After that, back into the warm bed with a jump, gasping and shivering like someone who just has taken an ice bath. As soon as the room had become sufficiently warm, I would get up and get dressed and fix my breakfast. First I would put the waterpail on the stove to melt and then put the water in the kettle to boil. While I was doing these morning chores, I usually saw Loophole's daughter, Jena, go to the school to look after and fill the heaters. This job brought her the capital sum of five cents a day.

Around nine o'clock the children arrived at the school, brought by their parents or bigger brothers in huge snow sleds. At nine thirty I began my daily teaching; a thousand times the same thing for sixty-four children from six to fifteen years of age. Some had very light and others very black hair, but all had the same sort of little stumpy nose in an otherwise well-formed face. I had one exception in my class, a little boy who had probably been absent when the noses were handed out and then had to do with what was left over.

He called me "Dummy"

It was very difficult to deal with these children. They had never learned any diligence, nor did they know anything about obedience. This was, as far as I can figure, the result of the coming and going of most of the Western schoolteachers, especially in the most northerly settlements. These, mostly young, teachers, just from the Normal School, moved from school to school, staying at each place for only a few months. In the last two years there had been six different teachers at my school. Each had done little more than repeat the work of his predecessor. Usually shortly after this repeat work they were either again prepared to leave or forced to. As a result the children were behind in everything. Luckily we are now going in a better direction, thanks to the Alberta Department of Education and that very useful institution the "Alberta Teachers Alliance."

When the noon hour arrived I would hurry to my shack to make some lunch and gobble it down to have a few moments of peace and calm. This was usually impossible as somebody was always knocking at my door, and upon answering a crying child would come in. If I then asked, "What's the matter?" it would be: "Sir, Rosie, took my pencil," or "Sir, Wasyl is hitting me," or "Sir, Pietro called me *caDusta* (dummy)," and so on until it was time to start the afternoon session. The work in the afternoon was usually a repeat of the morning efforts. In the evening when the children had left the school, I sat there preparing the lessons for the following day. Notwithstanding the fact that I had nearly been driven crazy during the course of the day by their annoying manners and the noise which they made, I still seemed to miss them when they were gone. Everything was so deadly quiet then. Long after their joyful shouts had died away over the hills, I would sit quietly in the dark room feeling bored and longing for companionship even if it was from those rough children.

After a real bachelor's supper, usually consisting of potatoes, eggs and some steak, and after the dishwashing and putting away of plates, I would sit down to an evening of reading, writing or dreaming. During the endlessly long winter evenings these things would soon bore me, and because I had nothing else to do, I would play some Patience or express my thoughts with a big question mark. I became very expert in sitting by the stove, peering at the wall, ignoring everything, like someone who only gets up to keep the stove going and then goes back to bed again.

Daniel Saganiuk and his Moonshine

Every week I would go the post office. Friday evening, right after school, I would leave my house and stumble through deep snow, over muskeg and hills halfway through the big Vermillion Valley, until I arrived at the little shack which served as a post office, about six miles from the school. The postman came from the village of Manville to this far in our district and then went back along another route. Sometimes he was hours late because the roads had suddenly become impassable, but he came anyway, the poor devil. While I waited, I usually made a visit to a teacher and his wife, who lived a little further on. Often I would stay there until late in the evening enjoying their cultured conversation and refined language. This couple had come to a homestead in northern Alberta from the heart of London. Their courage is incredible and there's no question but that they will succeed, like many Europeans before them.

Every once in a while I would also get a visit from people who lived in the immediate neighbourhood. The most interesting of them all was the hospitable Daniel Saganiuk. Because he had an artificial leg I called him "Peg-leg-Dan." On a certain night this lovable friend arrived at my shack and clumped inside with a big bottle under his arm. As is the general custom here, he came right to the point. He put the bottle on the table, sat on my bed, looked at me from under his bushy eyebrows and asked: "Do you drink?" I answered, "Every once in a while."

"Maybe you'd like one now?" he asked again. "That depends on what it is," I said, meanwhile looking at the bottle with some suspicion.

"Well," he said going on, "I've got a bottle of fine moonshine (a type of alcoholic drink with a despicable taste) which I've made myself. It's very good, exactly like the stuff you can buy in the store. It's also very old, I made it last week Friday, so it's three days old already. You've got to have a taste!" He filled up one of my cups with his "very old" spirits and drank it up, seemingly with great satisfaction.

"You can see it's good," he said.

In any case, he was still standing there healthy and alive, so I decided I might as well chance it and have a taste. Brrr…! It was awful. I had a taste in my mouth as if I had drunk a mixture of sulphuric acid and vinegar. It felt like a quantity of molten lead had taken my Adam's apple along with it. It squeezed my throat closed. I heaved and sputtered enough for three people while Daniel beamed with satisfaction.

"It's good, eh!" he said.

He seemed to judge the drink according to the effect it had on me. The more fuss I made the better it was.

"Yes," I said at last, "it's the best. How much do you want for it?"

"A dollar-fifty."

I paid him and got rid of him. When he was gone, I carefully considered having another taste but finally decided to let the poison neutralize itself in the bottle. In any case it was better there than in my body.

Salute your Lady

Most everybody there drank or made moonshine. Those that made a business of it were great competitors. A good method of lowering the production costs was dilution with water. Since this significantly diminishes the strength of the poison some thought had to be given to remedying this. This was usually done by the addition of a cheap kind of poisonous substance. In one case I knew of a man who used "Copenhagen Snuff" for this purpose. A significant quantity could be found in all his bottles. Even pure moonshine is dangerous to drink but the adulterated kind is absolutely poisonous.

Lately I've been at a number of different dances whenever they've been held within a distance of twenty miles. It's very common to go fifteen or twenty miles (mostly on foot or in buggies on rough or unpaved roads) to attend a dance, and one has to do it, if one wants to find a little entertainment. They're all exactly the same, so it doesn't much matter which one I describe. So let's take the first and the best I experienced.

One evening after school, a neighbour by the name of Onesim Myharo came to invite me to go with him to a dance which was being held about twelve miles to the west. After putting on my best clothes I walked along with him to his house, about two miles west of my school. In contrast to most of the families there, the Myharos were only five in total. There was Sam, the father, a straight, skinny (but muscled) old man, a former cavalryman in the Austrian army, the mother, a colossally big and friendly woman, and Pietro, Onesim and Nicolai, the three sons. During the whole winter they proved to be my best friends, caring for me during my initial period of unfamiliarity and regularly bringing me all kinds of things to eat which came from their own farm and Mrs. Myharo's oven.

After supper Onesim hitched two horses to a big old snow sled and he and I and Pietro got on our way to the party, right into a biting cold west wind. After having gone about ten miles through bush and over hills, we came to a small group of houses on the edge of a frozen pond. The dance hall was a small building, unpainted, and on the inside outfitted on three sides with rough benches and on one end with a somewhat higher platform. When there were enough people, the musicians on the platform began to make some incredibly loud and boisterous music. The fiddlers began to saw unbearably on their violins and a harpist began to hammer on his harp with all his might.

Three groups formed up and the dancing began. During the set they continually sang:

> *Salute that lady and that lady on the left!*
> *All join hands and circle to the left!*
> *All swing out with all-a-man left!*
> *Give your right hand to your partner left!*
> *Meet your partner, home you go!*
> *First couple out to the right!*
> *The ladies cross their lily-white hands!*
> *The gents their black, and then!*
> *Ladies bow and gents bow under!*
> *Swing 'em around, and you swing like thunder!*
> *Do you remember when...? ? ?*

The Ruthenian Dance

The men and boys were dressed in their best overalls and their multicoloured shirts. Some continued to dance with their coats on and nobody took their hat or cap off. The women and the girls twisted around their partners in the most fantastic steps and jumped and stamped with all their might, acting as if they were at a big city dance.

Besides me there was one other English-speaking Canadian present, a teacher from a school, quite a bit farther west. In spite of strong urgings from many young men to come and join them on the dance floor, we sat together in a corner sharing our gloomy experiences. Neither of us knew even one dance much less one of the heavy Ruthenian dances which were being carried on there. The urging of the people to dance along became so strong that it was very difficult to decline. Finally my friend made an agreement with one of the young men. If he could work it so that one of the young girls asked him, he would dance. When the music began again, practically all the women and girls came to our bench and presented themselves. My friend made his choice and there they went. "Poor guy!" I thought. It just happened to be a very fast and complicated (Ruthenian) dance. His arms and legs flew in all directions and patterns and every once in a while I saw an expression of complete fatigue on his face. When at last he was brought back to his place, he was a total wreck.

One time that evening I danced with the beautiful Zanovia. She was the prettiest girl in the hall. It was very difficult to capture her from the vigilant Michael Taschuk, her repugnant worshipper. While I danced with her, he stood in a corner looking at us with burning jealous eyes and drinking poor quality moonshine. Zanovia danced beautifully. She was like an armful of warm feathers. I felt sorry for her when I thought that all too soon she would be tied to a brute like Taschuk. The rumour was going round that their marriage was not far off.

Across the Bed

The night came on: the music got steadily wilder: the moonshine gradually flowed more and more; the noise got greater and greater and what was polite was at last totally forgotten. Everything pointed to a big fight. About three o'clock in the morning the scene began. Those who had come to dance gathered up their stuff and went home, for those who had come to fight their entertainment was now beginning. When we left the hall I saw a number of men lying motionless on the ground and others walking around bleeding violently. I was shaken at seeing this bestial behaviour but Onesim reassured me.

"That's nothing," he said, "that's just the custom. After a little while the moonshine leaves them and they're all right again."

This night I stayed at the Myharos.' The old people were already asleep when we came home. The mother slept in a small bed and the father in a bigger one with little Nicolai. Father and son got up to make room for the three of us and we tumbled into bed half dressed and lying across each other.

Sometimes people moved to try their luck in another district. Then they would hold a public auction to sell all their possessions. People would come from miles around out of the surrounding district bringing things of their own they wanted to get rid of. Sometimes whole families came. Some came to buy, some came to sell, but most came to have a pleasant time as they always make a little carnival out of an auction.

On one good day Eila Triska decided to leave to try his luck at getting in another place. He had made circulars and had posted them in the whole surrounding district. In the evenings he brewed beer and distilled moonshine while his wife and daughters made cakes and all kinds of other delicacies. When the great day broke, crowds of people began arriving from all directions.

A group of French Canadians, about twenty in number, arrived from the settlement on the Saskatchewan River. So it looked like another occasion for a fight, as these French Canadians never get along with the Ruthenians. They never wanted to understand or appreciate each other and this was reason enough for open hatred. The French were often duped by the Russians. The Russians had suffered many "bodily" losses on such occasions and were constantly looking for a chance to wreak vengeance on a single Frenchman. This time was to be no exception for the sport.

A Brawl

Everything went well until late in the afternoon. By then just about everyone was getting full of Eila Triska's moonshine, mixed with whatever they generally brought along themselves. A young Frenchman precipitated the crisis by leaving his friends and going to the barn on his own. In a blink of the eye he was surrounded by the Russians and knocked down. They hammered him with all their might with clubs and fists. His cries for help reached the ears of his friends who dove in and freed him. The group of Frenchmen assembled by a woodpile, surrounded by fifty or more Ruthenians. The latter were afraid and stood at a distance yelling and throwing stones and chunks of wood until the angry Frenchmen finally flew at them like wild animals. Some Ruthenians ran away, a few stayed, but quickly had to give up. It wasn't long before the battle was finished and the French had triumphed. The Ruthenians who could walk had fled and those that couldn't lay spread around the barn, unconscious or too badly wounded to walk away.

For several hours thereafter the pugilists toasted their victory with Triska's moonshine and ate what was left of Mrs. Triska's fine baked goods. When the Frenchmen went home, the Ruthenians came back to the barn to get their horses and get this or that ready for the trip home. The sale had been a great success. The French had won the fight: the Ruthenians had made a lot of noise: and Eila Triska had become richer than ever before.

A number of weeks later the school was closed for the winter vacation and I was free to come and go for a number of weeks. I had planned to make a trip through several French-Canadian settlements near St. Paul de Metis, but the suddenly worsening weather made such a journey very unpleasant, if not totally impossible. So I hired Loophole to take me to the village of lnnisfree and the C.N.R. From there I went to Edmonton where I could enjoy modern life and the association with more civilized people during my vacation.

Dagblad Van Arnhem,
1 December, 1928 to 15 December, 1928

AN AMERICAN SCENE IN THE FAR NORTH

1 December, 1928
The Pas

We just happen to be here at sled dog contest and carnival time. There's dancing and festivity everywhere. I'll be glad when it's over because it's a lot more tiring than a long canoe journey. Unfortunately I have an incredible number of acquaintances and practically the whole "North" is here at The Pas. White and brown, ladies and gentlemen and besides that you've met the majority "somewhere." During the year you've been, so to say, a guest of the fur traders, trappers etc. because when you arrive at a "post" they expect you to stay over for at least a day. They're glad when they see a white. In fact it would be an insult to pass a "whiteman's" house without stopping in. There are always letters to deliver or for you to take along.

And now most are in town. Dancing, eating well and drinking, are the things to do. The races are held during the day and from the evening until six the following morning the feet are flying off the floor. What's being eaten? The restaurant, where I eat, had, among other things, 300 big live lobsters and I don't know how many chickens and turkeys. The lobster was gone in four days in the lobster salad. And drinking? The Pas had a reputation for disliking prohibition and I can almost believe it now. "Carnival is only once a year," they say around here. It's a good thing it only comes once a year!

More than 3,000 dogs accompanied the great crowd here during the festive days. They're the little "pesky ponies" who've brought the revellers to town. One family, Father, Mother, son and six daughters plus two Indian helpers needed 55 of these "ponies" in 9 teams. A new suit for the son, six evening dresses for the "girls," etc. etc. Pa told me that the Carnival had already cost him more than a thousand dollars and that the bigger the girls got the more the brown brothers would have to trap. The difference between the purchase and sale price will also have to be greater. I agreed with all of this completely, especially when he opened a new bottle of champagne.

The day after tomorrow comes the finale; a masked ball. Jack Cullinan got a very bad case; he casually ordered the best dance orchestra from Winnipeg to assist the local one. Friday evening, closing dance. I'm going too and I have a sort of riding costume (Indian and cowboy clothes are not considered carnival costumes here).

Saturday I took the train and then the dogsled to Keet Lake, fifty miles west of the Hudson's Bay railway. I set out expecting to be away for about ten days and that's a good thing because I couldn't afford things as they were. A carnival like that costs a pile of money and if you're no longer a stranger you have to be involved.

Love lies in wait during carnival days and you see a lot of couples, who have "secrets" to tell each other, walking along the river. Too bad that it's too cold to sit on a bench.

When I returned to town, I had a very bad cold. I was in bed for three days. My maid fixed me up very nicely with hot lemon-rum punch. I could have floated away. A glowing stove, heavy blankets and warm punch. It's a patent medicine here but they make it oh so strong: 24 lemons and one big bottle of Hudson's Bay rum. I drank it all. It makes you very sleepy but it helps wonderfully.

8 December, 1928

I returned to The Pas yesterday and received a proposal from a mining company to go far, far away with a partner to a place where we will see our first Eskimo. I talked to the director today and the idea is to investigate the so-called Barrenlands for metals (copper and zinc) and other minerals, copper and oil. Very few people have ever been there, especially in the area where there are supposed to be immense deposits. The only white who's visited this country in recent times is an explorer by the name of Tyrrell, that was in 1898. Other people have been in the Barrenlands but the area is generally regarded as a hell, and why?

1) There's no wood (can you imagine no firewood in these icy temperatures?)
2) The lakes are never ice-free.
3) There's no life, no game, only lots of fish.
4) It's 600 miles north of Fort Churchill. That means that an airplane, which leaves from The Pas, can get there but can't come back because there's no gasoline. It's 1,000 miles from The Pas. The only way to get there now is by train from The Pas to Halifax or Quebec, from there to Newfoundland, Labrador, Hudson Strait, Hudson Bay. From Labrador on, the trip would have to be by fishing boat.

Mr. Flyn, the director, told me he could charter a good boat and crew there. Once we're in Hudson Bay we'll go on to Chesterfield, an inlet in the Bay. We would build a house there with the lumber we had brought along and have enough coal and other supplies for two years. Four men would overwinter there.

It has to be done before the railway reaches Fort Churchill in 1931 because then it becomes too easy to reach the place from there by boat. At present there's no water transportation and no chance to ship food, wood, coal, etc. Naturally this isn't possible by airplane. Another unusual problem is that the airplane leaves here with wheels or pontoons on, in the spring or summer naturally, but needs skis to land because the lakes never melt and there's no beach on the Hudson Bay coast.

The fact that the Eskimos make all their tools out of copper which is 98 per cent pure, indicates that it's not all that improbable that there are lots of metals there. If you saw the ore, you'd think it had come directly from the Stokvis Foundry. They can smelt it without purifying it.

If you figure that 15 per cent purity is regarded as wonderful here and that, despite high wages, they can make a profit on mining and smelting 1.5 per cent copper ore in the United States (the markets and conditions are of course better than here, due to transportation, etc. etc.) then you can imagine what 98 per cent copper ore means. Right, and now I could be one of those four chosen ones. I declared myself prepared to go there, in principle at least, or wherever the company wished to send me, with the exception of the tropics.

The discussion was very businesslike, as is the custom here, but not so businesslike that we didn't talk about Holland, Father, Mother, brothers and sisters.

Mr. Flyn has been everywhere in the world. He's a little man but very clever. He didn't have much good to say about the Dutch Indies government. They're afraid to let Americans get involved in anything there. A number of important gentlemen in The Hague, with inherited wealth, are sort of the boss there. The business of concessions, and a lot more, doesn't suit them.

Before I left I couldn't resist asking him how it was possible to assemble incredible amounts of capital in the United States just with a snap of his fingers for a basically speculative venture. He laughed, "You'll find out that it's not half as speculative as it appears. We don't get any cash payments for the venture, but a good profit on credit. If we can pay dividends in ten years, then we'll be happy. The four shareholders won't eat one slice of bread less in all those years and it's pretty difficult to spend a million dollars a year if you eat, drink, sleep or travel sensibly and have millions to spend each year." That's what he told me.

Well, I couldn't make any judgements, given the nature of the thing but I hope to experience even that sometime in the future.

If I don't go to Hudson Bay then I'll go to Reindeer Lake, North Indian Lake, Lac La Ronge, Nelson House or Burntwood River, but that's just a summer job. As for Hudson Bay, it's primarily the transportation problems which make it difficult. I told the "manager" that he could send me to the North Pole: it doesn't matter to me where I stand on God's earth. If we were to go, then they would take us there by airplane. They hang the canoe underneath between the chassis. They let us off somewhere and every four weeks they come to see how things are and bring us some supplies. That way I can send mail every four weeks. The company has four airplanes, one of them is a sister of Lindbergh's airplane and is named "The Spirit of The Pas." They also have four De Haviland "Moth' monoplanes.

It's a good thing that I'm not married because they don't like to send married people that far away and besides, married people would rather not go so far away. But what difference does it make to me if I'm in Canada, South America or wherever. As long as you can still get mail from your best friends on earth and you can send letters, it matters little where you are, and anyway you have a lot more adventure to enjoy than in the movies or from a nice book. On those trips you always experience something different and always something you can think about when you're out of there.

This was the case on the last trip to Reed Lake. As luck would have it, I met a rather immature Dutch fellow on the evening of my departure. He came to ask me if I knew of a job for him. We talked, and he was very keen to go with me the next day. Well, he went along but I've had enough. As long as we were in civilization it went all right but then we had two "pack days", that's to say, we had to carry our food, sleeping bags, tent, instruments and tools on our backs and walk across the lake using our compass.

We couldn't make a fire the first night but I had a big lunch of canned meat, sardines, canned cheese, etc., but he felt lonesome there, between the snow and the stars. I had made a kind of wall out of snow blocks and we had to sleep inside it in our eiderdown bags. I had been able to borrow one for him on the evening we met. Well, you sleep in them like you're in your own bed, and not at all cold, but he sat and complained about this and that and how he wouldn't take my job for a hundred dollars a week, etc. etc. etc.

Everyday he was a nuisance and I even had to cut the firewood myself besides cooking three times a day. So I had my hands full. But I'd better shut up about it. Never again in my life. Some people want to earn a lot of money, but in Canada, like everywhere else, you have to do a lot for a lot. As a result I have absolutely nothing to do with Hollanders.

When the railway construction began, a whole bunch arrived here and I talked to a number of them. I even got work for a few, but although it was good work, they came back. One was fired for fighting; one for laziness and two didn't like it. I also helped some fellows with money, but it's finished now. They think that someone who walks across the street in good clothes and knows good people is also immediately required to provide jobs, money, etc. because he's also a Hollander. I had to tough it out in the beginning and they only want to half believe that. No, I enjoy my Canadian friends a lot more.

Apropos, I received a letter from a certain Denkers from Chatham (Ontario) at the same time as a copy of the *Arnhemsche Courant*, which told about a Dutchman who had to walk 3,000 miles to find work. Well, that scribbling is so full of lies and stupidity that it's impossible to even begin to give an answer to it. We would call this "work-seeking" Hollander a vagrant in the Netherlands, and here they call this kind of traveler a "tramp." I had a letter ready for Denkers and was planning to help him but the newspapers arrived and I thought to myself, "that's not the right kind of brother to have close to you. I'll have nothing but unpleasantness from this." I didn't send an answer.

There's one Hollander here I do associate with. He's a carpenter from Hummelo. He was in the U.S. for seven years, went back to Holland for military service, started his own business with American dollars, went broke and has been here for two years. He's a first-class tradesman and earns $9 a day from, the railway contractors. He enjoys it here and is planning to begin on his own again in the spring. A big grain merchant from Winnipeg wants to help him. This gentleman owns a house which the carpenter worked on for nine months: the gentleman liked the carpenter and helped him with the work.

15 December, 1928

They do a lot of advertising here, an incredible amount, but the calculations are totally different than in Holland. As I've heard from different businessmen, one does it like this: Purchase price and expenses and advertising and profit, e.g. purchase 60 cents, general expenses 10 cents, advertising 3 cents, profit 20 per cent of the 73 cents, sale price 88 cents.

Advertising is not considered an expense in America, but something taken for granted.

What we don't have yet in Holland is the so-called "Groceteria"; the self-serve grocery store. It's very common here in the cities.

Everything is wrapped in America, you can't get much that's unwrapped, even salt and sugar has to be bought in 1-pound linen bags. I have never seen these goods unpackaged. A grocery store without a scale is entirely possible because meat such as bacon and ham are all packaged and you buy them whole. Butchers use the scales more often.

A girl sits behind a cash register in this groceteria; the goods are all priced and there are sometimes instructions on the price tag. As you come in you get a little basket and you pick out what you want to buy. You go to the girl, show her what you've bought and then you take it with you. No writing up, no service, no employee expenses; it's a low cost business. Apparently stealing is not a problem, in spite of the fact that a shopper could easily put a can in his pocket instead of the basket. They do steal here but it doesn't seem to pay for most of them under $100,000.

The newspapers here are also full of the stigmatization at Konnersreuth, that's something generally known around the world. And it just suits the nature of the American newspapers because it's very sensational. The *Chicago Tribune* had great big pictures and imaginative drawings of the poor sufferers. The text was sensational but not mocking or dubious but, as a result, the public naturally asks for more. You wouldn't believe what a scandalous, sensational and I don't know what, newspaper it is. Divorces, murders, financial scandals, etc. are the main dish.

Last night, a scene was played out here again which one could only experience in America. A group of friends were sitting in a shack. They had something to celebrate, what it was they didn't know. That happens quite often in the world. There were also two young "Magdalenes" there and that could only increase the joy. The party got very happy, too happy. Someone in the group suggested that one of the fellows should get married to one of the ladies. I don't know whether they flipped a coin or not, but Jim Steele, 29 years old, was the lucky one chosen to marry one of the ladies who had just arrived on the afternoon train. They all got in one taxi (we now have three old Ford taxis in the Metropolis whose only source of business seems to be... the intoxicated who just sort of drive around to get rid of the hard-earned dollars faster, which they have acquired in bush, mine or railway labour). They drove to the watchmaker-jeweler, who they got out of bed around eleven o'clock, bought two rings and a marriage licence (an absurd document, a marriage permit which you can buy in most stores) and then on to the Presbyterian minister. And this one was also hauled out of bed and for $10 the two lovers were united in legal matrimony.

Then back to the party to turn the interrupted "get acquainted" celebration into a marriage feast. I don't know what happened after that but there was a fight and the poor bride got a shiner and not a small one either. Klutz, the peace officer of The Pas, separated the two and the groom awoke in the police station this morning with a thick head.

He had to pay a $3 fine and walked around looking for his wife, which wasn't all that easy because he'd forgotten her first and last names (the acquaintance period had been too short) and he didn't remember where she was staying either. Luckily they found each other and this evening they were sitting together in the movies. The groom, however, looked like a bear with a sore head!

Mrs. Woodward told me this evening about more of these marriages. She is an Anglican and said that the Presbyterian ministers were more dangerous than bootleggers. They ask nothing and will marry anyone who slips them $10. She was scandalized.

To clarify: marriage by a minister is legal here; you don't have to go to the city hall. The Presbyterians and Methodists are the big pushers for prohibition and they can put a lot of pressure on the candidates for Parliament. Besides that, they control a great deal of money and yet they don't seem to be opposed to marrying drunken people.

You've probably already heard of the new South Pole expedition to be undertaken by airplane by Col. Byrd, the American. This afternoon he landed here in a big, all-metal Ford monoplane with three engines. Now, even I am almost beginning to believe that we're in a cold wilderness here; carrying on their trials here because the conditions are most similar to the country they are going to fly over. If everything goes well, they'll go on to the South Pole.

Just saw a movie scene in real life. There are waitresses in the restaurant where I eat. A travelling salesman made a smart remark to one of the girls, but she had just brought a big cream pie out of the kitchen and pushed it straight into the gentleman's face. A gale of laughter broke out because it was six o'clock, suppertime. The owner, Mac, a Chinese, was rolling on his stomach with laughter. The noise was indescribable and the guy couldn't open his eyes because of the cream. He learned you shouldn't joke with the Metis girls if you can't handle the response. By eight tomorrow morning, the whole town will know about it. It'll be very difficult for that man to do business here because he's lost his decorum.

Schuitemaker's Permerender Courant,
28 April, 1925 to
12 November, 1927

CANADA IS A FUNNY COUNTRY

28 April, 1925

Only those who are familiar with agriculture or cattle breeding are considered suitable for emigration to Canada. If these two vocations are combined, so much the better. Free information about Canada can be obtained at The Holland Emigration Central, Anna Paulownastraat 8, The Hague, and at The Society for Emigration, Bezuidenhoutscheweg 97, The Hague. Anybody will be given information, free of cost and as fully as possible.

A person should go with a determined will to work hard and bear hardships. Everyone is encouraged to study English as much as possible. I have found, by personal experience, how troublesome it is if you can't express yourself well. I've learned enough to look after myself, but there is a Dutch family on board who don't know a word of English. Usually I serve as their interpreter.

It is recommended to leave in the spring. Good weather and work begins in Canada at that time. One ought not to think that he will earn a great deal at first. Apparently about $25 a month, including room and board. If one can also speak the language, this will naturally change. If you know the basics, the language can be easily learned. They say that in three months, you can talk about work and the weather but you have to be there at least a year to be able to converse about other subjects.

To emigrate, if one has been in the army, one must apply at the Ministry of War for a release from recall exercises. This is usually granted. After that, you must apply for a certificate at the tax office, indicating that you have paid your taxes. Then you apply for your passport at the secretariat of the municipality to which you belong. It must be specially stamped with "for the trip to and stay in Canada," otherwise the Canadian official will refuse you a visa. You can travel with the Holland America Line, the Canadian Pacific, Red Star, etc. I chose to go with the Canadian Pacific because I wanted to see something of London. In order to emigrate, you should have at least 410 guilders (f.). The ship costs 280f. All the companies charge the same in third class from Rotterdam.

The train in Canada costs about 50 f. You should also have 75 f. for landing money and for your immediate expenses.

So we left for London at 7:00 p.m., Monday, March 30, on the *Batavier*. We saw the *Soerakartia* lying at the northern pier in the Hook of Holland. Sloping into the sea at the bow on the port side. The cabin was small but satisfactory. The food was good. The *Batavier* sails up the Thames as far as Gravesend. From there you take the train to London; one and a half hours by rail. The Thames is very muddy. The difference between high and low tide is 16 feet. We saw several ships high and dry. In London, you arrive at Liverpool Station at about 12 o'clock. The Y.M.C.A. on Tottenham Court Road is a cheap, good, hotel. As for the most noteworthy sights of London, let me just mention: Westminster Abbey, Westminster Cathedral, Marble Arch in Hyde Park, The Bank of England, the Tower, St. Paul, the British Museum, etc.

To identify the points of interest of each one of these places would be a little too much. I will only mention the beautiful interior of Westminster Abbey. (We happened to arrive just as a service was going on and we were able to listen to the beautiful voices of the boys' choir. You are permitted entry to the Henry VII Chapel for a sixpence). Of special interest in the Tower are the Crown Jewels and the armory, etc. You get a wonderful view of London from the Monument.

The traffic on the street is extraordinarily busy. You can stand on a street corner for over an hour without seeing more than a small opening in the long procession of trucks, buses and so on. If you want to cross over, you have to watch the traffic policeman very carefully. With just one movement of his arm, he stops the whole procession and then you have room to reach the other side.

We spent considerable time standing quietly on a corner of Piccadilly Circus. The activity was beautiful. Especially noticeable were the different lighted advertisements. Something new with every blink of the eye. Sitting on the top deck of a bus is always to be recommended. You can always see everything very well. It all roars and tears around you. "Haven't we run into another one of these wonderful crazy things yet?", we shouted at each other as we sat on the top of one of those buses as it weaved its way through all kinds of vehicles with great speed. We expected a collision at any moment, but, incredibly, everything always worked out satisfactorily.

We also quite often traveled on the "tube." This is the underground railway. You take a ticket, descend several metres and arrive in a
tunnel. Electric trains constantly whiz through here. As soon as you sit
down, the train whizzes away through pitch dark tunnels. In a twinkling
of an eye, you're transported from one part of the city to another. They've
dug corridors under the streets and squares, like moles. There's even a
tunnel under the Thames. A stairway on a corner of a square, where we
went down, carried us (much to our surprise) to an underground station
as big as the whole square. It had its exits on the corners of the streets
which came out on this square. So it did double service: first as a station
for the underground and secondly as a safe way to cross the square. It's
difficult to find your way around, especially in stations where two or
more lines cross. Fortunately the English are very amenable and give you
all the desired information.

Friday morning we took the train to Liverpool; a journey of
about 5 hours. Around five o'clock in the afternoon, we departed on the
Montrose. The ship displaces 16,402 tons, and for the voyage from
Liverpool to St. John (a distance of 2,915 miles) it carried 542 passengers
in first and second class, 1,262 passengers in third class and a crew of 386.

We didn't see much of Liverpool, a giant factory city with a
couple of big buildings at the harbor side. Just like in Amsterdam, com-
munication with the other side is maintained by ferry. Naturally, these
were several times bigger than those in the Netherlands, as was practically everything that we saw in England. The English landscape is very
changeable. One moment you're going through a tunnel and the next
you're riding over a high embankment. Remarkably, we found that there
were no level crossings here as in Holland. One either passes under the
train or up over it.

There's not much to say about the voyage. No other Hollanders
on board. Hooijberg was seasick for two days. I fought against it furiously
and successfully! I wasn't seasick but I caught a very bad cold, resulting
in a severe headache. This will calm down after we land. The sea was
quiet for two days and then turbulent for three, so I usually sat at the dinner table with six or seven men instead of with thirty. Saturday, April 1,
we'll be landing, so the voyage will have lasted 8 days, almost 3 days more
than I had estimated. We will arrive at St. John (N.B.). Then by train to
Toronto, IS hours more or less. We don't know where we will be sent
from there.

7 July, 1925

It's taken much longer than I had intended to send a follow-up to my first letter, but our initial experiences were so disappointing that I wanted to wait to write until I had seen life here from a sunnier perspective. The disappointments began with the realization that the Emigration Central in The Hague had done nothing for us at all. I also realized that the Central was again busily encouraging emigration to Canada in all the newspapers. So I ask myself if it isn't necessary to inform the larger community that those who apply to that organization should not expect to depend upon their information or help in Canada.

Cor and I had to go out and look for a job on our own and landed in a district called the "Mountains" here. It was so rough that when we were ploughing we had to continually pull big stones out of the ground with chains. Besides that, it was still winter there and so what we ploughed the one day, lay deep under the snow again the next day. People in Holland can't even imagine such snows. In the winter the houses are usually buried in it up to about half their height. Besides that, the farmer for whom we worked was poor. The sleeping accommodations and the other workers were dirty and the nearest store, five hours away. And so we soon left there, but not with any bad feelings as the farmer himself drove us to the station and would have gladly kept us on but it was not possible.

They regarded us with some mistrust at the employment agency in Toronto when we showed up there again, but the end result was that we got another, position. This time in Ingersoll with an Irish Canadian, Peter Shannon. A decent man of about 35. His grandfather came here from Ireland. He's a hard worker. While we're free in the evenings and on Sundays, he's still cutting wood or building sheds. As soon as he gets up in the morning, he begins working and doesn't stop until he goes to bed.

Cor is here for the horses and the field labour and I'm here to look after the cows, work in the stable, the garden and so forth. At present I'm painting the ceiling of the kitchen and according to them this is going so well that they've also ordered me to paint the whole outside of the house. We earn $35 per month (we've hired ourselves out for six months) and the board is excellent. My English is also coming along quite well. We work from five o'clock in the morning to seven thirty in the evening. By the time you've eaten your supper it's already eight thirty and by nine thirty you really want to go to bed. On Sundays we're free after ten o'clock. Then I get cleaned up and wash my dirty clothes because that's not done for us and sending it to the laundry is very expensive. This is a lot of work especially if, as in Holland, you're used to seeing your clothes lying in front of you all washed and ironed. As a result there's little time left for writing. I still owe letters to ten people. Even though my replies take a little time, I still hope that our friends in Holland will not forget us, because it's very nice to hear something from your homeland when you're in a foreign place. Cor is, at the moment, busy writing a letter home with a sketch of the 15-metre high silo in which they store the finely cut unripe corn for cattle feed.

This week we're ploughing turnip fields. We had hired ourselves out as "fully experienced" even though I had never held a plough in my hands and Cor had only ever milked one cow. Up until now we've managed to get through it all right and the farmer hasn't made a single remark. Ploughing is rather strange work around here. The land is full of stones and hilly and the ploughing doesn't have to be done as neatly as in Holland. If one furrow doesn't lay too well, you can always cover it with the next one.

The cows are driven into the stables for milking, so you never have to milk in the rain here. For that matter, it's rained very little lately. You really notice the very strange climate they have here, when it's so hot one morning that you sweat like a horse while you're milking and the next day the snow doesn't melt and there's ice in our wash pail. That's really something on the twentieth of May! According to our boss, the hay will remain quite short this year and there will only be about a third of last year's crop. The fruit trees also appear to have suffered considerably from the frost.

I'm continuing this letter on the 21st of June. I'm here all alone now because Cor left me and is working in one of Ford's factories in Detroit. As a result, we've gotten a lot busier around here and are now using a milking machine. That goes a lot faster. My work hasn't got a lot worse because of this, in fact, I've become a sort of foreman and take the horses out into the fields. This is a lot more pleasurable than housework. We have nice young horses which have already bolted three times, but not with me yet. The great activity of seeding is past and so we won't get another hired hand, but we will be getting help in the summer from a couple of sixteen-year-old students who will be spending their vacations on the farm.

It's exceptionally dry this year. While I've been here, we haven't had anything worth calling a rain. Therefore the crops are stunted, the haying is going to produce very little and the grain isn't half as high as last year. Last week we had a little foretaste of summer warmth: The thermometer in the milk house, just above the water reservoir, reached 86. This lasted for about five days. It rained a little last night and the temperature dropped a bit. We have 8 hectares maize (what they call corn here).

On warm evenings innumerable fire-flies fly around here. Especially close by in a valley. Cor and I just stood watching it in amazement. It's just as if they were turning little electric lights on, all around you.

Yesterday we began mowing. There will be unusually little hay this year due to the drought. We have a field of clover on a piece on which there was wheat last year. The clover is no higher than the wheat stubble and there won't be much left over. One of the students who works here in the summer told me unloading is very easily accomplished. They use a spike or fork, just like they use with ships, and they unload a wagon in 4 or 5 loads. A horse pulls it to its destination with a long rope. Luckily there's still a lot of hay left over from last year.

Our farm is about a mile from the little town of Ingersoll. So no farther away than fifteen minutes walking, but the road is very hilly and so I usually only go there on Saturdays. We go together in the car. When I have to go shopping I always have trouble with my name, so to make things easy for myself, I let them call me Shannon.

I received a letter this week from Cor. As I said before, he's working at Ford. On the picture postcard you can see, incredibly clearly, a great big courtyard filled with 50,000 employees. I said, 50,000 men together. They work from seven in the morning until three in the afternoon, with only twenty minutes for lunch at 11:30 a.m. It's nice that you're finished at three in the afternoon, but you have to work so hard that you first need to rest for a couple of hours in order to recover. Living in Detroit is supposed to be very expensive. You do earn a lot, but the money just flies out of your pocket. Yesterday I sowed about 3 hectares with grass seed. It was a real job, especially as the field was very uneven. Hill up, hill down.

The bull is put out in the field with the cows here. When the cows are two years old, their horns are sawn off at the skull. When the wounds have grown closed, it looks as if they have never had horns. Every morning and every evening, they're driven to the stable with the help of the dogs. I don't have to do anything except give the dog instructions. He grabs them by the tail. Our other dog (she just had four pups) nips them in the heels. When they kick, she ducks, so they always kick over the dog. A cute sight.

I finish, because it's almost twelve o'clock and at five my alarm clock will be rattling again.

29 August, 1925

I received a letter from the Canadian Pacific Railway Company about my last piece in the *Purmerender Courant*. In it, they advise me that they, through their extensive organization, can help all those who emigrate to work in agriculture, to find permanent employment or temporary work during the harvest time. The immigrant can also rely on help from its offices, which are spread across Canada. Those who have sufficient experience with Canadian methods of farming can, through this company, purchase land in an extraordinarily easy manner. The company's model farms and experimental stations are spread across the country.

It's difficult, given the nature of things, to make a fair evaluation. I did write the C.P.R. agent in Rotterdam, that I expected to write something about the C.P.R. in my next article but only about things that I had personally experienced. I can say very little about their colonization work in Western Canada when I'm settled in Eastern Canada. Some of the people I've talked to say it's good there, others say it's bad there. Employers around here naturally paint the conditions in Western Canada as poorly as possible. Hundreds of people leave Eastern Canada annually, to go "Harvesting" in the West and the railway companies have to put on extra trains (you're in Winnipeg for $15). This lasts from the middle of August to the end of October. The employers around here say that you never earn more than $2.50 to $3 a day there, but I've also heard $6 to $7. My plan is to go there and see it with my own eyes, next year. For now, however, I'll stay here this winter for $25 a month (plus room and board).

Now something about the money. Every dollar you save is naturally worth 2.5 guilders in the Netherlands, but you can't do more with it here than with a guilder in the Netherlands. So cigarettes cost 35 cents American for 20 (so-called English tobacco). Cigars are 10 or 12 cents apiece (3 for 25), not at all as good as in Holland. You can't smoke the five-cent ones! A 35-gram package of tobacco costs 15 cents and a new suit $15 to $30, etc. My expenses are very small because I always work and never go out. But if I went out dancing or playing pool on a Saturday night, then I wouldn't be able to save much of my salary. If one is industrious and frugal in Holland, then one can, as a bachelor, save some money as was the case with Cor, who managed to save his travel money in Holland.

Even though I like it a lot on the farm, I don't think I'll stay here in the long run because you can earn a lot more in a much shorter time in the factories. Sometime, Cor should write about how things are going for him in Detroit. We're working here for $35 plus room and board per month ($65 without). From five in the morning to eight in the evening and never free on Sunday. The lack of free time is the biggest objection, because I have so much to write in order to maintain my friendships in Holland. I would also very much like to study some English. Hopefully, it'll be better in the winter when the days are shorter.

It seems to me that Canada is a very good place for married people. You can start a little farm with very little money. Naturally, I'm talking about a couple with the man being willing and able to work hard and the woman prepared and able to do her own housekeeping. It seems to me that the U.S.A. is probably better for bachelors. Certainly, thousands of young men go there. It's true that malcontents continue to come back but opposed to that are the hundreds who stay. This is precisely why there is such a great demand for immigrants in Canada, because the native population moves to the cities and the factories. Hundreds of speeches are made by the authorities advising the people to remain in the countryside where it's so nice. And they're right, but they don't want to see the disproportionate relationship that exists between wages and free time.

Now about something else. We have two stations here; one Canadian Pacific Railway (C.P.R.) and one Canadian National Railway (C.N.R.). These are the two big companies. The locomotives deliver a screaming whistle at every crossing. This seemed very strange to us at first as it gave the impression that you were riding along in the middle of the wilderness and you had to chase a herd of buffalo off the rails. You can hear trains coming from miles away. You can walk through the cars from one end of the train to the other and all the cars are lined with folding seats on both sides of the aisles. You can sit one behind the other, but you can also turn the seats around and take your place opposite each other. No hard benches like in Holland, but all cushions.

Ingersoll is famous for its pork factory. Great export to England. Besides that, there's a broom factory and a dairy. The supervision is very strict here. Every month an inspector comes to see if the milking equipment is clean and that the stables have been whitewashed, etc. If things aren't in order, then it's put in the report. If the same infraction is repeated within a number of months, then you receive an order to fix it up right away or face the penalty of being prohibited from delivering milk. The milk cans are cleaned daily at the factory with steam.

Now something about the value of cattle. A newborn calf is worth $1.50 (the value of the hide). A fat calf (one that has been nursed by the cow for at least 6 weeks), 8 cents per pound. A good fat cow is only worth $50. Bulls are worth a lot less. We can't even get $35 for our bull (weight: 1600 lb.). They're not eaten here. It goes overseas. My farmer got $25 ($20 and $5) last year for two cows (one had two teats and the other was a little sickly). A cow that's just calved and is a good milker costs $75. A good workhorse around $100. Old horses and horses for the slaughterhouse can't be given away. They put them down and bury them. Sometimes they cremate them and grind them up and mix the powder with seed grain to combat grain diseases. You should have seen their incredulous faces when we told them that we ate horses.

This reminds me of another event. One time a can of milk came back from the dairy with a message that it was sour. I let it stand for a couple of hours and then made a tasty lunch out of a plate of sour milk with a rusk and sugar. You should have seen their faces. The woman of the house couldn't eat anything else. And even though I swore that it was very tasty and they should try it, they simply wouldn't touch it.

They also looked very strangely at the wooden shoes which I ordered from Holland, but I've found them very handy.

Just a little note that a farmer about a mile from here went broke. His ten cows were taken to market in Woodstock and sold there for $38 apiece (all in one sale).

Tomorrow I'm going threshing at one of the neighbours. This promises a big supper, etc. All about this another time. Also about The Holland Emigration Central in The Hague, to which I wrote a long letter and about which I discovered a lot of information here.

10 November, 1925

In my previous letter, I promised to say something more about The Holland Emigration Central (the office for emigration in The Hague) and about threshing. First about the H.E.C. I wrote them a letter in July, to which I have not yet received a reply and this is the beginning of October. My letter reads, in the main, as follows:

"Now that I've been here in Canada for a number of months, it strikes me that I could be of some service in relating to you one thing or another about my experiences with the Central in Toronto. My friend Hooijberg and I left for Canada at the end of March. We arrived in Toronto in the middle of April. We missed your representative on the day of our arrival, but we visited him at his office on the following morning.

It quickly became apparent to us that nothing had been done for us yet, even though your office had written us that such work had already been undertaken. We were taken to a recruiting office of the Canadian Government; from there we were sent to Terra Cotta. This is a terrible district, up in the mountains, three miles from the nearest store: a semi-wilderness. The soil was full of stones which we had to pull out with the horses. We stayed there only for a short while because things didn't agree with us and because we had asked for a place where we could earn $30 per month. In Terra Cotta, they asked for a couple of farmhands at $20 a piece.

"Back in Toronto we again presented ourselves at the office of your representative, who was very unpleasantly surprised to see us. He led us to understand that he did this work without any remuneration and that he really didn't want to be bothered with it. We should have stayed where we were and written him a letter. Sure!... Then he told us about a rich Finn who brought his countrymen over and how these then worked for him for room and board and the chance to learn English from him. So we trekked over to the Canadian office again and said that we wanted to return home but that we first had to earn our travel money. After they very carefully impressed on us that they didn't want any more trouble from us, they gave us an address in Ingersoll where I still am today because things are a lot better here.

"I'm sure that you'll admit that in this case, I've had nothing but harm from your involvement.

"Now something about the Canadian bureau. This office places labourers with farmers without setting any conditions. The immigrant can only wait and see how the farmer will deal with him. The farmer, if he fires his employee within the year, can be denied a new farmhand for a year, but the old employee is not taken care of and he doesn't get any compensation either.

"In my opinion, the first thing that's necessary is the hiring of a salaried person whose job would consist in remaining up to date on the circumstances of the immigrants you have placed. If you're not able to find anyone, I would be willing to take on the work temporarily for nothing more than the costs. This representative should have a good knowledge of the district, wages, working conditions, payment conditions and so forth. Furthermore, the immigrants should have already been placed by you. This can be easily done as there are hundreds of requests annually that cannot be filled.

"Until now I haven't heard a thing from your organization. In fact, I haven't received any of your publications although I am a member. Three Hollanders I spoke with in Toronto had similar bad experiences. If you want to do something to better the poor circumstances here, send me a list of your placements and I will undertake some investigations about them. My membership card number is 43.

As I said, I haven't seen hide nor hair of any response to this letter up to now and that's why I think it's necessary to have it printed for the benefit of those who want to emigrate to Canada and want some help from this office of the Dutch government.

Now about the threshing. This creates a lot of activity around here. Because they don't have enough farmhands of their own, the farmers trade work with their neighbours. One threshes right from the fields, the other stores the harvest in the barn in order to finish the threshing in the fall. The farther away the fields are, the more men you need, naturally. You have to provide the wagons and the pitchers, a couple of men to carry the cleaned grain away from the machine, another two men for the machine and two more for the straw. First you drive the grain to the threshing place and unload it with a Jacob's Ladder. Turning knives cut the binder twine. The grain is separated from the straw and the latter is blown away by a long pipe. It's all very easy. One man steers the blower and the other packs the straw with his feet and works it into the corners. While the farmer and his hands are working outside, the ladies on the farm are baking and broiling because they have to look after all the food for all the people and nobody wants to be outdone by his neighbours.

As with the threshing, the neighbours also come to help with the filling of the silo. This work is not at all as dusty as the threshing. But it is heavy work, especially with the pitching of sheaves and particularly this year when the corn is so thick and long. I've found stalks that were more than 4 metres long.

At the bottom of the silo you set up the chaff cutter, which cuts the stalks into pieces about a metre in length. These are then blown to the top of the silo. Here they fall into a cylinder which is attached to a moveable articulated pipe. Our silo is about 13 metres high and has a diameter of almost 4 metres. We filled it up in a day and a half.

Threshing and silo filling time is pleasant, not only because of the outstanding meals but also because you get to know your neighbours that way.

Now some jottings about all kinds of things all mixed together.

Although 1925 is not a bad year for the farmer (milk $1.50 compared to $1.00 last year), the manager of a big bank in Ingersoll declared that many farmers were "hopeless broken down" (sic). He should know because all the farmers have mortgages at his bank.

Money is everything here. A lot more than in the United States. At the border (Windsor-Detroit) the American Customs asks, "Who are you and are you registered with us?" The Canadian Customs asks, "What do you have with you and how can I relieve you of some money?"

Everything is heavily taxed. Different emigration bureaus in Holland say that the direct taxation isn't high but they forget to say that the indirect taxes are very high and that they place the greatest burden on the common rank and file. My boss still has to pay $250 in direct taxes this year. He's certainly not a poor farmer but he does have a heavy mortgage. I don't believe there are any rich farmers. As soon as they don't have any debt and can live off the farm, they hang up their farm clothes in the attic. Again this fall, there will be loads of farmers holding auction sales because they can't make ends meet. Honest competition is almost impossible because of all kinds of protection. The import duties are extremely high. They're a fountain of income for a spendthrift government. The total number of government buildings and civil servants is several times greater than in Holland, while the population is not much bigger (not even nine million). And of course it's the hard-working farmer who has to deliver the biggest part of the taxes.

Everything possible is done to keep the people in the countryside, but the great majority (not all) of the young people move to the cities and the best look for a place in the U.S.A. While the highest wage that can be expected on the farm here is $40 a month, with room and board, they easily pay $60 in the States. Besides that, newcomers don't count in things like this. They stay patiently on the farm because they're needed there and it's difficult for them to get work in the city. Canadians always come first and of them, always veterans first. It's all very cliquish. It's very different in the States. If you have a trade then you're all set there. Also, many foreigners can't get used to the English Sunday with its complete Sunday rest. That means you can't do anything on that day except go to church in the morning and sleep in the afternoon.

Our neighbour operates a farm for someone else. He gets 40 per cent of the net yield. His wife looks after the house and helps with the milking. He told me that his income for the month of June 1924 (the month in which his cows give the greatest amount of milk), without any major expenditures having to be made, totalled $16. Although this is not a criterion, one does have to keep in mind that a dollar is not worth more than a guilder. If you figure the dollar at 2.5 guilders then every-thing is so incredibly expensive that you don't dare buy a thing. Set the dollar at 2.5 guilders only on the things that you sell in order to reach a reasonable price; milk at three dollars per 100 kg (butter fat 3.5 per cent), wheat at $3 per h.l., oats at $1.50 per h.l., everything figured on the high side. Cows, let me take them high, $50 on average. If land wasn't so cheap here, you'd be finished in a year. But you have to work extremely hard here, from dawn to dusk. Imagine if you had a farm in Holland of 60 hectares, half of which was arable land, and you rented 10 hectares of extra pasture and kept 34 cows on it and you had to work the whole business with two men!

Dutch boys had better consider the fact that it's very unpleasant when you don't know English well. You feel very unlucky and like a stranger. I often notice that when the conversation goes a bit deeper, I have to search for words. Most people here think I'm Scottish, which is not a bad thing as Scots and Irishmen are held in much higher regard than Englishmen.

There's government involvement in every business. There's a lot of good in this, but it costs a lot of money and kills free enterprise. Take apples for example. Because of government involvement, the trade in a 12-mile area has fallen into one person's hands. As a result, the fruit can-not be handled quickly and hundreds of barrels are lost, especially in a bumper crop year. Our chickens, geese and ducks practically live on the fallen apples which they find in the orchard.

Whitsuntide is not celebrated here, nor Ascension Day. There are three official holidays; 24 May, Queen Victoria's birthday, 1 July, Dominion Day and 7 September, Labour Day. These are statutory holi-days for all businesses. But not for the farm (naturally). Free half days are also given in the city on special occasions. The farmer is also exempt from these. They're supposed to amuse themselves in the evening, after work is finished.

I've gone out once to the London Fair. The Toronto Fair begins the season and lasts for 14 days. The greatest exhibition of the world. One hundred thousand visitors. After this comes the London Fair, 7 days. This is the biggest Western Ontario fair and the second biggest in Canada. The exhibition, in itself, isn't much, but there are a lot of diver-sions. In the evening, I saw the *Ten Commandments* in the movie theatre, where they also showed pictures of the devastated town of Borculo. I also heard Sousa's band in a covered arena (ballroom in the summer and ice rink in the winter). The word: ice-rink, make me think about winter when it's not all that great to clear a path through the snow when you're just out of bed and the barns are 50 metres from the house.

The government of Canada is Liberal. Ontario is Conservative. The Labour party does not exist. They do try to put up labour candidates in the big cities but this is not successful. It's very peculiar that the cities are conservative and the countryside more liberal. On the 29th of October there will be a parliamentary election. A principal issue is the emigration of the indigenous population to the States. The Liberals indicate, in great headlines in the press, that under their administration 55,000 Canadians have returned from the States in the past year. I would really like to know how many of the 55,000 are still here at this moment and how many tens of thousands re-migrated to the States in the past year? (The Conservatives won a majority in the last election. – *Ed.*)

Although Canada has been richly blessed by nature, the population is growing very slowly. The majority of immigrants are Scots and Irish and as I've already noted, are more respected. The cheap eating and laundry places are mostly in the hands of the Japanese. These chaps scrimp and scrape their money together and when they've saved a pile they sell the business to a countryman and go back to Japan. They take money out of the country and for that reason are not well respected by Canadians.

Canada possesses huge coal resources, but due to higher political interests they remain undeveloped, and expensive American coal is imported.

After all this political fodder, let me return to the farm. The remaining corn is set up in big sheaves and every day a portion of it is given to the cows. They're crazy about it. Most of the farms have American windmills. These carry the well water to the house, to the tanks in the yard, to the stable and to the milkhouse. Nearly every farm also has a telephone, 12 parties on one line. This way you can listen to everybody else. But it does have a bad side in that the ladies spend half the day on the phone. If you want to make something generally known, you can't do it better than by telephoning.

My experiences with milking machines have not been wonderful. If you want to do a quick job with it, as if you had done it by hand, then you need two of them. If the cows are letting their milk down fully, then it does go faster. However, if a little later on they don't let their milk down as easily, then you have to remilk about a third of them. The easy milking cows let it down very well, but the tough ones hold it back. Especially this year, we had to do a lot of remilking! If you want to get the last drop of milk out of a cow (not only because it has the highest butter fat but because it keeps the cows in milk much better), you can't do it much faster than by hand. The two of us milked 30 cows by hand in 1-3/4 hours, while with two milking machines it took us 1-1/2 hours. With cold weather, the cows don't let their milk down easily and so the milking machines are generally only used here in the summer. It's a lot easier, but not cheaper. Besides that, if you want to keep your milking machine clean, you have to boil the rubber hoses every day and let them slowly cool. There's no time for that! I was present one day when the inspector came to check the machine. You can hardly imagine the filthy spoiled milk which came out of it! We always just shoved the rubber hoses in some cold water. Something that I do think would be useful to the Dutch farmers are the hay ladders and hay forks which are used to load and unload the wagons. Both save a lot of time and work. They also have big furnaces in the basements here. The warm air is directed to all the rooms through large pipes. Because of this central heating, you have dry warmth throughout the whole house.

To summarize, I don't want to discourage anyone from coming to Canada but my advice is: always learn good English ahead of time, don't stay on the farm any longer than is necessary for your adjustment and language skills, never hire yourself out for an entire summer, make sure you get your full salary every month. If I had to hire myself out again, I wouldn't bind myself longer than to the middle of August and would then go harvesting in the West. After that, if you want to stay on a farm at a lower wage during the winter, then there's always that opportunity here. Better than in Holland. As for myself, I'll be looking for work that leaves me more free time to study English and bookkeeping. In all the cities of Canada, there are opportunities to learn the basics of any trade in six to eight weeks, and a good tradesman earns a lot of money.

Last week, two missionaries preached here for seven days in a row in the Roman Catholic church. My boss slept at his in-laws' in the city and was able to attend services every morning and evening. In the mornings, he would join me in the stable at a quarter of seven. I had usually finished seven cows by then, so my total would reach 17. I was also in the church one evening, like a lot of other Protestants. All services were filled up.

I'm going to sleep, otherwise this letter will never get away. I close with greetings to my friends, many of whom still regularly write me. A person in a foreign country appreciates that much more than when he was in his homeland.

19 January, 1926

Quite a bit has happened, since I wrote you the last time. I left my boss, on good terms, on the tenth of December and made my way directly to the Hemphill School in Toronto. I enclose a brochure from that institution. It's something like Dalmeyer, but on a bigger scale. The business is, however, somewhat exaggeratedly described in this brochure. The bricklaying course, which I am taking, is very good because it is taught by an excellent instructor and there are only eight students in the class. As a result, there is sound supervision over your work.

After a week, I noticed that my studies left me sufficient time to earn something on the side. This seemed desirable to me as the course takes three months and I would rather not be at the end of my money at that time. So one day, during my free time, I walked into the employment office and was just standing there a moment looking around, when someone came up to me and asked me if I was looking for work. Naturally, I answered yes. He hired me to do kitchen work for $12 (f. 30) a week, plus free board. I'm still there and things are pretty good.

My work day alternates between a long day from 7:30 a.m. to 2:00 p.m. and from 5:00 p.m. to 10:00 p.m. and a short day from 10:30 a.m. to 6:30 p.m. As a result, I go to school in the afternoon of the long day and in the evening of the short day. I work as a dish and pot washer in the restaurant. Thus a distinguished vocation! But this doesn't matter because it's only temporary. At each meal, I'm allowed to eat 40 cents worth of food. It doesn't matter what I order, so right away you learn to eat everything. My breakfast is composed of oatmeal, two eggs (sunny side up with bacon), two pieces of toast, butter, coffee or tea. Dinner and supper: soup, meat or fish, potatoes, coffee, tea or milk, one serving of pie or pudding. You eat a lot of meat here and few potatoes. Shannon's was a good boarding house, but this is better. The proof of how good things are for me is that I now weigh 155 English pounds, in other words 140 Dutch pounds, while I never weighed more than 130 in Holland.

Until now, the Canadian winter has been rather mild. Except for a few cold days (but then it was so vicious that we've never experienced anything like it in Holland), the thermometer drifts around the freezing point. In fact, during the day the sun makes it warm. Furthermore, there is very little snow this year. There wasn't even any snow for Christmas. So we had a busy week in the restaurant because at Christmas people entertain each other. Just like our St. Nicholas feast. I received a Christmas gift from my employer, a tin of cigarettes (50), even though I'd only been working there a week. Nice eh? On Christmas day we had a huge Christmas dinner: turkey and Christmas pudding.

I'm still planning if possible, despite this, to cross the border in April to the United States, where life is better and the wages higher. The consul here informed me that they had requested a visa for me from the American consulate in Amsterdam for next April, when I will have been in Canada for a year. In order to be admitted I need a testimonial from a farmer in Holland for whom I have worked and a testimonial from my farmer here and a certificate of good behaviour from the mayor of Ilpendam, all translated into English and everything in duplicate.

It would really be worth it to me to be able to go to the U.S. because, even though I don't want to say anything bad about Canada, there are shortcomings to the life here. The main one is that it's difficult to make friends. Everyone lives for himself and as a result, I still don't have a friend or a girlfriend. Most of the Hollanders I spoke to here talk about nothing else but the ways in which they've first earned money and then squandered it. Once I went to the Dutch church, where I met another 25 people, but after the service everyone went his own way again. There's also a Dutch society here, but I've not been able to attend one of its meetings. Usually I go to the "Union Church." Diagonally opposite my room (I have a nice room in the middle of the city for three dollars a week) are two churches: the Roman Catholic, St. Michael's Cathedral and the Methodist (Union) Metropolitan Church. Both beautiful buildings. Inside and out. If you're an ordinary person, you'll find the Dutch service terribly boring after going to the English church. At least as far as I'm concerned, that interminable singing puts me off.

I'm writing this letter on New Year's Day in the Y.M.C.A. (Young Men's Christian Association), 40 College Street, of which I am a member for three months without cost. This is also my mailing address. The Y.M.C.A. is a big organization here. It owns a big building with swimming facilities, gymnastic and billiard rooms, etc. You can also rent rooms, but this is quite expensive. It was also too far away from my work. There's lots of activity around here today. "Open House" for all young men. All kinds of games with prizes, which you can participate in without any cost. I also heard a beautiful concert by a first class pianist, violinist, soprano and so on. I had a truly lovely day.

Last night (New Year's Eve), I felt homesick for the first time. The clocks struck; the sirens screamed at midnight and then I thought about Holland where I always waited out the old year surrounded by friends. Friends who were surely thinking about me so very much alone in that distant land, without a relative or friend. But this was only for a second. Now I think: who knows if I won't spend the next New Year's Eve at home. It's possible that I'll dash over to Holland for a few months next winter. But… these are castles in the air. For the time being, my first concern is to get into the United States.

16 March, 1926

I'm only calling on the hospitality of the *Purmerender Courant* again because of the great interest which Canada holds for those who are trained as gardeners and farmers and can't find an opportunity to acquire a self-sufficient existence in North Holland. This opportunity certainly exists in Canada, but one should weigh the pros and cons here as well. Especially since emigration to Canada is described as far too easy by the Netherlands government's associate, The Holland Emigration Central in The Hague, and by the agent of the Canadian Pacific Railway in the Netherlands (Rotterdam). Until now, I haven't met anyone who didn't complain about these organizations. Just like me, these others had expected that the H.E.C. or the C.P.R. would have helped them on. They soon realized, as I had, that everyone here is totally responsible for himself.

Because of the importance of this issue, I would like to look at it more closely. If my writing encourages others to say something about their experiences, I'll be very pleased. Especially, if others can relate better experiences. At the moment, I remain insistent that everyone who decides to make use of an agency or bureau should begin by asking for the addresses of people who have been aided by that agency, so that they can first ask for some information at these addresses. I want to emphasize this warning: Don't Hurry! Very carefully prepare for your trip and meanwhile learn good English.

Ultimately, even the best prepared person has to learn by his own experiences. But isn't this the case in the Netherlands as well? No one can really answer the question, "How are things in the Netherlands," without first asking, "Which part of the Netherlands do you mean, Beemster, the Veluwe, Drenthe…?" And if the answer is, "Beemster is prosperous, Drenthe is poor," that doesn't take away from the fact that you can meet poor people in Beemster and prosperous people in Drenthe! Well this is the case in Canada, to an even greater degree.

I hear that someone is presently busy in the Netherlands recruiting people for Saskatchewan. Now somebody asks, "How are things there?" I don't know a thing about it, because that part of Canada is a lot farther West. But there are people here who have worked there. Some of these say: "Manitoba is good, Saskatchewan poor." Others conclude just the opposite. Naturally! Because both provinces are so big, much bigger than our whole country, the question that ought to be asked is: "Which part do you have your eye on?" Besides that, there are as many people who succeed everywhere as people who fail everywhere.

I met a young Hollander, about my age, in the Y.M.C.A. building. He was attracted to Western Canada (against his family's will) through the efforts of the C.P.R. He had as bad an experience there as I did in the first place which I received from the H.E.C. He was stuck there, miles from the nearest city. He didn't have the money to leave. Finally, he didn't even shave any more. In a word, HORRIBLE HORRIBLE! How extraordinarily lucky I was at Shannon's.

As far as I'm concerned, immigrants should start out in Ontario. This agrees with what seems to be the most trustworthy advice, namely that of Dr. Henry Beets, Mission Director of the Christian Reformed Church,... and J. R. Brink, missionary teacher of the Christian Reformed Church... of Grand Rapids, Michigan, U.S.A. These gentlemen, also well-known in the Netherlands, have sent an open letter to Dutchmen in Canada and in our country. The following are condensed excerpts:

> Don't spread yourself across Canada, but begin by establishing yourself in Ontario, especially in the southern part. In Toronto, Chatham, Windsor. The winters are not too harsh and the summers are not too hot. Total crop failure is unknown here and the soil is very productive. 16,430 factories produce 1.7 billion dollars worth of goods. Ten million acres are already under the plough. More than 230 million unbroken arable acres remain.

The Province of Ontario covers a land area of 365,880 square miles. The waterfalls of Niagara produce her electricity. The university has 5,000 students and is the biggest in the British Empire. There are 7,000 public schools and seven Normal schools for the training of teachers. You only need to know one language, English and the population of Ontario is predominantly Protestant. In Quebec and Montreal, French is spoken by the Roman Catholics who make up the majority.

Toronto, the capital of Ontario, has 641,000 inhabitants. The Christian Reformed Church holds services in Dutch, behind St.

Andrew's Presbyterian Church at King and Simcoe Streets. 2,060 Dutchmen live in Toronto. Furthermore, there are: 700 Austrians, 2,000 Bulgarians, about 400 Chinese, 200 Danes, 470 Finns, 5,400 Frenchmen, 2,570 Germans, 1,000 Greeks, 152 East Indians, 1,100 Negroes, 500 Norwegians, 3,500 Poles, 200 Rumanians, 1,100 Russians, 1,000 Swedes, 300 Syrians, 800 Ukrainians and 40,500 Jews. In total, a little less than 75,000 foreigners.

Chatham has 17,000 inhabitants. Dutch religious services are held in the First Presbyterian Church on Wellington Street.

Windsor and district has 65,000 inhabitants and is situated close to Detroit, a city of a million and a half inhabitants. Many people from Windsor work there.

That's all the news from the two Christian Reformed ministers, who say that they're also prepared to provide information about other parts of Canada such as Vancouver, Winnipeg, Edmonton and Neerlandia.

As I said, these addresses appear to be completely trustworthy, even though, by the very nature of the business, they are more helpful to those who feel at home in the Reformed circle. Regardless of the fact that I value their work and their persons, as much as I've been able to become acquainted with it, I still feel (see my previous letter) more at home in the English church and the Y.M.C.A.

This is an appropriate point, to come back to the place that church and religion have in Canada. It's absolutely essential that anyone who's thinking about coming here accept the idea that he'll find an out-wardly very religious country. I won't judge the inward religiosity, but outwardly the society manifests a marked religious and church-oriented character. Very different from many districts in the Netherlands... Once again, how far these things penetrate into the inner life and how much similarity there is between theory and practice are questions that I stay away from. Perhaps the believer will be more struck by the superiority of the ideals which are preached to him, and the unbeliever more by the moral failures of the believer. However this may be, outwardly anyway, people are religious and church-oriented and there's a beautiful church building on just about every corner. (At the same time there are a lot of movie theaters which open as early as nine o'clock in the morning.)

Let me put it this way. You have to know religion here, just like you have to know how to speak English. It doesn't matter if you think

English is nice or not, or if perhaps you'd prefer to speak Dutch. You have to know and use English. In the same way, you have to know about religion and you have to become involved with it, or else suffer other people's lack of understanding and be regarded as uncivilized.

This is also evidenced by the position of the Y.M.C.A. I spend my free time at the Y.M.C.A. building at 40 College Street (this letter is written on free paper). On Sunday afternoons, we have a religious service here. Every month another preacher from a different church and with different opinions. For February we have Bishop Brewing of the Anglican Church. Always the best preacher in the city. Sunday afternoon, after the completion of the church service, we get together for the so-called "Fireside Club." We all sing together for a half hour, after which Mr. Knick, Secretary of the Senior Section and Relief Work, gives a short speech. After that, we drink hot chocolate and eat a sandwich. Mr. Knick is an exceptionally nice man. He was a chaplain during the war and so he's generally addressed as "Captain," just like Mr. Best. The latter runs a forty-five minute Bible discussion on Thursday evening. Although I don't generally have a high opinion of the inner, truly spiritual, life in Canada, where everyone gives the impression that they are only concerned with their own needs, these two people do, however, appear to be examples of true upright Christians.

No one should think, that as a result, there's less fun. While I'm writing this, I hear music from all sides. A phonograph, a piano, a chorus, every one praiseworthy by itself, but a little strange all mixed together.

After all this spiritual information and advice-giving, something a little more material. Those who travel here should not take too much baggage along. Two sets of underwear is sufficient, along with a couple of work shirts and three pairs of socks. Whatever else you need, you can easily purchase at Eaton's or Simpson's in Toronto. Eaton's is easily bigger than the Bijenkorf. In any case, don't bring along winter clothes. You can buy these much better in the Fall. So-called "overalls" are generally worn here as work clothes. You pull these over your ordinary clothes. I think they cost about two dollars a pair. You'll also require one or two pairs of work shoes. Everything all together, barely a large suitcase full. You send this one off with the baggage, while you keep a small case with you for washing and shaving equipment, shoe polish, writing materials, etc.

I'm still enrolled in the bricklaying course. The work still isn't as easy as it looks. The art is to do it quickly. I've now reached 800-1000 bricks a day, but a qualified bricklayer must be able to lay 1,500. As a result, I'll have to be satisfied with 70 to 80 cents an hour in the first months. Just to point out a few of the difficulties. You have to be able to spread a full trowel of mortar equally along the length of three bricks (about 60 cm). The next movement involves spreading the mortar equally across the width of the brick. You must then push the bricks into the mortar bed with the left hand, exactly along the line, absolutely horizontal and not higher or lower than the line and at the same time catch the pressed-out mortar with the trowel in the right hand and spread it on the end of the brick so that the vertical space between the two stones is filled up with the placement of the following row.

The time for bricklaying hasn't arrived yet, as it's still too cold. The streets are slippery because of the tramped down and frozen snow. Most people wear overshoes, the ladies wear overboots which aren't flattering, as far as I'm concerned.

In closing, I have to correct a mistake in a previous letter. I spoke about Japanese restaurants, but my Dutch friend, on reading this, remarked that the owners are Chinese. The Japanese, just like the Chinese, have been denied the entry of their womenfolk. Anyway, the above-mentioned little city can boast of about 20 Japanese (as compared to four or five thousand Chinese).

My writing about Canada is probably finished for the present and I'm surprised that people have been willing to follow my correspondence this long. My family and friends were able to continue hearing something from me in this way, while I felt that I was doing something useful for others at the same time. I had wanted to work in the bush for a number of months and would have written about this, but the wage there is $25 to $30 a month and because the forests are far from here, the travel costs are too high. My plan now is to work here this summer and go to the United States in the Fall. Naturally, with the legal papers which I've already applied for and will surely be able to get. Everyone should be warned against sneaking into America without good papers.

Who knows, maybe I'll spend a winter in Holland after that. If so, then it's possible that I might trek to our East, to which my oldest brother invited me. In that case, there would be lots more stuff to write about.

Next week, I hope to speak about the immigration question at the Dutch club.

But for now, that's the end of it. Many thanks to the *Purmerender Courant* for its hospitality, and to my readers for their interest.

1 March, 1927

Around Christmas, I left Drummondville (French Canada) where I had been laying bricks until that time, and returned to Toronto. At the moment, there's nothing to do here in the building trades (besides that, it's way too cold in these districts in the winter), but we expect a busier time in March because there's supposed to be a lot of construction: a hotel of $8 million, another of $3 million, a factory of $5 million and other buildings as well. A considerable number of building lots have been prepared along the waterfront for warehouses, along with marshalling yards for the L.P.C. and the C.N.R. At the same time, there are plans to make the St. Lawrence navigable for oceangoing ships as far as Toronto. This will also cost millions. This last plan was already approved before the war, but due to the unhappy circumstances of the time, it had to be postponed. Now they see the light of day again.

The belief that the outlook is fairly good can be seen in the fact that, as of May 1, the wages will rise from $1.125 to $1.25 per hour. These better prospects are of special interest to average bricklayers like myself. It's the same in all the trades, the best always have work, but after the poor ones are gone, the average ones are also quickly fired. They pay a high wage, and as a result, they don't keep anyone at work a day longer than they have need of him. The one who doesn't do his work well is soon out. If there's a lot of work, even the average ones are kept and they then have the opportunity to practice and work themselves up to first quality workers.

I've now advanced farther than the Hollander with whom I first worked and from whom I learned a lot at that time, because I've got three things going for me that he doesn't: I'm younger, I can speak better English and I'm not conceited. I'm writing this with a special purpose. I want to point out to those that have a desire to emigrate to Canada that as far as I'm concerned, in order to succeed you have to be young enough to accommodate yourself, you have to know enough English and you have to be prepared to carry out the required work promptly.

Earlier, I wrote that I had become a member of a trade union. Last week, thanks to the union, we had a so called "smoker", a convivial evening with recitations, etc. I felt very proud, as an accepted fellow member, to celebrate with my comrades in an association that stands for something in this world. Here in Ontario, it has 700 members. They are mostly over 30, although I did see a number of younger fellows. As Ontario is still dry, we had to be satisfied with beer that had an alcohol content no higher than 4 per cent. It was impossible to drink too much of it. The snacks consisted of "hotdogs" (a bun with a Frankfurter sausage in it) and crackers with cheese. A friend of mine, who hasn't made it to bricklayer yet and earns 50 cents an hour as a hod carrier, thought that he would be allowed to attend this meeting but, as he didn't know the password, he was tossed out right away.

This friend came from Hemphill's bricklaying school. More than 30 poor devils, who have paid a 100 or more of their hard-earned dollars for tuition and who now think that they can handle a trowel and hammer pretty well, go to school there. Poor wretches, as soon as they come out to go to work, they'll discover that they still don't know anything about it and then they'll have to go back to the farm, for want of anything better to do. It's a shame that something like that can still go on. The union can't do anything about it. The boys could probably do it themselves, but they don't yet understand that they're being plucked and once they do, it's too late and then they don't have any money to take it to court. Those that have been there and still get into the building trades later, in another way, keep quiet about it because they don't want the union to know that they've been there.

Canada is a funny country. You live free here, but everyone you meet is as poor as a church mouse and out of work. If you work, you have a good time until you're suddenly out of work and then you haven't saved a penny. At least that's the condition of the majority of young people I meet and also of those at the Y.M.C.A. I had managed to save $150 from the Drummondville job, but a couple of the young fellows who worked with me in Quebec told me that they were already broke after the first week.

One of these friends, with three years of high school, got work again in a factory on Monday. He plans to take the provincial exams in a few years and then go to university and so he goes to school four nights a week. Most of those who prepare themselves for the university do this without support from their parents. The most they get from home is room and board. They have to provide clothes, tuition, books, etc. for themselves. As a result, they have to work as waiters, etc. in the evenings and during their vacations. An acquaintance of mine, who is studying to be a minister, had a job in a movie theatre as a commentator on a film which he had helped to produce. A Baptist minister, Dr. Cameron, holds his evening services in the largest movie theatre in Toronto (three thousand seats) while his church is being rebuilt. Every Sunday evening it's filled to the rafters and hundreds have to be turned away.

Last week, I spent a very pleasant evening with a Dutch family. Next Saturday, I'm planning to go to Niagara Falls. Last summer, I was too poor to travel there and so I want to do it now, before I get too poor again to do it. It's supposed to be a beautiful sight. Especially when the falls are frozen.

I still haven't heard anything from the American Consulate. It doesn't much matter, if it gets good here this summer. I still hope to get my visa for the Fall, so that I can be in the United States by the winter.

George Young, a 17-year-old Toronto boy, swam the Santa Catalina Channel. Apparently, this was reported in the Dutch newspapers. He had to make his own way to California, as no one believed he was capable of doing the deed. Now he's the hero of the day. You can't read a paper that doesn't have something in it about him.

Last week it was very cold here. 20 degrees below zero. Three days later it was 40 degrees above. Quite a bit of difference, eh? In general, I'm getting quite used to the winter. Much better than last year.

When I came back here at Christmas, I decided to spend my free time in what I considered to be the best way, that is by sending some twenty letters to the Fatherland. To these, until now (Feb. 2), I've received only one reply, from my friend Cor Hooijberg. If you, dear editor, are willing to publish this letter in your paper, there may be those among your readers who will remember that they belong to the remaining nineteen. And when they consider that a letter from the Fatherland is doubly welcome and let me hear something from them, then I will be very obliged for your help.

8 November, 1927

I wanted to write you earlier, but the questions in your last letter were not that easy to answer, and because I first wanted to discuss them with as many people as possible. I let quite a few read your clippings about Canada from the Dutch newspapers. They were very interested in them, and the warnings were greeted with general approval.

It's very hard to say if emigration to Canada is to be encouraged or not: the country is so big and the emigrants are also all so different. If I had to give a general impression, concerning whether they've been lucky or unlucky here, the majority would frankly answer: "no", in reply to the question if they would like to return to Holland for good. But married people should be strongly advised against emigration.

However, it would be better if I related what different people have told me: firstly what I learned from the A. Family. The husband is a gardener and works for a landscaping company here in Toronto. They're doing quite well now, but they've just gotten through a difficult time, especially in the West. He wrote up his experiences, upon my request, and they'll be included in my letter. His conclusion is that Canada perhaps offers better life opportunities to people like the peat cutters of Drenthe, who endure desperate lives in Holland, but that married people are better off with a humble existence in Holland, surrounded by relatives and friends, than eating and drinking well here but living completely isolated on some farm in the West.

Now, let me tell you what I also heard from unmarried people. I know a whole group of them. They've worked at different factories and companies, anywhere from six months to four years. Most of them have worked in the Western harvest, when there was no work or future opportunity here. The trip to Winnipeg costs $10, and the return $15, and they earn $2.50 to $6 a day there, plus room and board. On rainy days, they only get their board. When they return the following month, if they've been frugal, they can have saved about $150. Then comes the misery of trying to find a job in Toronto. Some can return to the factories where they worked before the harvest, but most remain unemployed or, now and then, find a little job for a short time because you're summarily dismissed here without notice: five minutes before quitting time, the boss comes to tell you to go to the office and pick up your wages. Furthermore, it's the rule here, for the big factories to close for two or three months per year.

Naturally, there are those who have better luck. I know such a young man, a mechanical draughtsman who arrived in Canada this spring. After he had gone around to different factories for work, he finally decided to go to the farm, but one day before he was to leave, he got temporary work as a draughtsman at a newly established washing machine factory. Things went well, and now he's hired permanently at $125 per month. Another young man has been here since April. His profession is decorator/painter. Because an incredible amount of advertising is done here, he has continuous work and earns from 50 cents to $1.25 an hour. Next year he hopes to start up for himself. Another young man has been here for three years. He's been in lumber camps, until finally last year, he got a job as an elevator operator at Simpson's (something like the

Bijenkorf). He worked his way up, so that now he has a very good position in the "house furnishings department" with a good chance of promotion, wages about $25 a week. (If you earn $20 to $25 a week, it's regarded as not doing badly.) Another fellow has been here for two and a half years. After first having worked on the farm, he went to learn bricklaying. After a couple of years of ups and downs, he's now had a very good summer and fall, an average of 35 dollars a week since the middle of June. He probably has work until December and maybe longer. In order to succeed you need: professional knowledge, stamina and luck.

This applies, however, only for people living in and around the city. However, Canada doesn't want them: it wants people to populate and to work the land. The chance of owning your own farm in the foreseeable future is very great. Whether or not it's worth giving up many conveniences, friends and acquaintances in order to acquire a farm is a question which I wouldn't dare answer.

Things are going well for me. Every day I feel more competent in my job and I get along well with my colleagues. At present I'm working in Oshawa, a place with about 20,000 inhabitants, 32 miles east of Toronto, headquarters of General Motor Car of Canada. They manufacture the Chevrolet, Oakland, Pontiac, Buick, Oldsmobile, G.M.C. truck and a couple of other makes of automobiles here. It's Ford's greatest competitor. G.M.C. is expanding incredibly this year, they've added eight buildings. I've worked on three of these, the last of these will be finished next week. It goes without saying that a significant number of houses will now have to be built, so we'll be working a little while longer. Toronto is fairly dead, besides that, the conditions are quite strained, the carpenters are on strike and now its rumoured that the bricklayers will strike out of sympathy.

I usually spend the weekend in Toronto. There's a regular bus service between Oshawa and Toronto. This journey is definitely a pleasure trip: beautiful roads through a uniquely pretty district. For example, you come past a hamlet, Rouge Hill. The highway crosses a valley here on a long, slanting uphill bridge (unlike any I've ever seen before) and the view over the flame red, fall tinted, glowing woods is exceedingly beautiful at the present time.

Last Friday night, we had a banquet for the bricklayers in Oshawa, organized by the local union. There were 50 of us. The dinner was tasty and the evening passed pleasantly with recitations and songs by the members. I was quite surprised when I heard the chairman say: "And now we'll have a song from Brother Dutch." So as not to embarrass myself, I took up his challenge, and sang a Dutch song that was quite well received. We had a convivial evening. Cigars and cigarettes were served all around. No rough or vulgar word was heard. Absolutely no alcoholic beverages. The banquet was opened with prayer and we ended at about eleven o'clock by standing and singing the "Internationale", followed by the national anthem "God Save the King." Would something like that be possible in the Netherlands? Imagine if the S.D.A.P. (Social Democratic Worker's Party) opened a convivial gathering with prayer and closed with the Wilhelmus (the Dutch national anthem)! And just the same, we had a very pleasant evening, during which not a discouraging word was heard.

On Sundays, I visit the museum and other attractions. Public amusements are not available on that day. We go to church every Sunday, to the big Uptown Theatre in the evening, religious services which I've written about earlier, 3,000 seats and full up every time.

12 November, 1927
(Prepared by Mr. A. of Toronto at the request of J. R. van der Meulen, Toronto, Y.M.C.A. 40 College St.)

A lot of propaganda is made to encourage people to emigrate to Canada, primarily by the Canadian railways but also by the Canadian government. There is, without a doubt, a lot of good to be said about Canada but this is just a bit overdone, as the not so good and bad points are concealed as much as possible.

To give an example of how the Canadian Pacific Railway office on the Coolsingel in Rotterdam gulls people, I will relate my own experience.

Around February 1926, I went to the C.P.R. office on the Coolsingel in Rotterdam to get some information about Canada. I had worked in fruit in Holland for three years and in nursery work and landscaping in the United States for five years. During the last five years, I had been a bookkeeper. Naturally at the C.P.R. office, Canada was most highly recommended and was described as a land "par excellence." Originally, I wanted to go to Ontario but I was told that the West was the very best place for me. There were a lot of gardens, of every sort, around Winnipeg and by the time I stepped on the boat, they would already have a position for me. I wasn't married yet but they told me that if I went there married and if my wife wanted to work in the household for the same employer, then we could easily earn 60 dollars a month year round. In any case, I alone could earn enough to support my family.

Everything was so nicely explained that I even decided to get married and go to Canada. So we left on the 22nd of April, naturally with a C.P.R. ship, and arrived in Winnipeg on the 5th of May. The first disappointment was awaiting us here. Because of my stay in the United States, I had a good command of the language and was able to notice all kinds of things which escaped the others in my party. In the first place, there was as yet no work for anyone and at the C.P.R. office they had yet to begin to telegraph and telephone to their different agents if they could place people. I was told that at that moment there was nothing available around Winnipeg. But if I wanted to wait a few days, something would turn up. On the street, I had already noticed that there was significant unemployment in and around Winnipeg and that there were thousands walking around without a job. The only thing I could do was take a job on a farm.

Along with another couple of Hollanders, we were sent to a little place in Saskatchewan where we could work for a farmer, my wife in the household and I on the farm. The wages for the two of us amounted to 35 dollars a month. The other Dutch couple got the same wage. We could earn a living there until after the harvest, about October 1 and after that there was nothing to do and we would have to see how we would get through the winter.

Now, I wasn't totally green as far as farming was concerned. I could milk, handle horses and had some experience with farm work, and besides that, I spoke the language. You can understand then what a totally green Hollander can earn when he's just arrived. We had to work from five o'clock in the morning, when I began the milking and my wife prepared the breakfast. I worked in the fields until seven o'clock in the evening, after that I unharnessed the horses, then supper and when everything was finished, I still had to milk nine cows.

Now, working hard and making long days is not a bad thing, if you're earning something. But all that, for just a little more than a dollar a day, it's just a little too crazy. The other Dutch couple, with whom we regularly associated, discovered the exact same thing. When we hired ourselves out to that farmer, we made it a condition of employment that we could leave at any time. Shortly before the harvest, we had had more than enough and we departed for Winnipeg. When I asked for my wages, I was shorted 35 dollars because, according to the farmer, I should have given a month's notice. He denied that we had an agreement that we could leave at any time. There were no witnesses, so I couldn't do anything but watch my hard-earned pennies disappear. Later in the village, I heard that this farmer always has difficulty with his employees when it comes to payment.

That's the kind of people that the C.P.R. sent us to. I've heard from many different people about the shameful manner in which the C.P.R. tries to get rid of the immigrants. Meanwhile, they tell you in the office, that the C.P.R. first gathers information about the employers before they send anyone to them.

Well anyway, we went to Winnipeg and found very little work. Strictly speaking, we found no work at all. The many gardens that are there, according to the C.P.R., are owned by truck farmers who only supply the city (Winnipeg has a population of 290,000) and there's no export. You can't find tree nurseries because the climate is unsuitable for this and many other agricultural endeavours.

Work was impossible to find. So with my little bit of money, I bought a horse and wagon to peddle vegetables. My wagon was mounted on a sled, covered with a tarpaulin and carpentered inside with planks. There were two holes in the front wall for the reins and a stove inside. Often it was so cold that the vegetables froze by the time I reached the door.

Well, even in that there was no money to be earned and so in the spring of 1927 we went to Toronto. Here, I had the luck to find a job in my own trade; the landscaping of gardens. Now at least, I can look after the needs of my family. For that matter, Toronto isn't such a booming place at the moment. It's the 1st of October and there are thousands walking around without work. It's true, many of them don't want to work, but there are certainly enough who do want to but can't find anything.

A number of weeks ago, the newspapers reported that the city of Toronto had supported 13,000 families last winter. This certainly indicates that things aren't rosy here. A few weeks ago, *The Evening Telegram* reported that the government of 1921-26 had spent more than thirteen million dollars to bring 6,000,000 immigrants here, while in the same period 500,000 people left Canada for the United States!

Now, a thing or two about the so-called, and by the C.P.R. and C.N.R. highly touted, "GOLDEN WEST."

I have already described what awaits you if you go there as a labourer: extremely hard work in the summer and no work in the winter. So, after you've spent your hard-earned pennies, you have to go hungry.

Now people are going there to buy farms. That's just the kind of victims that the C.P.R. and C.N.R. are looking for because they (being the only railways here) possess great landholdings which they would very much like to sell. They offer them at all kinds of easy payment terms and make it as simple as possible for people to start up. The greatest objection, which is usually recognized too late, is that the farms are practically impossible to sell. I spoke with a great number of farmers in the West, who stayed on the farm for 15 to 20 years and really didn't have much money and would have very much liked to go back to the civilized world, but couldn't because it's almost impossible to sell a farm. And isn't it wonderful to be condemned to waste your whole life away on the prairie. The climate doesn't help! For five months it's summer and very hot and then seven months of winter with minus 30 to 40 degree days when you can't work outside.

A little while ago, I read that the total acreage sown to grain in two of the three prairie provinces had decreased, while the total empty and abandoned farms in all three provinces had risen. If you look at the map, there seems to be a lot of villages along the rail lines. A village like that is usually only composed of a railway guard's house and a store. Many farms lie miles away from these stops and stores. In the winter, when the snow is two metres high, you sit there shut off from the whole world. Not for nothing is it said in the West, that the insane asylums are full of farmers' wives.

Leeuwarder Nieuwsblad,
4 April, 1927 to 11 April, 1929

THE LAST ILLUSION

Into the world!
4 April, 1927

I have, in my short life, cherished a considerable number of illusions, more than I could now possibly remember. Most had a brief existence, and died out by themselves only to be quickly replaced by new ones. Others took possession of years of my life. Again and again they formed the theme of my deepest thoughts and were the cause of many dreams. But slowly and surely I got older. I came to understand the reality of life... and that reality shattered my most beautiful illusions into shards.

There's one fantasy which I've carried with me practically all of my life. I wanted to leave Friesland's flat countryside which (even for the Frisian), becomes (after a while), a monotonous landscape. Away from this little part of the world where everybody is the same. I wanted to have adventures. Into the world! I wanted to see strange people, Indians, Chinese, Arabs and even Hottentots, as long as they were different from the people who crossed my path every day. Wild mountainous landscapes, thundering untamable waterfalls, primeval forests, where the lion and the tiger are still masters. Into the world! That was my great dream. Now my dream, at least in part, is going to become a reality, a harsh drab reality, with necessity as its background. Now I have to go into the world. Now I have to: in order to find a decent existence.

How many are there in these districts who, like me, find the struggle for existence increasingly difficult? How many are there like me who longingly envision a land where one gets the opportunity to work and through that work a decent existence? I'm going to give it a try in Canada. I believe that Canada offers a man a chance, a chance to show what he can do, a chance to roll up his sleeves, a chance to succeed. Oh, that success must be wonderful! Here I notice the sympathetic and, more often than not, contemptuous glances of my acquaintances. I hear their scornful gossip and scheming, niggling whispering about "that Frans, who can't get into his stride." That's the terrible torment which I'm now going to escape. I'm going into the world!

Canada has no use for dreamers, only people with a practical spirit and a pair of strong hands. It needs those people for its agriculture. In Canada there are not just thousands, but millions of arable hectares of land waiting for the industrious hand to liberate them from the wild bush and tree cover, from the dry woody prairie grasses. The soil must come in contact with the air, bringing to it the marvellous nitrogen which causes the grain kernel to germinate, and magically transforms it into a mighty, heavy, bending grain stalk. With tenacious patience and concentrated work the arid, but by nature fruitful, Canadian prairies must be changed into rolling seas of grain. Agriculture: there lies the future of this young land.

I shall test myself in only a small branch of that agriculture. For about a year and a half now I've worked in market gardening in the vicinity of one of the Frisian cities. I have dug, planted and picked, carried pails of water for half-days at a time and toiled away pushing untold barrows of manure. My arms have become stronger, my hands sturdier and I can display great calluses with pride. I can walk in wooden shoes and not even complain anymore when my socks are soaking. I've learned to get up early and to go to bed early. In short I've mastered farm work. In that far-off land my hands will be my capital. They'll have to be put out to earn interest.

I'll settle in the area around Winnipeg. The manager of the Canadian Government Immigration Office in Rotterdam will give me a letter of recommendation which should help me find a job. A trip of about ten days or so and then to work. In a series of future letters, I hope to show my fellow countrymen what happens and what conditions I will encounter in my new fatherland.

Frans van Waeterstadt

Auf Wiedersehen!
11 April, 1927

As soon as I stepped on the Leeuwarden station platform, on the last Monday of March, I recognized my traveling companions. A group of men and a few women were standing clustered together, surrounded by a large number of suitcases and packages which seemed to form a fence around them. There were some new suitcases but most had seen better days. Perhaps they had been quickly rustled up for this occasion from generous family or friends.

They weren't a happy group. Most of them stood silently and looked depressed, sometimes calmly talking with the few family members who had come to see them off.

Then the train arrived and there was a bustle and commotion to find the right coaches. There was also a young woman. "All aboard! All aboard!" cried the conductor, in his usual and everyday manner. To that young woman it meant that the last family ties were now being cut away. To her younger sister, who stood beside her, it meant that in a few moments she would see her dear sister's trusting face, perhaps for the very last time... "Now Griet, it's the best thing hear, take care of yourself." The last words were forced out in a shrieking sob. "Goodbye Sjouk... Goodbye Sjouk"... Very sadly and almost tonelessly came the reply. Then into the coach. With an angry push the porter slammed the door closed after her.

Because of all my looking and fooling around, I had to run to find a place and that wasn't that easy. There didn't seem to be any empty places, but it all worked out. A couple of doors down a pair of heads were stuck out of the window. "Direction Halifax! Direction Halifax!" We— my traveling companions and I—dashed towards them. "Are you fellows going to Canada too? Everybody who's going to Canada can get in here!" Five, six voices yelled and bawled together and several pairs of hands lifted my baggage and myself inside.

There we sat—but not comfortably. We had met five future Canadians, all about twenty years of age, farm hands and all incredibly boisterous and profane. Immediately they began to sing, in five different keys, that "they had lost their heart" in a notorious Leeuwarden cafe. They certainly could have lost that organ in a better place! Apparently they realized that they were acting in an unusual manner. "You'll have to excuse us, today is a rather special day!" There was one who was obviously much relieved when the train slowly started to move because he loudly proclaimed that he had half-expected a number of creditors to arrive at the last minute. Then one of his friends remarked, "you'll probably never pay your debts." He replied, "you know darn well I'm honest. They'll just have to wait. Look at it this way, today I'm running weighed down by debt, but in a couple of years I'll be running weighed down by dollars." Then they began to fantasize about how large the money chest would have to be which they would take back to the fatherland in five years or so. Their ideal seemed to be to earn a lot of money, to drink a lot of beer and to have a lot of fun. The pittance which could be earned working for a Frisian farmer seemed to upset them.

They counted up a whole series of farmers they would have liked to have thrown into the ocean on their way to Canada. If you believed them there were a lot of evil farmers in their district. It wasn't a restrained orderly discussion. Songs and snatches of songs echoed wondrously confused in the little room. There were pleasant songs, sentimental love songs and happy-go-lucky songs. At every station stop, the heads were stuck out of the window. "Direction Halifax, Direction Halifax!" The pronunciation of their English was proof of its scanty practice.

We breezed through Peperga and soon reached the Frisian border. "Up with Friesland," shouted the group. "Up with Friesland: but down with the farmers!"

As for me, I can't judge the farmers. I know that the Frisian farmer doesn't live in luxury either. But I agreed with my companions... "Up with Friesland!"

In Rotterdam our first task was to go to the Holland-America Line offices. As soon as we stepped off the ferry and onto the grounds we could see our destination. Groups of Poles and Hungarians were milling around, the women wore large multicoloured kerchiefs tied over their shoulders and white ones on their heads. They looked poor and unpleasant, the clothes were grey and sun-bleached, the shoes down at the heel and without a trace of black. And the faces! Ugly, extremely ugly, sallow and dirty and unusually dumb in appearance. But the eyes, mostly half-closed, flickered with a strange cunning shine. Sometimes we saw very old people and it was hard to understand why they would emigrate.

There were many strange people outside the office building and even more inside. I was surprised when I got inside. A great hall had been allocated for the public and it was packed full of waiting people. Of the whole series of ticket windows not one was uncrowded. In long rows along the walls stood the Slavic women and children waiting for husbands and fathers who were busy paying their baggage money. These people were quiet and calm, without that hurried agitation which is the hallmark of every other emigrant. But they certainly talked enough, so much that hearing and understanding were destroyed.

The waiting wasn't all that bad, it seems that paying out money isn't that difficult and generally takes little time. In return for my money I received a transportation contract with a series of regulations printed on it which I was obliged to obey. I was prohibited from transporting diamonds, jewels and valuables other than for my own use. The only gold I possessed was in the nib of my fountain pen!

I also received a railway coupon for the Halifax-Montreal route.

After having weighed the pros and cons for a considerable time (just like a Leeuwarden council member occasionally does), I chose Montreal as my final destination instead of Winnipeg. [The ticket costs $9.58 (23.95 guilders).] A ticket to Winnipeg costs $25.

Finally I was given an introduction card which I was to present at the placement bureau of the Canadian National Railways in Montreal and I also received a "doctor's card."

With the "doctor's card" in hand I went to the "American doctor." After waiting very patiently for about an hour, he spent about a half minute very quickly examining me while a helper offered another five seconds in which he stamped my card. At the eye and skin specialist it was the same, only the wait was longer and the examination shorter.

At last—after another long wait (this tale is becoming monotonous) I received the visa on my passport from the Canadian immigration officer: the Monday jobs were finished. I had begun the process at two o'clock and reached my hotel at six-thirty.

S.S. *New Amsterdam*

P.S. halted because of signs of seasickness.

Washed Ashore
12 May, 1927

On Thursday evening, April 7, the bulletin board in the dining room of the *New Amsterdam* carried the following message printed in large letters:

BREAKFAST, 1st TABLE, 6 o'clock.

2ND TABLE, 6:45.

It meant that we were going to reach Halifax the following morning and that those whose destination was Canada ought to get up early to pack their suitcases. I had waited for that moment for a long time, but now that it had arrived I wasn't looking forward to it. I had become used to ship life. I had formed a circle of acquaintances and the last days had been exceptionally convivial. But one doesn't live simply for pleasure alone and all good things must come to an end. I went to say goodbye to a number of people. A Polish beauty, bound for New York, asked me to wake her the following morning so that she could be present at my departure. Naturally I took that little job with rather great pleasure.

At four o'clock I jumped out of my bunk and fifteen minutes later I was standing in the... snow! A welcome greeting from Canada!

Snow and thick fog. The warning voice of the steam whistle sounded hoarse and dismal. "Here I am," it called, "here I am and I'm bringing Frans van Waeterstadt, who had expected fine sunny spring weather in his new homeland in the middle of April! Look there he is, walking on the after deck, his cap pulled down over his head and his coat collar high up in the air, hear him swearing." Of course the steam whistle was lying, I wasn't swearing, just muttering. What weather! A fine snowdrift whirled across the deck, the mist hung clammy and wet on my nose. "That's the way it always is here, sir," said a sailor. "You get one good day a year here, and on that day you have to plough, sow, harvest and take your vacation!" I gave him a dirty look and went down the stairs.

They could have let us sleep a little longer as we didn't catch sight of land until about eleven o'clock. And what a land? The steep bluffs of the Nova Scotia coast lifted themselves high above us on both sides and were still thickly buried in their winter dress. Snow, wherever you looked! The cone-shaped fir trees stood unmoving and densely packed. The first impression was one of deep winter rest. It looked like the country in which Curwood had his characters hunt for furs, fir trees and snow and a rolling land. The Canada of the romantics, but I didn't fall into a romantic mood at all. Winter meant that farm tasks could not yet be started. It meant that I might have to wait a while before I could get going. I thought about my tiny stake with just a touch of fear. But there was more than enough to see so I didn't think about that question too long. Slowly we neared Halifax and the spruce trees gave way to a few factories and warehouses, which certainly didn't give a very prosperous impression. We heard someone say, "everything is poverty-stricken here as well! They build their factories out of wood!" He'll have to wait a while before he sees a brick house. In eastern Canada everything is built out of wood. Little wonder as the forests have a rich future potential.

We remained outside of Halifax in the stream and in the afternoon the immigration authorities came on board. They arrived on a tugboat that was completely decorated with garlands of icicles. The formalities got under way quickly. First we passed by an eye doctor, who rapidly examined us and held back an occasional one in order to take a more careful look at his eyes. After that we were dealt with by another official who checked our papers and asked how much money we had. He was delighted with any answer. A Limburger had two dollars left in his pocket and he declared three hundred! All you need is a little nerve!

That's how we got permission to enter Canada, but the possibility to do so was not yet at hand. It appeared that the wind or current or both prevented our ship from finding a place at the wharf. The earliest opportunity was on Saturday morning. Around eight o'clock I trod on Canadian soil and came into a large shed. First the baggage was placed on a long cart train and after that it was paraded into a great hall where the rail coupon, paid for and acquired in Rotterdam, was traded for a ticket.

Then back on the road to the wharf where the *New Amsterdam* still lay waiting, ready to proceed on its journey to New York. All the remaining passengers had gathered together on the decks and I and about five others stood on a high platform in the middle of an ice cold wind. But I didn't care about the wind, I wanted to see that drifting little piece of the Netherlands up until the last moment, the very last moment. I wanted to see the "red, white and blue" wave in the wind.

Friendly greetings were exchanged, jokes and quips were bantered back and forth. One of our group began to shout angrily when he saw his newly acquired love interest in the arms of another passenger. Love was sometimes quickly given on board but not always retained. The Polish girl called to me, "Be lucky." And honestly, she hid her face in her handkerchief. "Be lucky," I believe she truly meant it.

The gangways were taken in, the steam whistle blew for the last time. Slowly the ship began to move. In a few moments my temporary home disappeared around a corner.

And So to Work
25 May, 1927

I climbed the flight of stairs up to Mr. Monette's house with just a little bit of nervousness. What kind of person would he be and on what conditions would he offer me a job? I felt a little guilty as well. The manager of the placement bureau had asked me, "Do you speak French?" And with a substantial dose of *braggadocio* I had assured him I spoke French. Indeed they had pumped a load of French into me in school but the ten following years were sufficient to diminish my knowledge of that beautiful language to a minimum. At that moment, "bonjour" and "bonsoir" and another ten words made up my whole stock of French words. Just suppose that Monsieur Monette spoke only French, then I would really be in for it and would have to take myself and my whole kit and caboodle back to Montreal.

I plucked up my courage and firmly pulled the house bell. After a wait of several moments a head appeared behind the window of the door: a very fat head, with a tangled mass of hair on top and a double chin on the bottom. The large eyes in that head swivelled first towards me and then towards my baggage. I pulled my letter of introduction from my inside pocket and waved it in front of the window. The eyes twinkled satisfaction.

Then from behind the window came a storm of strange sounds: French naturally. The man could just as well have spoken Greek or Russian: I didn't understand a word. I remained standing with an open mouth and an apparently dumb look on my face. Albert Monette changed his tactics and tried English, "Go to the back," he called. At the same time he made a waving motion with his arm. Now I understood him better. I put my gear together and began looking for the back door of the house. The door was open and my future boss was waiting, leaning against the door post. The fat head was attached to a fat body with a very fat stomach. There, in living, breathing flesh, I saw the "Canadian cousin." I didn't yet know if Mr. Monette had accumulated a lot of money by farming, but I did notice that he had never lacked regular and overabundant meals. "I've been sent by the placement bureau of the Canadian National Railways, sir, they told me you could use a man. My name is, etc., etc." "Absolutely correct!" said the boss and extended a meaty hand which I very carefully pressed. The first thing he then asked me was whether I could plough. Naturally, I had to answer in the negative. I don't believe there are any gardeners in Friesland who use a plough on their 3 or 4 hectares. "Do you know how to work with horses?"

In the past I had a friend who worked as a deliveryman at Van Gend and Loos. One day—I was about nineteen—I ran into him and his wagon at the head of Spoorstraat (Railway Street) in Leeuwarden. It was warm, hot really, and the sun's burning rays were only partly absorbed by the half-grown trees. I had to be at the other end of the street, a rather long walk for which I had little desire. So I climbed on the driver's box of the Van Gend and Loos vehicle. The deliveryman remained walking alongside in order to deliver his boxes and packages here and there. With a pompous air, I picked up the loosely hanging reins and let the ends dangle in my hands. The heavy Belgian slowly and sluggishly trudged forward. When we reached another stop the deliveryman called, "Ho!" And before I had a chance to shout "ho!," the horse stood still, glad to have a moment's rest. When we had to move on things went a little differently. The deliveryman then shouted "forward," and the beast pricked up his ears. I also yelled "forward" and he lifted one of his hind feet. As far as my friend was concerned things didn't move fast enough because as soon as he was finished delivering his package he could begin his lunch hour. So he yelled angrily, "get up you damn...!" The Van Gend and Loos horse was one of a very cultured breed, and in order to avoid more rude words he again trudged forward. In this manner we neared the end of the long straight Spoorstraat. During all this time I had held onto the reins. Furthermore my friend had told me how to drive. If you pulled towards the left, the horse went to the left, if you pulled to the right the old crock would go right. And thus I told Monsieur Monette that I knew how to handle a horse.

As a result this gentleman began to boast. With great verbosity he told me that I would have very pleasant work with him, that I would learn all the necessary things and that I would have good food and an excellent bed. That was all very well but I was sitting and waiting in great suspense to find out how much heavier my wallet was going to become either every Saturday or every month. But we hadn't progressed that far yet. First I had to describe my trip to Canada: whether we had had good weather and how much that pleasantry had cost. I began to find Mr. Monette's behaviour increasingly annoying.

But the answer came quite quickly: a farmhand was called. He was instructed to take me to the boss's foreman who was to inform me of any further necessary things.

After a short walk we entered that gentleman's kitchen, and after I had again undergone the same interrogation as with Mr. Monette, came the question, "What is your price?" Now it was up to me to say how much my wage ought to be. It was a difficult question: what did I know about the wages being paid in this district? I decided to try and get the lay of the land first and I asked the old fellow to make me an offer. "Fifty cents a day!" I was truly surprised. Fifty American cents a day equals one guilder and twenty five cents in Dutch money. It was much below my expectations. They had told me that I could always figure on twenty-five dollars a month with free room and board and now I was being offered less than fourteen. And so I said, "It's an awfully small amount." "Yes, but I have another young man working for only fifty cents per day. Furthermore you mustn't forget you've got year-round work here and holidays and rain-days are paid."

I thought it was excessively generous of that other young man to make his skills available at such a moderate wage and a year's employment was indeed very desirable, but the fifty cents did not agree with me. I put on a sad face and said I had better get on my way as I felt the

offered wage to be too low. Then Mr. Decarie—the name of my opponent—showed his hand. Well, he'd be willing to try me for two weeks at
75 cents per day. During that time we could get to know each other and
at the end we could talk a little more. If my work was acceptable he
could perhaps offer a little more. The bargain was agreed to.

I accepted my first position in Canada.

And So to Work (II)
28 May, 1927

I went to look the place over, the stable and the fields. The first
impression wasn't all that good. On the last day I had worked for my boss
in Friesland all you could see in his gardens were young plants. The tender young spinach beds stretched out like a thick carpet, the new lettuce
stood up lively in long rulerstraight lines. The young beans poked their
noses out in a sprightly and forceful manner. A delicate green veil lay
over the gooseberry bushes. Only a few more nice days and the apples
and pears would display their beauty of snow-white blossoms. Yes, the last
days of work in the Netherlands had been a pleasure. Spring, the most
beautiful time for a gardener! A time full of promise.

And here in Canada? The ground lay dirty-brown, still
unploughed and full of weeds. Drifts of snow still clung in several shad-
owed places.

The tenth of April and not a scrap of green! The fields were separated by strips of grassland on which no grass had yet appeared, only
dead haylike stubble from the previous year. A man was busy ploughing
with a tractor. "How pleasantly the life of the peaceful farmer rolls on"
wrote the poet Poot. Now, I know that our friend Poot traded "the life
of the peaceful farmer" for one in the city, and that he profited exceedingly well from that life, but still, much poetry lies hidden in farm life.
But as the tractor appears on the farm scene, poetry disappears. The
whirring and sputtering of the heavy motor is an annoyance. Bring
machines on the farm and sooner or later it will become a factory. And
I hate factories....

Slowly the evening had come. The sun disappeared and left a
flame-red western rim behind. The full moon glimmered quietly in the
sky, surrounded by a few ephemeral little clouds which seemed to drift
like fairy boats on a deep blue lake.

The stars shone vividly. The surroundings, the barren fields, the house and the stables—everything disappeared. Only I remained, together with the moon, the stars and the little clouds.

Oh that sky! It shone the same as at home. The same interchange of light and dark, the same constellations. The moon with her beaming face looked like an old acquaintance, my only friend in this strange land. Quietly I sat on a pile of planks, thinking.

The trip with all its many diversions was finished. Life had now tossed me quite alone in the midst of people whom I could only partially understand and who would regard me, for the present at least, as a stranger. Now I had time to put things together for myself, time to think about the past... and I thought about it.... It was a difficult moment.

Next morning, at about five thirty, a couple of resounding blows landed on the door of the small room I shared with another employee. Naturally on the first day, you're always exceedingly diligent and so I very hastily jumped out of my bed. In a twinkling of an eye I was downstairs ready to begin. My roommate and I made our way to the stable where a pail was shoved into my hands and I was asked to water the five horses. I'm a friend of horses, I find them to be beautiful and exceptionally intelligent, but they're also very strong and not always gentle. And to be honest, I didn't feel much like twisting myself in between a wooden partition and a strange horse. But you can't always have what you want and so I put on a nonchalant, brave face and with an agile turn I stood at the head of number one.

After number one came the four others and with a lighter heart I went to tell my fellow worker that the water business was finished. But now I went from the frying pan into the fire. Curry them! I had never done it, in fact had never seen it done.

Well I did it, even though it was with a lot of fear and trembling. There was one horse which seemed to be extraordinarily ticklish in the legs. As soon as I touched them a heavy hoof would go up and then come down back to the ground with a resounding plop. It's very disturbing when you're currying a horse for the first time in your life. It didn't get any better when the boss came to have a look. After he had stood watching my work very inquisitively for a while, he began to speak.

"Say," he said "that horse never kicks"—a load of worry dropped from my shoulders—"but if he kicks"—I pricked up my ears—"but if he kicks, then it'll be towards the back. So stand a little differently—a little more to the side."

Since that time I haven't had a quiet heart when I've had to clean up that crock. I always handle his back feet with extreme caution and I always keep myself at a respectful distance. I wish that my annoy-ing boss had never warned me.

After the horses were cared for, we took the planks off Mr. Decarie's cold frames. It may sound a little strange to Dutch gardeners that cold frames still have to be covered against severe night frosts in the middle of April! At seven o'clock we had breakfast, followed finally by the beginning of the day's work until twelve. Then from one o'clock straight through in one piece until seven. It was a long haul. I really missed the 15-minute tea break which is customary among the Friesian gardeners at midday. But anyway: "When in Rome..." There are other strange customs here which one must get used to. But more about that later.

P.S. In Rotterdam, at the Holland-America Line, I received a card with the instruction to guard it well. It's a so-called "identification card." The following momentous Dutch instruction is emblazoned on the reverse side.

This card must be retained at all costs.
This card must be produced when an empowered official desires the same.

All of this simply means that you have to show your card to every Canadian official who wants to see it!

The Language, the Girls and the States
13 June, 1927

A retired person has nothing to do; otherwise he wouldn't be a retiree. And doing nothing is just a little boring after a while, so some-one like that is tempted, quite quickly, to do all kinds of little jobs for others. That's the way it is with Mr. Monette. Now that I've been here a week or so I've discovered that the gentleman achieved financial securi-ty and then rented the farm out to my boss's son. And now, to kill time, he does service as a kind of helpful guest. He goes to the village for the neighbouring farm wives and orders meat and other foodstuffs. He takes shoes to the shoemaker and dirty collars to the laundry. And if he isn't too tired after all this busy work, he chops a little firewood.

He went to the placement bureau of the Canadian National Railways for my boss and his son and requested two farmhands. And that's why I was sent by the bureau to him and why I was mistaken in the belief that he was the boss of the business. Indeed, I have nothing to do with him, the old gentleman Romain Decarie is my only boss.

He's not a bad boss, at least I've had no trouble with him yet. It's a very different situation with my workmate, the young gentleman Joseph Perron. This young fellow is nineteen years old, comes from Montreal and speaks hardly a word of English. And I have to work with him most of the time. Oh, those first days, when all the jobs here were still strange!

Every morning after breakfast, friend Joseph stuck out his small skinny chest, composed his face and called out in a bossy tone, "Come here!" What else could I do but stand up and meekly follow the lout. And then the stinker winked at the boss's daughters, who in turn snickered. At the time I thought they were laughing at me, but now I believe that they were making fun of the kid who was too dumb to say a word in company, was deathly afraid of the boss and who only dared to order around the newly arrived Dutchman, who didn't understand anything anyway.

Then together we'd go out to the field and when we had reached our destination, Perron would shout, "Stop!" He would begin telling me what we had to do, in French naturally. In spite of immense concentration, I was never lucky enough to understand even one word. Mostly that was my own fault (why hadn't I kept up my French better?) but he was also at fault because the French they speak here is incredible. There's a new farmhand at our neighbours', fresh from France, and he told me that he can barely understand his French-Canadian boss, and his wife not at all. That's how peculiar the language is that's spoken here. Added to that is the problem that a lot of English words are mixed in with the French.

Every morning I'd have to repeat again, "*Je ne comprends pas*," "I don't understand." Then the kid would pull an ugly face and deluge me with a flood of words; swearwords as I understood it. Oh, why didn't they teach me a repertoire of swear words at school? Then I could have answered my colleague in fine fashion. At that particular moment you want to throw out all your knowledge of other French and simply desire to know a few strong, sturdy, and to-the-point, swearwords. But that's the way teachers are, after all, they don't teach you what you need in everyday life. *Was der Schuler weisz das braucht er nicht und was er braucht, das weisz er nicht.* (What the schoolboy knows he does not need and what he needs he does not know.)

But eventually everything worked out, Mr. Perron demonstrated what I was to do and I began working.

I've been here about six weeks and I'm beginning to understand the French names for the daily chores fairly well. But there's still a lot that I don't understand and then someone has to demonstrate what I'm to do. You get the feeling, unwillingly, that you're only giving half your labour—an especially sad and awful feeling.

When I began to think about moving to Canada, I naturally read everything very eagerly which was written about this country in the newspapers or in pamphlets. Regularly I would read the injunction, "learn English before you set out." You require French for the province of Quebec but most of the Dutch trek to the western provinces anyway and English is the general language there. For the thousandth time I repeat the advice: "Prospective immigrants, learn English. Spend all your free time on that." And for the thousandth time it will be given in vain: much to the sadness and injury of those for whom it was meant.

I had worked at Mr. Decarie's for eight days and was busy feeding the horses when he came looking for me. "Tell me Francois" (as you can see my name is already frenchified), he said to me, "tell me, are you planning to stay here?" With great interest I asked him why he wanted to know. "Oh, there's another farmhand here who's offering his services, so I want to know if you're going to stay, If not, I'll hire the other fellow, but I'd rather you stayed." You have to strike while the iron is hot so I began to fish for a little higher wage. I flattered the boss a little and assured him that I was very satisfied in my situation with him. Naturally I would prefer to stay with him, but what did he think of the question of wages. Would he perhaps give me a little more (after the agreed probationary period)?

"Beginning the first of May I'll pay you a dollar a day," was the answer. The agreement was sealed with a handshake: I had contracted to work for Mr. Decarie for a year. I had begun work on the 12th of April for 75 cents a day, as of May 1, I would receive one dollar: a raise of 33-1/3 per cent: such occurrences stimulate hope and desire in your heart.

While the work with my colleague wasn't all that pleasurable in the beginning, things went a lot better with my boss's daughters. He has three—all three are especially friendly and fairly good-looking—but only two work along on the farm. Weeding, transplanting and all kinds of other light jobs are reserved for them. We, the male workmen, have little to do with them, sad to say. Let me tell you, work goes like a breeze when you have a cute face in the neighbourhood. Every now and then you rake up a few French words and you carry on an irregular conversation interspersed with smiles on both sides and blushes from the lady.

Cecile, the eldest, is helping me with the cabbage planting. She is the biggest and the boss of the others. She is the boss of the poultry department, and you'd be amazed how handily she grabs a chicken by the wings and shoves the insect powder sprayer under the feathers. Saturdays she takes a fork and shovel and cleans out the chicken coop.

A few minutes before I began this letter, she came into the room with a triumphant look on her face and a fork on which was spitted a great big rat. She had seen the beast running, had thrown the fork at it and had hit it. Most women would surely have run to the house to get help.

As I said: this sturdy young lady of twenty-six is my companion in the cabbage patch. It's her duty to throw a plant down in front of me, which I set in its place with a little shovel. The work is quick and hard, and about 3000 plants are handled per day. Time to talk or make a joke simply doesn't exist, but sometimes Cecile makes a mistake and drops two plants instead of one. Unaware I grab two plants. Cecile, who quickly realizes her mistake, also grabs for them and—before we know it—we're holding each other's hand.

Then my female helper mutters a "pardon!" I say: "excusez," and on we go. A thing like that makes a nice distraction.

My *friend* Perron also helped me on one occasion. Once in a while he'd make a mistake and we would grab each other by the hand. But then I would say: "Watch out, stupid." Besides that I couldn't work as quickly with Perron. But that's the way men are, they always put the best foot forward in the company of a member of the fair sex. As for myself, at least I can honestly say that I never work harder than when I'm working with Cecile.

Probably a good piece of advice for the down-and-out Frisian farmer would be to send the farmhand and farm girl into the fields together: about twice as much work would be done, or perhaps none at all.

I once said to Cecile, "this is the first time in my life I've ever worked with a girl." "And how do you like the job?" "Delightful." She said nothing more.

When I was a boy of about thirteen or fourteen and approaching the age to choose an occupation, my parents said, "Son, you have to choose your own occupation, whatever you want." And they didn't just say it, they meant it too. They didn't put the least bit of pressure on me. There were two exceptions: under no conditions would they permit me to become either a baker or a butcher. The first occupation was too unhealthy—this was still in the time of the notorious night, work—and they thought that the job of a butcher was too bloody, too brutal.

Luckily neither appealed to me, so that the prohibition created few problems. As far as I'm concerned they could have added a third prohibited job; they could have easily forbidden me to become a barber.

I hate barbers. First, their work is exceptionally childish. When I'm in their hands I always have the feeling that they're just playing around with my hair. Secondly, they're mostly gossip mongers. Whether you go to a home for the aged or a barber, the conversations are identical. You can hear all the local gossip and they know something about everyone. Besides the barber is usually involved in politics.

The Dutch and Canadian *hairstylists* are birds of a feather. I went to one in a neighbouring village and of course he automatically knew I was a stranger. Then he began to pump me for information. What country did I come from: Holland? Wasn't there enough work there or were the wages too low? And did I work here in Pont Viau?

I told him that I worked in St. Vincent de Paul and answered his next question by telling him that Mr. Decarie was my boss.

Then he began to warm up. Was he a good boss—how was the food and the bed? I said that I got along well with my employer, that the meals were excellent and that the bed was quite good.
But the wages probably weren't very high?

At first I wanted to tell him that he shouldn't be so terribly curious, but I found it impossible to remember what "curious" was in either English or French. I didn't want to remain silent, so I told him that I was getting a dollar a day.

Then he stopped his work on my head and kicked the barber chair so that I turned like a top and was able to look him in the face. He had a very surprised look.

"A dollar a day?"

"Yes, one dollar a day.

"Now, that's no money for such a great big strong fellow! One dollar a day! There's a gardener here in the neighbourhood who pays three dollars a day!"

Well, I had thought myself pretty lucky with my job, and now somebody had already come along and told me that I had contracted myself for a pittance. But it wasn't all that bad because when I told him that I would be employed year round and rain-days were paid, my barber said that that changed things. At the three dollar boss, rain-days were unpaid and employment was only for the summer months.

"Am I in a good district of Canada?" I asked. "Oh, what shall I say," was the answer. "Montreal and its environs have already had their best times. That was about ten, twelve years ago. That was when things were really good. I was just a boy then and on holidays I would get a dollar for pocket money. And now? A child who receives a dime nowadays should be extremely satisfied as most only get a nickel and some nothing."

So slowly he satisfied his curiosity about me and he began to tell a little more about himself. The barbershop wasn't really his but belonged to his father, who, because of sickness, couldn't carry on the business. He used to work for someone else but had quit his last job. "I only got $18 per week and what can you do with that if you have a wife and two kids? No, a married man needs $25 here."

I asked him which was the best place to be in Canada. "The best place? That's Windsor!"

It just so happened that I'd heard about Windsor when I was aboard the *New Amsterdam*. It lies on the border between Canada and the United States and its inhabitants are almost all factory workers who work across the border in adjacent Detroit. In the mornings they cross the border to the automobile factories and in the evenings… they are supposed to come back. But every now and then one fewer comes back than went: then one more has seen the chance to smuggle himself into rich and prosperous America without papers. It's a big gamble: if someone like that is caught, he first gets put in prison, sometimes for half a year, then he's sent back to his native land. The steward on the *New Amsterdam* told me that they had had a Czechoslovak on board on the previous trip who had sold all his property in Czechoslovakia in order to emigrate with his wife and family to Canada. From Canada he crossed the border to the States, all alone. He was arrested in Chicago, did five months' time and was sent back to his fatherland. Now his family was in Canada, practically penniless, and he was on his way back home, flat broke and without a hope of finding a job, at least a decent one.

When the barber told me that Windsor was the best place in Canada, I asked him directly: "The States?"

"Exactly," said he, "over the river and you're there. If you can speak pretty good English and you're not too reckless, the chance of being caught is pretty small. If I didn't have a wife and kids… well, I'd know what to do!"

The United States. There seems to be something magical in those few words. If someone hears those words, then he automatically thinks of abundance, of wealth. The Golden Land! The majority of people would love to go there but only a few get permission to settle and so it's no wonder that many take the chance and try to get in without papers.

But even if the States is the 'best" country, there are still "good" countries. I believe Canada is one of those. My first impression is that most of the people here have a comfortable existence and it appears that the farmers, in particular, do well.

I don't think I'll go to Windsor, a bird in the hand is worth ten in the air!

Hodge-podge with an Interesting Conclusion
5 July, 1927

Spring has finally arrived in Canada! When I arrived here, about the middle of April, the weather was beautiful. We had clear skies during the day with a delicious warm spring sun and a little frost at night. "It's much too nice," said the barber. "Spring's arrived much too soon." At the end of April, the bomb dropped; rain and more rain. May came in with a cold drizzly Sunday and it stayed that way until the 27th when, for the first time, we saw the sun for an entire day. However, by the evening, it was so chilly that all the cold frames had to be covered. The boss was expecting a night frost—*on the 27th of May*! Well the night frost stayed away and a beautiful Saturday followed. Today is Sunday, and spring is full-blown.

I went to Montreal and came back around dusk. For seven cents the tram dropped me off in neighbouring Ahuntsic and to get home I had to walk for just over a half hour.

A walk on a calm, quiet, spring evening through a beautiful district! What a delight! It's incredibly beautiful here. The land rolls in great waves; the road goes up and down. The pastures are already coloured dark green, sown with bright yellow dandelions.

The partially bare fields are intersected here and there by little groups of trees and bushes. Wild cherry, lilacs and may thorn trees are everywhere; along the fields, around the houses and along the road. Everything is in full bloom now.

From the road I can look down on the river. It is called the Black River in English or Riviere des Prairies in French. It's a left-hand side shoot of the great St. Lawrence and a paradise for campers and fishermen. The steep bank is covered with thick bush or orchards. A white flower veil covers everything. Here and there the roofs of the summer cottages of the Montreal well-to-do stick out above the green.

On the other side, the bank isn't quite as steep. It rises steadily and slowly becomes built up, until finally the widely separated houses merge into long strung-out blocks. There lies Montreal, the foremost harbor and trading center of Eastern Canada! In the background, like a huge dirt pile, rises Mount Royal, the mountain to which Montreal owes its name.

It's not a beautiful city. Many neighbourhoods and streets are definitely ugly and it's no wonder that the population climbs into the car on Sundays to see something of the outside world.

The car is very popular here! Anyone who has a fairly decent job has one, and the farmer doesn't want to be left out. If he's just begun farming he probably has to do without one, but as soon as he's saved a couple of hundred dollars he buys a Ford on the instalment plan.

It's easy to see which farmer has just begun and which one has been farming for a longer time, just by going to church on Sunday. On Sunday the new farmer cleans the wagon that he used during the week to carry his produce to market. He hitches up the work horse and goes to church with his wife. If he's farmed for a couple of years then he buys a little carriage and appears as a "gentleman" at the weekly promenade.

If he's had a few more years of patience, then the automobile finally appears. No "Rolls Royce," no "Overland," not even a "Ford" touring car. No, the business comes first and so he buys a truck. Meanwhile his family has undoubtedly expanded. Most of the farmers in this district have been richly blessed with children. The children are big enough to go along to mass and the carriage has become too small, so the truck provides the solution. It's packed full of chairs, the children, the hired men and a few of the neighbours take their place, and the truck proceeds down the dirt road. You see a lot of them on Sunday. Dressed to the teeth, the girls well-powdered (some with a touch of rouge on their faces), packed together on a muddy, rattling truck.

Once the business is doing well and the sons have taken the place of the hired men, then comes the luxury car. Papa has made it! In front of every church in this district is a big square, usually too small to provide room for all the wagons, carriages, trucks and automobiles.

Pedestrians are few and far between in the countryside. When I walk to the village on Sundays I always feel as if I don't belong here. Someone usually takes pity on me and I squeeze into one of the many vehicles, often times into a car. Sometimes I meet my special friend: the driver for the Montreal Ice-Cream Company. He's always busy on Sunday, trying to supply the many restaurants with his delicious ice-cream.

Ice-cream! It's a Canadian's favorite delicacy. Not a Sunday goes by that he doesn't stop at least once to treat himself at a restaurant. What can he do otherwise? A "refreshment" and Sunday belong together and the choice of stomach coolers on that day isn't very great. The sale of alcoholic beverages is prohibited throughout the province. The "taverns," the places where beer and wine are served, are closed. Strong drinks, such as whisky, gin, liqueurs, etc., are only sold in provincially controlled stores and then only during the week and not for consumption on the premises.

As a matter of fact, I got the impression that very little alcohol is consumed here. Comparatively speaking Hollanders are a bunch of *drunks!*

There aren't very many "taverns" (our cafés) here, and they have few steady customers. However, there are an incredible number of restaurants and eating places and they do a good business. The Canadian eats outside the home quite often. The bachelor doesn't live in a "pension" or a boarding house, but rents a room and eats in a restaurant. A great many Canadian ladies refuse to cook on Sunday so they go with their husbands and children to eat dinner in a restaurant. It's not as expensive a business here as in the Netherlands. For instance, I regularly go to a very neat and pleasing place on Sundays where I get soup, meat, potatoes, bread, butter, pudding and coffee for thirty cents.

So as you can see, dining is not expensive here. It's cheap, and good, at least at my boss's. They set out warm food three times a day; meat, potatoes, bread and tea. I wasn't used to seeing potatoes and bacon on my plate at seven in the morning. In the afternoon and evening there's soup as an entree, potatoes and bacon, and tart or pudding as dessert. The Decarie family is also addicted to sweet and sour. Pickles, preserves, or syrup to dip your bread in are the order of the day. The only thing I haven't tasted all the time I've been here is milk. However, tea without milk is nothing to complain about.

What do I object to? The fact that I, besides being a farmhand, have to function as a washerwoman and seamstress. Only for my own clothes you understand. The ladies here make sure that I get my meals on time and that my bed is made. As for the rest, they don't lift a finger for me. I take my wash to Mr. Charles Wong, a fat and very dirty Chinese. He takes the worst dirt out and returns it weekly, still half clean. This business with the laundryman is very simple. You hand over your package of clothes and in return get a piece of paper with some mysterious Chinese chicken scratches scribbled on it. After a week you come back, turn in the slip and receive your goods. That little prank costs me

40 to 50 cents a week and so it's understandable that I occasionally sneak into an out-of-the-way place to wash a pair of socks or handkerchiefs.

Forty cents (Canadian), that's a whole Dutch guilder! One tends to convert all the prices into Dutch money, especially in the first few months. That's not very intelligent because you regularly end up shaking your head over the very high prices of everything here. You can't buy as much for a dollar as you do in the Netherlands for a "rijksdaalder" (2.5 guilders).

Before I left home, I read somewhere that a dollar has the purchasing power of 1.8 guilders and I believe that the figure is correct.

To play at being a washerwoman isn't all that bad, but seamstress! My overalls looked rather battered with their three-cornered tears and repair was necessary if I wanted to use them a little longer. Luckily a rainy day arrived and at noon the boss said that he didn't know what else was left to do, so I asked for and got permission to fix up my kit a little.

So then I went up to my room, sat down comfortably, and spent five minutes threading the needle. Then I picked up the overalls and stretched the ripped place smoothly over my knee. Then I began. It went well. Regularly and neatly the stitches appeared, one following the other. I began to enjoy the job. The needle moved up and down, faster and faster: until I pricked my knee. The desire to do any more work was suddenly gone and I angrily grabbed the overalls to throw them down, but couldn't. I'd sewn the whole thing onto my pantleg. I had to take everything apart again, stitch by stitch.

"Self-reliance!" That's the slogan around here. Speaking about clothes, you regularly read in emigrant articles in newspapers, "If you go to Canada, don't take too many clothes because different clothes are worn here." Childish advice!! What does it really matter if people can see you're a foreigner. Why is it necessary that you look like the majority. As for me, I'd say, take everything that you own, and if you have any money left, buy clothes with it before you leave. Even though they're cheap here in comparison with other things, they'll always be more expensive than in the Netherlands. Just don't get upset if you don't wear what other people do. That's what I did.

Once in a while I wear a so-called "butterfly" (wing) collar which is quite, a rarity here. Most of the men here wear it only once in their lives: when they get married. What do I care? I find it an easy thing to wear, much easier than the high double collars which are the fashion. On a Saturday evening, when I was parading my 'butterfly" again, I caught what Madame Decarie said to her spouse. "Look, he's got his groom's collar on again!" Nobody had caught on that this time I had understood the remark all too well.

I said, "This collar is good enough for me." The whole family was in a state of shock. I laughed last and best. As a kind of protest I walked around in my groom's collar for three Sundays in a row.

I believe in retrospect that it turned out to be an expensive joke, as my strange appearance attracted the attention of a clever young Montrealer.

I've always said that someone who lets his money roll out of his pocket is a dummy. Apparently I'm also one.

Today—I'm finishing this letter a week after I began it—I went to Montreal again. I was very calmly strolling Rue St. Denis. It's a decent street with a fair amount of traffic, in short, a street where you don't expect to meet pickpockets or other such vermin. Just for a moment I stopped to light a cigarette, when, from behind me an English voice said, "Hello, sir, do you have a cigarette for me perhaps?"

I looked around and there was a young man in work-clothes. Graciously I held out my cigarette case, and generously found a match in order to provide him with a light. A few words were exchanged, after which the young man said, "Don't take it unkindly but I've got to go." I didn't find that hard to believe because his clothes seemed to indicate that he was working today. He disappeared in a flash.

A little while later my wallet and $8 were missing. At the police station they gave me the following advice. "If somebody asks you for a cigarette again, don't give him a cigarette but a punch in the face."

The loss of $8 is neither here nor there, but the fact that I so generously gave that thief a cigarette and a light makes me livid when I think of it.

Dempsey-Tunney and the Emigration Question
10 October, 1927

On Thursday afternoon three of us were sitting around in Montreal when someone said, "Say, are you going to listen to the fight on the radio tonight?"

"*The fight.*" That could only mean the one between Dempsey and Tunney and it would take place in Chicago that evening. All of Montreal was agog over it. The newspapers were going to print extras and send them out as soon as the result was known. Dozens of pictures of the professional boxers had been printed and hundreds, no thousands, of dollars had been wagered. All of the United States and even all of Canada was in a state of anxious anticipation. That evening fortunes would be won or lost. Boxing! The most popular sport in North America, and the most bestial.

"Yes boys," our friend said again, "we've got to go there! You'll be able to hear the blows they give each other and the crowd in the arena yelling and shouting until your ears ring!"

We went that evening to a restaurant, where the fight was to be broadcast on the radio. We were allowed to listen to the commentary for the reasonable cost of a ten cent cup of tea.

With great anticipation we waited for the broadcast which was scheduled for ten thirty p.m. (Montreal summer time). The restaurant owner was already busy trying to tune in the radio. Nervously he fiddled around, turning a knob here, and unwinding a couple of wires there, tinkering and fumbling—until finally he became totally confused. We heard a lot of blaring jazz music, but to our great disappointment we didn't hear any of the hard blows landing on Dempsey's stomach or Tunney's nose.

We weren't the only ones; several other customers asked hopefully when the fight was going to start. The owner shook his head sadly and began to take the radio apart. Sniggering contemptuously the visitors left.

We also left and walked to the nearest park. Something seemed to be going on. A closely packed sea of people—probably several thousand—were all shoved together. We went towards them and when we got closer we heard—*the radio!* A restaurant had set up a loudspeaker outside and the voice of the announcer echoed far into the park as he described the progress of the "big fight" in Chicago. The crowd listened quietly and even the trains seemed to be traveling with less noise than usual. In any case, the drivers rang their bells in a much quieter fashion. Imagine if even one word concerning this earth-shaking event should be lost to the listeners!

When we arrived the boxers were in the seventh round. We had just found a place to stand when the echoing voice of the announcer said, "Dempsey knocks Tunney down!" The people went crazy. From every side came yelling and cheering. "Hooray Jack! Hooray!," and "Dempsey's going to win!" echoed everywhere.

Because Dempsey was the favorite here, just about everyone bet on him and it was practically impossible to find anyone who would take a chance on Tunney. Watches were pulled out of pockets and everyone stood there counting him out with great swings of their arms. A paperboy took advantage of the momentary silence to peddle his papers at the top of his voice. A "BUG... OFF" was the only reply he got.

Finally, in the ninth second—and nine seconds lasts an eternity, when ten decides the loss or gain of a small fortune—it was reported that Tunney had stood up and the fight was on again. The majority sighed disappointedly, while the little group of Tunney supporters took the opportunity to cheer.

So the fight went on. In Chicago 140,000 people satisfied their bloodlust and watched the two pugilists in a barbaric display. Here in Montreal, at a distance of hundreds of miles, thousands upon thousands were gathered in different parts of the city listening to the loudspeakers. As the announcer spoke, everyone listened breathlessly. As for me, I had an awful cramp in my feet but I hardly dared to move them out of fear that the gravel would crunch too loudly and disturb the listeners. Sometimes, if something important happened in the fight, loud hurrahs would sound, but they would be instantly cut off when the radio voice resumed.

A policeman on a motorcycle kept the roadway clear. He rode back and forth as carefully as possible, but one couldn't expect the man to glide past like a ghost without a noise. The people gave him all kinds of dirty looks, sometimes jeers could be heard. Not the least little noise was wanted.

An army of police officers was on foot patrol because they were afraid of the disturbances which almost always occur after events like this. Generally they arise when someone, who has bet and lost, is not able to pay.

Slowly but surely the fight was ending and the crowd was getting more and more restless and nervous. Most realized how it was going to end. More and more the announcer said, "Dempsey seems to be tired." The ex-champion seemed to have lost his chance and Tunney would retain his title for a little while longer.

Finally, the decision was announced. "Tunney wins." Only a small group greeted it with hearty cheering, most of the crowd had lost their bets.

Everybody began to leave, and were fairly orderly at that. It was already 11:30 and so we hurried to catch a tram for home. It was quite difficult. St. Catherine Street was suddenly inundated with people storming the trains. Young people were hanging on the trains like burrs. Wherever there was a place big enough to put a toe, we could see someone holding on. Dozens rode along that way and we held our breath expecting them to fall off at any moment. We decided we'd rather walk. We weren't unhappy with our decision as we arrived at out destination much sooner than would have been possible on the streetcar, because the street was plugged. The cars stood in four long endless rows, without room to even crawl ahead an inch. Ever so slowly the side roads to the neighbourhoods swallowed the innumerable cars. The streetcar, which usually chugs through everything, now also had to wait patiently. All that commotion and all that noise was brought about by two individuals, who were going to bloody each other's noses... of the population of Montreal, which has about one million citizens, had gone out into the street that evening, to the cafes and restaurants and the newspaper offices to follow the radio blow-by-blow description.

Strangely enough I happened to meet an acquaintance, an American, an ordinary factory worker. He had bet and won $50—125 Dutch guilders! His wife had also become richer by $50. His fifteen-year old son had lost $5 from his already "none too large" hurrahs. The father tried to cheer up the little fellow. "Next time you'll have better luck, boy."

An ordinary worker and his wife, who together gamble a hundred dollars, and a half-grown squirt who's already beginning to follow the great example of his parents. That's a typical example of the American betting lust. "Monkey see..." A Dutch boy wouldn't want his parents to know that he even gambled for a dime. Not for all the money in the world.

It remained busy on the street for several hours. An hour after the fight a number of papers appeared as extras, containing a comprehensive account of the match: American journalism!

Many people stayed to wait for the papers and at one o'clock in the morning you could see people on the sidewalks with the extras glued to their eyes, while here and there groups were gathered, talking about the results. I only heard about that, as I was already snoring away.

In the last few years an active propaganda campaign for Canada has been carried on by the Canadian government, the Canadian railways and especially the steamship lines. "Help us to develop and exploit our land, our natural resources." They barrage the Dutch farmer with advertisements and brochures and one would almost expect to be greeted in the far West with open arms and a loud "Welcome Stranger." It's true, the immigration policy of the Canadian government opens the country's gates wide for everyone, from whatever nation—if he wants to work with the farmer. But... the policies of a government don't always receive the undivided agreement of its subjects, certainly not the immigration policies of the Canadian government.

There are three objections which have been particularly brought out by the leading men in the last little while:

1. Not enough is done by the immigration authorities to make sure that the admitted immigrants are (*truly*) farmers by occupation and are willing to work on the farm.
2. The country is too easily exposed to political intriguers of the communist bent.
3. Comparatively speaking the total number of immigrants of non-English blood is too great.

The first two objections were recently made by the mayor of Winnipeg at a conference of municipal councils (certainly not a case of the first being the best). He complained that the Western provinces were annually flooded by a great number of non-farmers.

In many cases these people are a total failure on the farm, and trek back in groups to the cities to find jobs in the factory or as casual labour.

That's not so bad in the summer, but in the winter...! Thousands of strangers arrive to beg the city council of Winnipeg to help them in their need. So it's understandable that Winnipeg's mayor presses for a more careful selection of the kind of immigrant to be admitted. There is also one more reason.

A significant number of the immigrants who go to Canada originate in the eastern states of Europe: Russia, Poland, Czechoslovakia, Rumania, the Ukraine, etc. In general they come from the Slavic countries, the center of communism. The communists in Canada, and also in the United States, carry on little or no public propaganda, which is probably the safest thing for them, as the authorities here are not at all as long-suffering and patient as in the Netherlands and other European countries. However, you can be sure that a great amount of communist activity is being carried on, behind the scenes!

Everyone is deathly afraid of that here. There's nothing an American or Canadian political leader hates more than a communist. That's why Winnipeg's mayor insisted that the recruitment of immigrants be limited to the importation of *proven* farm labourers. This is a category in which active communist propagandizers are seldom found and which likewise is not compelled to come knocking at the door of the city council in winter for support.

Now the third objection. Too many non-English are coming in. This was discussed in the synodical convocation of the Anglican Church of Canada. According to the press reports some members of that gathering were especially interested in the settlement of Englishmen in Canada; that is the settlement of people, who, for the most part, would belong to the Anglican Church. According to some speakers, "The present-day immigration policy of the government strengthens the power and the influence of the Roman Catholic church in Canada and it brings the English character of Canada's West into jeopardy."

Serious protests have been made against the fact that 25 Catholic priests are employed as immigration officials in the province of Ontario. The conclusion reached is that the laws should be changed in such a fashion that at least 50 per cent of the recruited immigrants are English.

One sees that the immigration question, which by its nature is pre-eminently an economic question, can also be viewed from another perspective.

When the Winter Comes
3 December, 1927

The summer has been very bad in the Netherlands this year. That small, low country nearly drowned in the almost daily deluge of rain. Storm and thunder battered some districts and in one blow destroyed the farmer's hard labour, sweeping away trees and houses, chasing people off the streets, leaving them disturbed and homeless. The summer was *extremely* bad there.

No doubt we had it much better in Canada! Just about every day this summer you could see the golden sun, shining and radiant in the clear blue sky. Once in a while, a rainy day would bring enough moisture so that the flowers and fruit could continue their luxurious growth and benefit the farmer who had spent his care on them. And following that: the sun, and with the sun the summer warmth.

But now the summer is past and it's already the middle of November in this country. The winter hasn't come yet—at least not here in eastern Canada—but it's coming. When you step out of doors early in the morning you can see it and feel it. The puddles in the street have a thin layer of ice on them and the morning wind blasts around your ears in a most disagreeable manner. You pull up your collar with just a hint of a shiver.

That awful, miserably damp weather that we have at home was only in evidence here for about two days. Two interminable days of rain and slush. It's nice again now. The sun is right there at daybreak and the sky is clear. The only thing is that it's getting a little colder. The clothing stores are now displaying bulky fur coats and men's heavy cloth coats: weighty in price too. You see men's boots, thick with wool or fur linings, fur hats, all kinds of warm underclothing, even Christmas cards are already being displayed: mostly landscapes, the little houses are almost buried in the snow, the fenceposts all with high caps on their tops, the branches of the pine trees bending down like the limbs of a weeping willow, everything, absolutely everything bearing a heavy load of sparkling white snow. When you look at all of that... then you begin to shiver.

I like the winter. I've seldom had as much fun as I had on the ever-popular "Tollhouse Flats" in Leeuwarden. I could spend a whole afternoon on skates, swooping back and forth across the ice. The rhythmic zig-zag of those hundreds of pairs of skates is music to my ears. Oh, it's extremely pleasant on the ice, especially if a certain someone is also there, someone with whom you are secretly in love. Where else, but on the ice, do you dare to talk to her with such freedom.

My roommate is sleeping and snoring at the moment: he worked last night, otherwise I would yell at the top of my voice, "Hurrah for the Flats."

I also like snow. I can sit happily for hours watching the slow and stately whirling of the flakes: from a comfortable chair beside a red-hot stove.

Here in Canada the winter is different. In reality the winter isn't much different but the circumstances in which I have to get through it are. If I'm very lucky I'll be able to remain employed as a general labourer at a construction site. That's not all that bad as they do most of the inside work, such as finish carpentry, in the winter. But there's not much chance of that and to be honest I expect that before the winter arrives—usually about Christmas in this area—I'll be given the "sack" along with most of my companions. What then?

Well then I'll be bound for the romantic life. I'll follow the example of the late Tom Thumb's father and swing a great big axe onto my shoulders with a jaunty flourish, watching out that I don't drop it because that might cost me a couple of toes or a piece of my heel, and go to the bush. Then all of you, even in faraway Friesland, will be able to hear the echoes of the tremendous blows in the quiet, clear Canadian air. A swing! A blow! Another couple of swings and blows! Snow, the soft rustling and scraping as it comes falling down from the branches, a loud crack, a dull thud... Your humble servant has conquered another one of the huge Canadian wood giants.

But all silliness aside (that's probably what will happen) I'll have to go to a bush camp to chop trees during the winter. It's very difficult to find a job in the city then and doing nothing is rather unprofitable after a while. But will it be a pleasure to go to the bush? On the contrary. I don't look forward to it at all. Up to now I've heard nothing but bad things about it.

The cold isn't the worst thing. You're completely surrounded by the thick Canadian woods which shelter you against the cold, cutting North winds. Besides that, don't think that during the whole Canadian winter the thermometer will stay at 30, 40 or 50 degrees below zero, day in day out. There are a couple of weeks in the season when your ears can freeze off your head if you don't have them properly covered, and when it's so chillingly cold that outside work is virtually impossible, but the rest of the time it's fresh and cold and everything lies covered under ice and snow and it's bearable.

Bush work is heavy and only healthy, relatively strong fellows are suited for it. Swinging a heavy axe for an entire day or pulling a saw back and forth is no child's play. But even that can be overcome. With a healthy and strong body and some fervent desire you can learn to do a lot that you've never done before.

Much worse are your companions. You aren't alone in the bush or in little groups, but jammed together with hundreds of other men in one camp. There are Russians and Finns who have never seen a bar of *Kwatta* chocolate but always eat a raw onion for a snack. You can smell them before you see them! There are Poles who always carry little parasitic passengers with them: you don't make friends with them! There are Italians who are too cheap to buy handkerchiefs and who find their thumb and index finger much handier—besides, they have colds much more often than the others! There are Indians who are much dirtier than the rest and usually drunk besides! There are... but I'd better stop. I'll make it short and sweet. It's dirty, extremely dirty in the bush.

The food isn't bad. On Monday you get beans and pork, Tuesday pork and beans, Wednesday beans and pork and Thursday pork and beans again. I don't know what you get the rest of the week but I suspect that the cook puts beans and pork on the table. As you can see, there's not much variety, but still good food.

The wages in the bush are quite good, besides bed and board you get about $30 or $40 a month. You can also do contract work and if you're the least bit handy as a steady worker you can earn $60 to $70 a month. Last year there was a Dutchman here in Montreal who worked for a farmer for $30 a month and room and board. So, not very much. This gentleman—he had been a "gentleman" in the homeland—wasn't all that satisfied with his income; he heard talk about the wages in the bush, the Dollar (with a capital D) wafted in front of his eyes. He invested about forty dollars in his outfit (a pair of boots, a leather vest, extra warm underwear, heavy leather gloves, etc.) and he left for the bush—in spite of many warnings from others.... After four days he was back, a great deal poorer than when he had left and desiring nothing more than a nice warm bath with a huge bar of green soap.

Winter's coming: and then much of the work in the city will be finished. Your humble servant fears with great trepidation that he, within a few weeks, will also have to go to the bush.

But first I'll look for a job as a dishwasher and if I have no luck there, well: "Keep smiling!" Then, with a laugh (like a farmer with a toothache) off to chop the woody giants of the Canadian forest! After all, it's only for a few months.

When the winter comes... then life becomes less pleasurable for an immigrant.

We Dutchmen generally come here with work-clothes which are somewhat distinct from the Canadian style and when you're working everyone quickly notices that you are a foreigner, naturally even more so because of your miserable English.

When you're a foreigner, you're a "Polack," at least that's what the French Canadians think as they've generally had little geography and have most likely never heard of Holland. So the foreman on my job thought that I was a "Polack," a compatriot of the many true Polish workmen who were labouring with me. One fine day he came to me and said, "Well I can't talk to those damn Polacks! Pick a couple of them and put a wire fence at the back of the property." I puffed out my chest, much honoured by my temporary appointment as crew chief (for which I had my very minute understanding of that strange language to thank) and chose my men: two Poles and a Hungarian. All three were greenhorns, having been here only about eight months and hardly speaking a word of English. If they had only understood German—such is the case with many of their countrymen—but they didn't know any of that language either.

I called number one first: the Hungarian. I wanted him to hammer a pole into the ground in the corner of the property. This is the conversation which followed: "Say John, go right to the corner and put a big post into the ground." "Yes!" "Be sure you get it deep enough, take a shovel and dig a deep hole first." "Yes!"

I wasn't completely satisfied with that interminable "yes," because I was afraid that he didn't understand my orders very well. So I asked him: "What are you going to do now?" "Yes!"

At that point I went along and demonstrated what he had to do. "Yes" is an easy word to pronounce; as a result, it's often used whether it's suitable or not.

To the Bush
4 January, 1928

Well it's happened! I left the big city to bury myself in the bush for the winter. Things were getting progressively worse during the last little while in Montreal. I remained at work with the same construction outfit, but more often than not I would be sent home again in the morning because there wasn't enough work that day for the whole crew. Besides that, winter was coming and it began to freeze during the night and in the morning the streets were covered with a layer of snow. In short, Father Winter was sending out his messengers. When the Old Man himself appears—usually around Christmas in Montreal—you know that construction is finished. So I took the necessary steps to make sure that I had a place for the winter.

The employment office of the Canadian National Railways was advertising for bush workers. The immediate destination was North Bay, Ontario, and from there you would be sent on to the camps. The trip to North Bay cost $10.55 and was at your own expense. Earlier in the season, in September or October, when there's lots of work available and nobody really wants to go to the bush, the travel money is usually paid by the employer. But now, with the winter coming and a lot of people with very little money in their pockets and a great deal of fear in their hearts, the companies can find an ample supply of men for the bush and it's rare that free travel money is offered. I asked, "If I go to North Bay, can I be assured that I'll get a job right away?" "Absolutely, at most you'll only have to wait a day and you won't have to spend a penny more. The trip to the camp will be taken care of by the company that employs you."

I dismissed my uncertainty. I had very little desire to spend the winter in Montreal living on my diminishing savings. It would be much better to go to work in the bush where you get room and board and where the pay isn't all that bad. I bought a ticket, counted out my ten and a half dollars and stepped on the train at 10:15 that night. The train goes from Montreal right across Canada.

That was the second time I had made a long journey on a Canadian train. The first time occurred when I was only eleven days from home and everything was new. Then we were stuffed in a full carriage, all Dutchmen together, all filled with great expectations. Now it was different.

I'm still a little "green," but not quite as much. When I speak English I don't stutter any more nor do I blush when I begin a conversation. Now nobody could send me to a farmer in the spring for $25 a month, not even with a club, and not eight months ago I was happy with my job. I've also learned to keep my hat on my head when I go to visit this or that official at his office. I'm not sure if that's an improvement.

The train was nearly empty this time. The only occupants were an Italian family, a couple of people who were also going to the bush and a Chinaman who immediately lay down to sleep and was still sleeping at ten o'clock the following morning. There were very few people, much to the chagrin of the young fellow who, throughout the whole train trip, tried to sell newspapers, snacks and cigarettes and finally whispered in my ear that he could supply me with some whisky if I wanted it. I refreshed myself with a soft drink for which the bootlegger charged three times the going price in Montreal. Two rather ordinary apples cost me 15 cents (37.5 Dutch cents). I don't think that was very cheap.

I went to sleep. It was pitch black outside and you couldn't see the moon or the stars in the sky. Swiftly but silently the train glided on. It was easy to sleep on the seat since it converted into a bed. And I dreamt... I was on the slow train from Heerenveen to Leeuwarden, we had already passed Grouw-lrnsum, Wirdum followed and in an instant (everything goes fast in a dream) we were under the smoke of Leeuwarden. The train began to go slower and slower. I peered and peered... Hooray! Hooray! There they were! Father, Mother, brothers and sisters. The whole family was there, cheering, cheering as loud as they could. My arrival in old Leeuwarden looked like a victory celebration. The train stopped and I grabbed my baggage. I had at least five suitcases and I wanted to get down the stairs as quickly as possible. But one of the damn suitcases wedged itself between my legs and the door frame and with a resounding smack I fell flat out on... the floor of the C.N.R. coach.

It seems I hadn't slept all that quietly and slowly but surely I had pushed myself to the extreme edge of my improvised bed and had dramatically lowered myself one level. I didn't hurt myself but the pants of my best suit had gotten hooked up and the result was a rip through which you could drive a team of horses.

I woke up at an opportune moment. Daylight was just beginning to break. We were already deep into Ontario and quite a bit north of Montreal and the difference was very obvious. Everything was deeply buried in snow and the roofs of the cabins which we flew past were decorated with an icicle fringe. The odd farmer we passed was warmly dressed. For that matter, we didn't go through that many populated areas and in great part everything was still bush interspersed by lakes and rivers set in a hilly countryside. Every once in a while the train would go through a hollowed-out cut in the rocky bottom. On both sides huge rocks were piled perpendicularly, making you look up and secretly fear that one of them would break loose and smash all of us, just like what always happens in a Wild West film when this or that bandit decides he wants his ill-gained riches.

All things come to an end: even my trip to North Bay. After eleven and a half hours on the train I stepped down into that little place.

I had expected nothing less than that my stay in North Bay would be of short duration, in any case no longer than a day. But I had forgotten one thing. It is of course of great importance to the officials of the placement bureau of the C.N.R. whether the company transports many or few passengers. Apparently the information which is given to those who inquire about job possibilities in this or that place is neither very carefully checked nor evaluated. To make a long story short: on Wednesday the 23rd of November they told me that I could immediately find work in North Bay with the help of the Ontario government placement bureau. On Wednesday, the 30th of November, exactly a week later, that bureau sent me to an employer. Furthermore, they had said that I wouldn't have to spend one more cent in North Bay. The truth is that I had to pay for a week's room rent and board and another $3.50 in order to travel to New Liskeard, the home of my future employer. Just imagine what would have happened if I had had little money or even none at all. Would the C.N.R. have paid my room and board costs? I rather doubt it.

But that's not all of it yet!

As I said, on Wednesday November 30 I was sent to New Liskeard by the placement bureau of the Ontario government. First of all they solemnly had me sign a contract in which I declared that I would do such and such work for Mr. So and So for this and that price. Besides that I declared I would, in any event, stay working until such advances as had been tendered me had been repaid. These were printed documents, which accounts for the last clause. After all, they hadn't extended any advances to me. So far, so good.

I surrendered my $3.50 and departed for New Liskeard. I might as well have thrown my money away. By the time I found my employer, who had incidentally asked for ten men, he had received eighteen on the previous day and now three more (I had met two other Dutchmen in North Bay). Mr. Hall, the director of the placement bureau, had sent twice as many people as requested. By mistake? Hardly! The man in New Liskeard told me that he had received a telegram at nine in the morning in which Mr. Hall apologized that he had sent too many men "by mistake." At ten—an hour later—the same Mr. Hall sent another three men.

Apparently all those who came to him every day asking for a job began to annoy him. He got rid of them in a very handy manner. But Mr. Hall ought to consider that I had to work very hard, from five in the morning to eight at night for three and a half days, for the wasted $3.50 travel money. He also ought to remember that I did not leave my fatherland to waste my money on the Canadian railways or to have Canadian government officials treat me like a snotnosed kid.

We left New Liskeard and went to Cobalt, where there's another placement bureau. I found a job then and at present I'm busily cutting trees into pieces. All about that in a following letter.

Back from the Dead
22 May, 1928

A little surprised to see me again, eh?

No wonder, it's been almost five months since my last letter was printed. One of my old acquaintances wrote me a letter in which he said: "See, I told you so, I was right when I warned you that Canada wasn't a good country. Things must not be going well, otherwise you would have continued writing." But my friend was wrong. First of all he knew nothing about Canada, except that which he had heard; a most unreliable source. Second, things went well this winter, very well, so well I couldn't find time to keep on writing.

I hadn't expected that at all five months ago. As some will probably remember, I went to the bush to cut trees on the 2nd of December. I wrote a whole epistle about an "axe which glinted keenly in the clear winter sun and came down on the hard tree trunk with a dull thud." I wrote how, after a few blows, the trunk would begin to crack until finally tree after tree would fall down in the snow.

But the reality was a little different. The axe glittered keenly above my head, at least I assumed it did as I had no time to watch it, and the thing came down with a dull thud, but never where I wanted it. If I chopped at a tree trunk twenty times, I would hit it ten times in ten different places and the other ten times somewhere deep down in the snow often so close to my toes that I'd jump backwards in terror. Finally the tree would fall, but never where I wanted it to. More often than not it would remain hanging in the crotch of a still standing tree and it would cost me considerable time to get my victim down safe and sound.

The worst thing was the snow which fell from the branches when I hacked at the trunk. It always fell down my neck and quickly turned into water which then ran in ice cold streams down my back, a very unpleasant feeling in the winter.

I did it for a week, until I couldn't do it anymore. I had fallen through the deep snowdrifts in the bush and had ended up with my feet in ice cold water. Instead of going directly back to camp and putting on dry socks and shoes, I had continued working in the fierce December cold and my footcoverings had quickly turned into hard ice clumps. It was then that my feet were frozen and a week later they were in such a condition that it was impossible for me to walk. I couldn't even bear the weight of the blankets on my feet. I won't even try to describe how much pain I suffered; suffice it to say that now, after 4 months, one of my feet still isn't completely healed.

The solution to this problem came about rather quickly. My boss realized that I definitely wasn't an experienced lumberjack and so he hired me on at his farm to look after the cattle and the horses, to chop wood, carry water to the house, in short, to do all kinds of odd jobs which aren't tiring but still keep you busy all day long. It certainly wasn't a profitable position; besides my room and board I earned nothing but my tobacco. However, at the time, I was happy to have a place where I could pass the winter.

When my friend reads all of this he'll say: "I can't see that things went 'so very well' for him." Be patient and wait! By the beginning of January things had improved to the point that I could walk a little again. At the same time my boss began to ship out logs; logs for firewood and for papermills. He made me the foreman at the distribution station which was on a small sideline. I had to measure the freighter's loads, load the flatcars with a Finn, measure the flatcar loads and ship them out. In short, I did all the shipping and acted as paymaster for the freighters who were paid by the load. Besides that, I kept my employer's books up to date in the evenings and wrote his letters (slowly but surely I'm becoming a fairly good Englishman). I kept this job for 2 months, at the end of which there was no more wood and all that time I earned $2 a day above my room and board. I believe that this was a particularly good position to have during a Canadian winter.

I'm a gardener again now, or rather, I soon will be again. Here in the Temiskaming district (northeast of Lake Huron) the winter is a bit longer than in the more southerly districts of Toronto and Montreal and considerably longer than in the more northern vicinity of Winnipeg.

It's now the sixth of May and great drifts of snow are still spread over the fields. We have had a week of beautiful weather but last night it snowed once again. My employer said that just after he'd arrived here he asked someone what the summer was like in this place. "Well," he answered, "I personally haven't experienced the summer here. I've only been here eleven months and haven't seen July yet." I don't believe that it will be that bad. We'll obviously have a little more than one month of summer, but in any case the spring is very late here. My neighbour told me that no one plants anything before the 24th of May. We'll have to wait and see!

My wage is now $40 a month, come rain or shine. A rather great difference from last spring when I began for 75 cents a day. But now I'm not so terribly green anymore either.

I believe I've satisfied the curiosity of my old friend with all of this. I would very much like to keep doing this if the editor will once more make a little room after my desertion. Will someone please request it for me?

It's absolutely unnecessary! We have welcomed Frans van Waeterstadt's first letter, after nearly a half year's silence, with great joy. We might remark that whatever parts of him may have been frozen, his head and his writing hand have stayed intact. We would be exceptionally pleased if, in the future, he continues to inform us, in his direct and inimitable way, about his experiences in Canada. – *Ed.*)

A Greenhorn's Complaint
5 June, 1928

"I'm not so green anymore now." I wrote something like that in my previous letter and I wrote the truth. It's remarkable how almost a year of living in a foreign land among foreign people changes a person. When I had just arrived I felt foreign and shy, my English wasn't all that great and I could barely make myself understood in French. I remember when I first contracted out my services to a farmer, a French Canadian in the vicinity of Montreal. "What's your price?" he asked me. I, the big fool that I was, replied that I was a newcomer and knew nothing about Canadian wages but trusted that my future employer would give what was reasonable. Well, he was reasonable, very reasonable. He offered me fifty cents (F. 1.25) a day with room and board. I was too smart to accept that but still crazy enough to take on that fairly heavy work for seventy-five cents a day.

That's the difficulty for every newcomer here. His first job is always with this or that farmer who's looking for cheap help. I believe, in fact, that the Canadian farmer who wants good help and is prepared to pay a decent wage seldom goes to the placement bureaus of the railway companies. Without a doubt, a great number of those so-called "experienced" farm labourers from Holland (or whatever country), who the newspapers have so bombastically clarioned, have never seen a farm in their lives. Everyone in Holland who requests a visa for Canada has to fill in a long list of questions about his agricultural experience. As far as I know, no one checks to see if the answers are truthful.

In the final analysis that's probably a good thing. I know quite a few people who came here and knew nothing more about a cow than that it had horns, and had never seen a plough in their lives. Now they're farmers whose business compares very favourably with that of many who have spent a lifetime among horses and cows. They had a couple of sturdy hands and a healthy set of brains—that's all.

The only thing I knew when I left for Canada was something about vegetable growing. I've kept my ears and eyes open this past year and tried to do my best. The result was that this spring I had my choice of six different jobs, each with a decent wage, at least I call $40 (F. 100) a month with room and board, laundry and mending, very satisfactory.

I had a great advantage on my side, I knew a little English. Not much mind you, but still enough to make myself understood and to make it easier to learn some more quickly. It makes life considerably easier if you can talk to the people around you; when you can understand a joke; or even tell one or two.

It was so different a year ago. I was living with French people and in the evenings after supper we all sat together in the roomy but very proper and uncongenial kitchen. Everyone talked and laughed and it was obvious that jokes were being told. Quietly I sat in the corner not understanding a word. I thought about home then; how we all used to sit around the big table, some with the newspaper or a book; the female members of the group comfortably slurping up the remains of the coffee. We masculine men, puffing and smoking with a vengeance, especially my oldest brother, who, as his boss always said, "smoked until the soot flew in my hair." We never said much, except the youngest who was always having a busy conversation with her dolls.

That was the kind of picture that materialized in my head every evening. I saw everything in perfect detail. I saw the furniture in its usual place. I even saw the scratch which I had put in the cabinet with a nail when I was a boy: a deed which bothered me a little and which I would rather not have thought about.

On such evenings homesickness crept into my heart. Then I usually went outside and sat on the stoop, peered at the old familiar moon and stars, sang this or that song, clenched my teeth and went to bed early. Now it's different. I live in a district where English is the principal language and I speak it well enough to spend a whole evening talking and chattering. I get invitations to card parties and dances and I even had the great pleasure of accompanying a young member of the fair sex to a party and then escorting her home: the most satisfying part of the program.

Actually the greatest advantage of my English is that I can understand thing much quicker. My boss only has to say a word and I know what to do. He doesn't have to demonstrate everything for me, as was the case a year ago. So I'm worth much more than someone who can't speak English, no matter how good a labourer he may be.

I'd better not boast too much. I'll have things to tell in a following letter which are not all that pleasant. I may not be as green as I was but I'm certainly not a Canadian yet.

Life on the Farm
20 September, 1928

"Well, how's life treating you on the farm?" That's what one of my old friends asked me in a letter and to be truthful I often ask myself the same question. I really don't know. Sometimes I think it's fine and sometimes I think it's... Well it doesn't matter. The truth is that in the early morning I always curse the farm.

About four thirty I wake up with a start. That's when the boss hammers on the wooden wall of my bedroom. Every morning I think he's made a mistake about the time, but a quick glance at my clock gives the disappointing assurance that it's truly time to get up. There's no sense grumbling about it so I jump out of bed and pull my clothes on. With a pair of sleepy eyes and a totally sleepy brain I grab some kindling and paper and build a good fire in the stove. After this little domestic chore I put my cap on. It looks pretty dirty and greasy because my boss often utilizes me as a mechanic and lets me crawl under his car where two drops of oil always drip down, one on my hat and one in my right eye. As I said: I put on my cap, grab a milk pail and go out to milk one of the two cows.

It's taken me a lot of effort to perfect that art! It wouldn't be so bad if a cow was an intelligent animal, instead of a cow. My cow—I always call her mine because I have to look after her—is called "Queenie." I don't know why, the fact is that she doesn't look like a queen at all and she has habits which often cause a whole stream of unrefined words to roll from my lips. In the past I would put the pail on the ground when I milked since the cow was always docile enough. That is until the pail was almost full when, with one kick, the beast would ruin almost all of the milk. "Wisdom is achieved by trial and tribulation." The next time I milked I held the pail wedged between my knees until the pail got heavier and neatly slipped away. Another pail gone to blazes! Anyway, that affliction has now disappeared and I can find employment anywhere as a farmhand who can milk fairly well.

There's one more thing about cows: They aren't clean, not half as clean as the family cat was at home. In the evenings I scrub them until my fingers are black and blue and their black and white hides finally glisten like a "tinned donut in the moonlight." I throw down a layer of straw in the stall which is almost deep enough to bury a half dozen cows and then my boss says: "I bet you $100 that they'll look nice and clean tomorrow morning." And the next morning I take a pail of water and an old sack, give a sigh and begin the perpetually miserable job of cleaning up our cows again.

Then there's our horse. A sight for sore eyes, but what a disposition! He's not bad for our buggy, perhaps just a bit too hasty. I take him out quite often and I haven't broken my neck, at least not up to now, but

I'm not so sure it won't happen soon. Before you've had time to step in, he takes a jump and trots ahead. He doesn't give a darn if I'm sitting safely in the wagon or lying under the wheels with a corpse-white face and a half-broken body. My only chance is to jump before he does and to fall on the cushions. So you see, getting the animal going is easy enough but stopping him is a little bit different. Every once in a while we try to use "Buddy"—that's the name of our trotter—as a workhorse. A little while ago I had him hitched to the harrow and when I was ready to begin I said "Giddyup." Buddy took a jump, stood still with a jerk and looked back over his rear at the harrow with a rather surprised look on his face. He's basically opposed to all hard work, just like our neighbour's farmhand who told me the other day: "I really like working. Yes I like it so much that all I want to do is to lie down next to it and sleep for the rest of my life." In any case, Buddy displayed none of his usual hurry. I got him moving with considerable difficulty and after ten passes he took a rest and then made a couple more passes.

That's the way the whole morning went; ahead a little bit—15 minutes rest—ahead a little and a little longer rest and then one pass. Finally, I was so angry that I would have sent Mr. Buddy to his eternal rest if I had had an axe or other weapon handy.

All kidding aside, farm life isn't all that bad. Often it's hard work and usually thankless too, but the farm gives you variety. It's not like an office where, day in day out, year after year, a person has to add and subtract the same books until he begins to get a feeling in his head as if his brains have turned into a pile of sawdust. It's not like a factory where the same machine makes the same monotonous movement in front of your eyes every day. Sometimes you work in the rain, but usually there's golden sunshine spread over the multicoloured fields and also over your face, which quickly browns like that of an Indian. You feel healthy and mostly satisfied too.

And you don't work all the time. Sometimes my boss and I quit a little early and go to a dance at a small nearby restaurant. They have a good open-air dance floor where a half dozen goats dance around the floor when the couples stop for a little rest to drink a soda or greedily down an ice cream cone. It's not the big city and you have to be a little careful where you put your feet because besides the goats a whole herd of cattle grazes around the platform. There's no first-class orchestra, only a couple of characters who play the violin and take their turn scraping on the strings. I and a couple of others who aren't that good at dancing make ourselves useful by stamping our feet to the beat, as loudly as possible.

So we have fun, a lot of it, and the following morning we have stomach cramps because Mr. Joy sometimes uses soured cream in his ice cream. But it all passes and it certainly doesn't stop us from going. Tonight I'm going again.

An Unfortunate Harvest
9 October, 1928

It's the 23rd of September here in New Ontario and a real fall day. The first thing I heard this morning when the boss woke me up was: "it's snowed!" Snow!

Finally a change after a summer which brought nothing but wind and rain. Our neighbour, who's been in this part of Canada for 27 years, has probably told me a dozen times that "this is, without a doubt, the worst summer I've ever experienced here." It must be so. I remarked that the weather is worse here than in the Netherlands and it's usually bad enough there. The twenty third of September and whole fields of hay are still lying outside exposed to the rain and now to the snow. The barley and oats are ripe, the heavy-laden heads are deeply bent but there's no possibility of harvesting them, since the heavy binders would sink over their axles into the soupy dirty slick. "It'll take at least two weeks before the ground is dry enough to go over it with the machines!" I've heard that remark from almost all of the neighbours.

We—I mean of course my boss and I—are no luckier than the rest. We have just enough hay in the barn to feed our animals during the long winter, but nothing more. About three tons of hay is still lying outside waiting for a little bit of sunshine which will last long enough to dry it for the threshing machine. Clover and grass seed are the primary products which put the money in the farmer's till.

Fifteen acres of grain is waiting for the scythe. That's what we concluded just this morning. We're not going to wait until the ground is dry enough for the binder. Early tomorrow morning, snow and weather permitting, we're going to take the scythe and try to mow the whole field. To be honest, I'm not very enthused about our undertaking. I have a vague suspicion that swinging a scythe for a whole day is very tiring, especially for someone like me who barely knows what a scythe looks like, let alone has ever used one. But anyway, I'll clench my teeth and no doubt we'll succeed in cutting it all down. Then we'll rake it together, pile it, give it a dose of salt and the whole business, oats, grain, thistles and all, will be used as cattle fodder. It's surely not the most useful way of handling expensive grain but it has been a completely useless, unpleasant, dirty, discouraging summer and fall.

As I said, there was snow this morning, not in the air but on the roofs and in shaded places in the fields. Everything was frozen but it began to melt rather quickly under the beautifully warm rays of a wonderful morning sun. I yelled out, "Hooray, snow means a change in the weather, better weather from now on!" But it was the same old tune again. After a couple of hours a tremendous wind appeared carrying hail and snow and rain, all mixed together. It was extremely cold.

It's a couple of hours later now and the sun is shining again. Airy, frayed little clouds drift across the sky and the ink-black, threatening, piled up pillows of snow and rain and hail have disappeared. Will we really get a beautiful, clear, sunny fall, that so-called "Indian summer"?

I hope with all my heart that we do, because my fate depends on it. My employer is behind with the payment of my wages and the grass seed, which I mentioned before, would, at least partially, pay off my bill. An employer who is behind in the payment of his workman's wage is a fairly common phenomenon in New Ontario. As far as I'm concerned I don't get the least little bit worried about it as my boss is absolutely trustworthy. Without a doubt he'll find a way to enlarge my small savings account with the expected amount.

My time here will soon be finished. After a couple of weeks most of the work will have been done and I'll have to look around for some kind of winter job. That won't take too much of an effort since a number of people have already asked me, mostly for bush work. Most likely I'll go and chop firewood, working with my boss for an equal share. After such an awful summer as this past one, he has little choice but to try and earn something during the long winter, in one way or another. My bush work last winter was a virtual failure, but my chances weren't all that rosy then. They put me out in the middle of the bush all alone with a very poor saw and didn't tell me what the easiest method was to cut and saw the greatest amount of wood in the shortest time. It's not hard to understand then, that my pile of wood was small and that I made relatively little money.

This time my chances are much better. I'm going with an experienced bush man; the type of wood is easier to handle and during the past year I've learned a considerable amount by listening and looking. At least now I know that I don't have to be so painfully exacting. It doesn't matter in the least if a piece of firewood is an inch longer or shorter than four feet. Even now I get a sour grimace on my lips when I remember how I used to measure my firewood last winter as carefully as a cabinet-maker who's making a chest drawer. This time I go to meet the winter with confidence. My feet won't end up being frozen because now I have the right kind of shoes and an overabundance of heavy warm socks. I certainly learned my lesson last winter!

A couple of days ago I received a letter from a *real* Friesian who complained that he didn't hear enough from me. He asked me if I didn't place any value on keeping up the ties with the fatherland and old friends and acquaintances or had I already become so "Canadianized" that I didn't give any of that a thought?

My old friend is wrong. I'm far from being Canadianized. I wouldn't want to be. I'm a Netherlander and a Friesian and I hope to stay a Friesian. A couple of months ago my boss introduced me to someone. That "someone" naturally didn't grasp my name. Nobody here can pronounce it until I've made the effort to spell it out at least ten times.

In this case the person said: "Pleased to make your acquaintance Mr. er..." And there he was stuck. "Oh don't bother," I said, "it is difficult enough to remember my name, much less pronounce it. It's foreign. I'm a Dutchman."

We—my boss and I—came home and he said: "You make me angry! Why do you broadcast the fact that you aren't a Canadian? You're a Canadian now!" I didn't say very much, only that I wasn't a Canadian, but a full-blooded Hollander and I concluded: "There's absolutely no shame in being a Dutchman. In fact, just the contrary!"

**"And the golden grain
We'll bind again."**
8 November, 1928

These are two lines from a rhyme printed on one of our calendars. About six weeks ago our grain shone like gold. Our field was completely gold-coloured and the heavy stalks were tightly packed together. It was like that all over Northern Ontario. "The best harvest we've had in many years", everyone said. They comforted themselves with that thought since many hadn't been able to save all their hay. One of the most important products which the farmer can sell here is his hay. Thousands of dollars worth of hay was left lying. Rain and more rain had totally wrecked it and it wasn't even worth hauling away. Next spring the fires will be burning everywhere again: not festive fires. The results of many hard hours of work and a lot of sweat will disappear and the only thing that will be left will be countless round blackened spots on the land.Very few farmers got all their hay in and nobody got it all in good condition. A lot of that so-called "rescued" hay has so often been alternately dry or wet—as the sun baked it or the rain drowned it—that finally it took on a dirty black colour and was unsaleable, just about half good enough to feed it to your own young cattle or to keep one poor milk cow alive. Many farmers don't even have enough for their own cattle.

"Old Charlie," the Swiss, besides being the butcher here, is a farmer, veterinarian, woodsman, and general factotum, and he takes pleasure in the rosy possibility of many future sales in and around February. At that time many of the less fortunate neighbours have a shortage of money and feed and—like it or not—will have to sell part of their herd. "Yes Frans, you buy cattle, bring to my stall and pasture, double money, we go together to Holland and Switzerland, a lot of fun, Munich beer."

That's what Charlie said last night in his bitten-off English. He speaks that way because in the twelve years he's spent living in and among the English population he still hasn't learned to express even one idea completely in English. I'm about the only one who can understand him well because the considerable amount of German, which Charlie mixes with his English, is not totally Greek to me. It's always very difficult for our host of last night to follow his speech. Especially last night. His three-week-old daughter had been very restless and disturbed the previous night and her poor father had to pace the floor half the night with that little bit of humanity in his arms. As a result, he stepped on a collar button in his bare feet: a button for which he had looked half of Sunday morning.

In any case, the man was quite sleepy last night and less able than ever to understand Charlie's language stew. However, as a polite host should, he expressed the required interest, nodded yes every now and then (whenever Charlie seemingly expected some commentary on his story), became more and more sleepy and didn't understand a word, until at last he guessed horribly wrong.

Charlie was telling how a neighbour had accused him of selling a tainted steak. "Now I ask you," said Charlie to our sleepy host, "do you think that I would ever, in my whole life, sell spoiled meat?"

"Yes-yes"… nodded our host, "yes-yes… Charlie…"

"Never!" thundered Charlie, and slammed his fist on the table and said something more in German. The host rubbed the sleep out of his eyes and found it a difficult job to explain to Charlie that he had not understood him. Charlie will not believe for a moment that his English isn't absolutely flawless.

With all that I'm wandering away from the subject at hand. As I said: not all hay could be saved, because there weren't enough dry days. Luckily the grain was very promising. It had grown very well and was quite heavy in promised yield and would certainly put some money in the till! The same thing was true for that part of the hay which most let stand in order to thresh out the seed. Everyone had a heartfelt hope that the grain would be cut and threshed in the fall and raise the minuscule annual profit. But that hope was not realized. The summer was even wetter, most of the grain lay flat on the ground and began to sprout like anything. If it always did that well in the spring the farmer would have few real reasons to complain.

There was grain that still stood up neatly, but no one saw a chance to get it off the land because the horses sank to their bellies in the slimy goo. So, everything considered, 1928 was a failure here in Northern Ontario when compared with the so-called "West" (the provinces of Manitoba, Saskatchewan, and Alberta) where they've had the best harvest in years and where good weather favoured the harvesting.

But we in Northern Ontario know there's more than one way to skin a cat. If the summer work on the farm puts no money in our pocket, then the long winter and the thousands of acres of bush will give us some results. The sawmills are sending men into the bush again to cut down the bigger evergreens. Meanwhile, many farmers have bought parcels with light trees in order to cut these into four foot lengths and to send them to the surrounding cities as firewood. Wood is the fuel here, only a few of the well-to-do are able to indulge themselves in the luxury of a coal fire.

I myself am now a bush owner. (Here my chest swells out and I puff a little harder on a fat five-cent cigar stuck in the left-hand side of my mouth). I bought it with someone else from the province and within a few days I'll give it a try with my new axe and saw. We hired one man to help us: it's my boss from the past summer, in this way he can "work out" the wages he still owes me.

To the Bush, Again!
8 December, 1928

"To the bush! To the wonderful green bush!" I sang those words many times before I'd ever worked in a bush. Now I don't sing those pretty sentiments anymore. Oh no! I know darn well that our bush isn't all that wonderful and certainly not green. Practically every pine and spruce has been robbed of its green attire. The long, thin trunks stand straight up, candle straight and bare to the very tip top. Even more are lying flat on the ground, unable any longer to withstand the screaming north wind, because their tough burly strength was taken away by time or fire.

Fire! The most dangerous and insidious enemy of Northern Ontario. Fire annually ruins hundreds of hectares of Ontario's beautiful tree splendor and leaves behind a multitude of bare half-burned and fire-blackened stumps.

In this neighbourhood there have been a significant number of forest fires, but when the people talk about "the fire" then they always mean the one which put the population in peril and out on the street six years ago. Its origin was very innocent: a couple of hunters boiled up a cup of tea in the middle of the bush and afterward "thought" that their campfire was out. A little spark that remained smouldering, then some wind, a little bit of dry grass that caught fire, a blueberry bush, dry as a cork after a hot Canadian summer that caught on fire very easily, then the surrounding pitch laden pine trees. Finally, up went a blaze, swept ahead by an ever-growing fire storm which burned everything to the ground in a path which was five kilometres wide and almost forty kilometres long.

Not only the bush burned flat. Sparks were driven through the air and fell on a little pile of hay that had been left lying in a field around a farm. That little pile of hay blazed up and the wind took it and blew it ahead and let it fall on the roof of a house or barn. As I said, the summer had been hot and dry and the houses were built of wood and covered with tar paper. Where a spark landed there was fire. The poor farmer who, with his wife, had chopped a few acres of ground out of the ancient forest, at a cost of an incredible amount of sweat, and who was so very happy and proud of the house, which he himself had built out of wood which was sawn out of his own tree trunks or had been built up with the rough logs, that poor farmer saw his home-made estate burn flat to the ground in a flash.

Some were barely able to save their own lives. In groups, they fled to some deep ravines where the ground was still slightly damp. They lay there for hours, their faces buried in the cool moss, while above their heads the flames and sparks were whirled in a terrifying, wild blast through the air. Everyone took his turn to expose his face and eyes to the scorching smothering smoke and heat in order to extinguish the sparks which were falling on his companions' clothes.

People told me much more about the terror which a forest fire brings with it; much more than I could describe in one letter. The blackened stretches of burned forest give me an idea of what it was like.

However, the bush is not the only easy victory for the fire-devil. The poverty-stricken, poorly built wooden houses are a constant fire hazard. They often don't even have a brick chimney, a hole in the roof lets the stove pipe through, and in the evening you can see the sparks of the blazing wood fires come sweeping lustily out of and around the pipe. When it's so bitter, bitter cold in the winter, it's so pleasant to throw an extra chunk of wood in the stove and stoke up a fine, cosy, hot fire. The stove becomes red instead of black, and even the pipe glows from top to bottom. Then there's danger, terrible danger.

Our nearest neighbour, that means a half a mile from us here, came home thoroughly soaked one evening about three weeks ago after he'd walked in the rain for an hour and a half. The man is as poor as a church mouse and he probably had no other clothes to put on the following morning. Anyway, a fire was quickly started in the stove and within a few minutes the man's pants and jacket were on the line to dry. Before he went to bed, the stove was stuffed with dry pine so that the fire would burn long enough to dry the clothes. In the middle of the night the woman of the house woke up. The attic, where the whole family slept, was full of smoke and the flames were licking along the walls in the corners. Fire! The five children were awakened and everyone fled to the stair-opening in a frenzied haste. There were no windows in the attic of the self-built house and the stair-opening was terribly small. A ladder, which had a few missing rungs, had to be used by everyone trying to scramble downstairs. Most of them got downstairs. Not all. When I came to look in the morning, they had just found what was left of the four-year-old youngest child in the hot ashes. A wooden house, the inside walls of thick cardboard, no chimney, the attic an absolute trap: and then the fire.

A week ago, another house, a couple of miles from here. The attic, another trap. A small window in that one, about big enough to let a cat out. The husband and three of the nine children so badly burned that they had to go to the hospital. The man has now succumbed.

That's two fires in the last three weeks in this neighbourhood. I haven't been here a year yet, but there have been almost a dozen fires.

Fire! The most dangerous and stealthy enemy of the people in Northern Ontario, the land of forest and poorly built wooden houses.

The Bear in the Bush

15 January, 1929

Rrrring - Rrrring - went the loud voice of the telephone. "Hello! - Yes - this is Abbott - who? Is Frans here? Yes. Just a moment please."

"Frans - there's someone on the telephone who wants to speak to you," said my host.

I went to the phone and asked who wanted to talk to me. "Is that you Frans?" "Yes," I answered, "and who are you?" I was very curious as it was a woman's voice at the other end of the line.

"Me", was the answer. If it hadn't been a woman's voice I would have said, "Go to H...!" Instead I asked very coyly:

"And who is 'me'?"

"Me" turned out to be the amiable niece of my partner. Then came the message.

"Say Frans, when Uncle left the bush tonight he saw a bear. What did you say?"

"Oh, nothing", I answered, although I had mumbled something like "good grief."

The girl went on. Yes, her uncle had seen a bear, not all that far from my shack. Couldn't I borrow a rifle from Abbott when I went back to the bush tonight? Maybe I would meet the animal and get a chance to shoot it. It was full moon and there was light enough. A bear skin was worth quite a bit of money and wouldn't it be wonderful if I managed to acquire one?

"Yes, yes," I mumbled, "certainly... naturally... it would be great... eh... was it a big bear?"

"Oh no, only about two years old." Two years; l didn't think that a two-year-old bear would be all that small. In any case, I said that I would borrow a rifle and do my best to put a bullet in the beast's heart.

My host asked me what all my talk about a bear meant. I told him the story and immediately asked him if I could borrow his rifle. Naturally, naturally, I could take his rifle along; did I know how to shoot? I answered him in the affirmative; it wasn't the first lie I had told in my life.

We began to talk about bears. Mr. Abbott knew a lot of stories about bears; most concerned ones which he himself had shot. Was a bear dangerous? Oh no, not at all, as long as you left it alone! They wouldn't think of attacking a human being. They'd sooner run away, as quickly as possible. But, watch out if you shot them and didn't finish them off with one shot! A wounded bear was a very dangerous animal. And a whole slew of stories followed, all about wounded bears which had attacked people and torn them up terribly, yes, even killed them.

I quickly recalled that I had only shot once in my life, with an air rifle, at the Leeuwarden carnival. I had chosen the easiest target on the shooting range: a cast-iron drummer, which would play on its drum with tremendous energy, if you hit the copper target. I shot five times, after very careful and very tedious aiming, and I never hit it.

I came to the conclusion that I was not the suitable type to acquire bear hides and that it would be perfectly alright if I did not meet that bear. I don't like wounded bears.

I walked back to my shack in the bush that evening with the rifle, which I carried very carefully. I did not meet the bear even though I imagined, at least a dozen times, that I saw him and I landed safe and sound in my shack. That evening I didn't forget to lock the door.

This incident occurred about four weeks ago. Meanwhile, winter has arrived and the ground is covered with a deep layer of snow and hopefully all the bears in Canada have now gone into hibernation. I wish them pleasant dreams. The bush is truly a lonesome place! At least I find it so.

Most evenings the whole gang leaves, and I'm left all alone in that little shack in the bush, about a kilometre from the nearest human being. All alone in the middle of a bush which is always full of noises. Noises which I, having been a city dweller all my life, have no way of explaining. Usually it's windy and the trees grind and peep, the branches rattle and crack and the wind whistles, or moans, in any case it makes a terrible sound. Sometimes it's calm around the shack; dead silence; not a breath of wind; not a single moving twig. Cold, frosty nights bring that kind of silence. Suddenly—crack!—the frost splits a tree open. That's the way it goes the whole night: that deadly silence broken every now and then by the cracking and splitting of the trees. The bark is never silent! Everybody is probably laughing at me, but I don't care! I don't feel at all comfortable all alone in the bush.

Every evening, as I sit smoking my pipe next to my kerosene lamp, I'm intermittently startled by this or that noise and then I stand up and look out the window or go outside to see what's going on. Naturally, there's never anything but I'm only partly convinced and curse the bush, and my pipe, which has gone out in the meanwhile.

Well, I guess I'll have to get used to it. It'll be quite a while before we get all our wood cut and I'll have to endure that long at least. I'll endure, but I do wish the wind would blow a little less often.

Bachelor Cooking
29 January, 1929

I wasn't the only bachelor in the neighbourhood living in a poor, usually not very warm, wooden shack in the middle of the bush. A young Englishman had dragged his few earthly possessions to an abandoned hut about a kilometre from mine in order to pass the long winter as a lumberjack. If anything, he was in a worse situation than I was. At least I had company during the work day, while he was all alone both night and day. I had a bed with a fine spring mattress and enough blankets to keep myself warm during the coldest Canadian winter night while he had spread evergreen boughs over a wooden crib and had to go to bed with his clothes on because his stack of blankets wasn't sufficient. And his shack! When he arrived practically all the panes of glass had disappeared from the windows, a very unpleasant circumstance when you don't have any money to buy more. But no problem! Our friend grabbed some lumber and nailed the windows shut. The cracks in the walls let enough light in, along with, every now and then, a goodly quantity of northern wind; something which is fairly cold here in Northern Ontario.

Being next-door neighbours, both bachelors and both fairly new arrivals in a strange land we very naturally often came to visit each other. Our visits were seldom short and in any case we always talked long enough so that we could eat together. There was always something wrong with our meals. His tea was too strong or too weak, and his potatoes were never done and I don't really care for raw potatoes. On the other side of the coin, my meat was usually too dry or burned, and my carrots were never very soft. However, an Englishman is always polite and so my friend would say that I was truly an excellent cook and thus I couldn't say anything but that his cooking was much better than mine.

The first time I complimented him he replied: "Baloney! I know that I'm nowhere close to being a restaurant cook, but that doesn't matter. Up to now I haven't poisoned myself and I'm not getting any thinner. And I'm getting ahead, I'm progressing. Every meal I make is better than the previous one and in a whole week I've only once forgotten to put salt in my potatoes. Tonight I'm going to try to bake bread."

"What?" I asked.

"Yes," he replied, "I'm going to bake bread. I'm no longer prepared to pay a whole quarter for two loaves of bread."

I agreed that store bought bread wasn't cheap. Sixty-two-and-a-half Dutch cents for two 4-ounce loaves is fairly expensive. At the same time I gave voice to my doubts that the youthful Londoner would be able to bake an edible loaf of bread.

He, however, remained confident. Oh, baking bread was simple. He had acquired the art by watching the Canadian farmers' wives, who, practically without exception, bake their own bread. What they could do, he could do! And so we made a bet that if his bread was edible he would get a dollar from me, if it was inedible one of his hard-earned dollars would move over to my pocket.

The following Monday evening, I looked him up. How was the bread? The yeast had not worked enough!

Tuesday evening, in the middle of a heavy snowstorm, I again went to my neighbour. Was the bread ready? The dough hadn't risen yet!

Wednesday evening, finally! When I arrived he had just shoved a half dozen dough-filled bread pans in the oven.

"Now forty-five minutes in the oven and they'll be ready," said my friend. And then, "I hope that they won't turn out too bad."

That didn't sound very hopeful: apparently he had lost his confidence in his ability as a baker. I didn't say anything and he didn't seem very talkative either. Silently he took the teapot from the stove (a real Englishman always has tea ready) to pour each of us a cup.

I heard him mumble, "Damn...!"

"What's the matter," I said.

"Damn...!" he said again, "the pot's full of water but there's no tea in it!" And then he began to chuckle about his own forgetfulness.

"I really believe I'll never be a good cook. I always forget something—salt in the potatoes, half a dozen times, and now tea in the pot."

"Did you put salt in the dough?" I asked.

He thought for a moment. "By all the devils," he said, "now you mention it: there's no salt in it. That bread would drive a man crazy. Last night I set the dough pan between the cookstove and the heater and wrapped my heavy winter coat around it. When I got up this morning both stoves were out and the dough was frozen. And now I forgot the salt…I'm afraid that bread isn't going to be that great."

Meanwhile the 45 minutes had passed and we opened the oven door. In there we saw the six loaves of bread, each about as big as a bun. We put them on the table and took a knife to cut one open but we were eventually forced to resort to the axe.

We weighed one: it was 4 pounds.

"It's a good thing that I didn't waste the salt," said the baker.

We're going to buy ten-cent cigars with that dollar.

Sawmill
2 March, 1929

It's delightful to sit around a nice warm stove during a cold Canadian winter with no other responsibilities than a couple of cows and a pair of horses who regularly need their water and their feed. It's delightful and most of the neighbouring farmers would like to do nothing else. But what's delightful isn't always profitable. And besides that, it's impossible when almost all of your hay and grain has been drowned the previous summer. The Canadian farmer can't live on air either.

And so it was that almost everybody in the neighbourhood left the milking to his wife and children last fall and left for the bush. Some went with their horses to the sawmills to transport the logs or the sawn lumber, but many others bought a piece of bush from the provincial government and chopped and sawed it into firewood.

You could hear the echoes of the axes and the cracking of the falling trees everywhere, and every little station and sideline was packed full on both sides with huge piles of firewood. The firewood dealers in the neighbouring towns had filled up their yards. Besides that: the winter had been fairly warm so that the housewives had not needed to have such hot fires.

The result: few sales and low prices for the wood which my partner and I had chopped with much effort and diligence. Add to that we didn't always get along that wonderfully well and the reader will understand why I—for this winter at least—said goodbye to wood cutting.

That's five weeks ago now. All at once I came to the conclusion that I had had enough of chopping wood, but I didn't ask myself if finding another job would be all that easy. Luckily it wasn't that hard.

I said goodbye to the axe and saw on a Wednesday morning and

Thursday morning I began working at a nearby sawmill—and learned, before an hour had passed, that you have to be careful with a circular saw. Luckily I only sawed a cut in my leather mitts, which isn't as bad as one in your thumb, even though it wasn't very nice that I had to throw away a pair of mitts which had cost me $1.50 after only having worn them for two days.

I've never had the opportunity to wear the uniform of a Dutch soldier and I only know from hearsay that our defenders of the realm spend many a pleasant hour in their lodgings. I don't believe that they ever have more fun than we do here in our log camp in the middle of the woods. Our beds are perhaps not as luxurious as those in the armoury in Assen: a bed for every man is an unheard-of thing in a Canadian bush camp! Wooden planks with an armful of hay and a number of woollen blankets, along with an overcoat as a cushion, is our bed.

The first night isn't that bad, but after a week or so the hay is so compressed that it almost seems as hard as a plank. I told the boss about it and said that I was going to steal some hay from the horses to make it a little more pleasant to lay in bed.

"Oh," he said, "one of the men hasn't got much to do today: I'll tell him to shake up your bed." That night I found only planks in my bed instead of the promised hay. So the following day I opened up a bale of hay and fixed up my nest. That night I lowered myself down with a sigh of contentment only to hastily jump up again. A certain part of my body had come in contact with the point of a cow horn which had been hidden in the hay.

You hear some very strange tales sometimes when you listen to the older lumbermen gab at night. About the Indians for example... who were setting out a graveyard and shot down an old one-eyed Redskin so that they could inaugurate their new installation in the most appropriate manner. And about the old sawmill boss with a name I can never remember, whose wooden leg was trapped between two tree trunks and was stuck for five hours, until help arrived.

The poor boss's other leg froze and he now walks around the neighbouring village on two stilts, "where no doubt you must have seen him." Up to now I've never seen that stilt walker: but maybe I didn't have my eyes open enough.

And then they told me about the sawyer who lost his right index finger to the circular saw. One of his workmates rushed up and wanted to know how it had happened.

"Well," said the victim, "It was very simple, that damn... thing cut it off!" And he pointed to the swiftly turning saw, and pointing too closely, he lost his left index finger, "so that now he has no index fingers at all to point to saws," concluded the fat machinist who was telling the story.

The fat machinist tells the greatest number of stories and the most lies, and I never know for sure which they are, true stories or lies. Whatever they are, true or not, his stories are very pleasant to listen to.

Emigration
21 March, 1929

February 28 today: four more weeks and it will be two years since I climbed into the train at the Leeuwarden station and took the first step on the thousands of kilometres long road from the Fatherland to Northern Ontario.

It had taken a long time before I was personally satisfied that emigration to Canada was truly such a desirable thing. It took a lot of head pounding and then when I finally decided to go, it remained a risky enterprise. My knowledge of the new fatherland was very vague; wait and see was the only answer. If things went well, so much the better, if not, well the whole move would be a mistake.

It's not difficult to understand that I was nervous, when I climbed into the train on the 28th of March: nervous as well during the preceding weeks.

I searched all the papers that came within my reach, from A to Z, looking for news about Canada, and I also read a lot of brochures.

Naturally these were always in agreement in their praise: It's not profitable for railway and ship transportation companies to criticize the immense, half-populated country on this side of the ocean.

It was different with the newspapers. Often articles appeared which had been sent in by different young people who had already sometime ago put their feet down on the western prairies or in the Ontario bush.

Some were satisfied, didn't have the least regret about their decision, were progressing and felt at home in Canada. But others, well, one even wrote that a ship company had "lured him to this land with false hopes."

All this didn't clarify anything for me: the only thing left to do was go myself, look and judge for myself.

And I went...

And now many potential emigrants will ask: "And what do you think about it?" To tell the truth: It's not very easy to become a millionaire in Canada. And very few will ever achieve moderate riches here. But: Canada offers a good living to anyone who has a pair of hands and some brains, and uses them. You work harder there than at home—but your wage is higher—and you don't have to be unemployed very often, especially not if you're an experienced farmhand.

For example, our Friesian farmhands, who have spent their whole lives on a stockfarm, are sure of a permanent job in Ontario, and I believe in all of Canada. Experienced gardeners and their colleagues the florists would have little difficulty finding a well-paid job in southern Ontario—especially around Toronto.

The man who has a profession—especially a carpenter—can get a job in the big cities right away—if he knows sufficient English.

In conclusion: anyone who wants to work has a chance in this country, which is progressing quickly and has room for thousands.

But let no one set too high expectations for himself, don't think that you're going to get luxury or an easy life here. You have to work hard and in return you get a good living with few worries and the possibility of saving something, which at the moment is practically impossible in the Netherlands.

On my Own
11 April, 1929

Thank goodness—the winter's gone! As long as you're in the bush where the thick spruce tree army catches the sharp winter wind, it's not too bad, but when you go back to the settled districts, where there are hundreds of hectares of open land: BRRR... then it's cold. And not only cold, but boring too. The farmers here don't have their places as well fixed up as their Friesian colleagues. It's only the odd one who has a few trees or bushes around his house and the house itself: it's always made of wood and hardly ever painted. So the countryside in Northern Ontario in the winter doesn't look very cheerful and lively. Poets can talk very prettily about "the white snow blanket, spread upon the earth" and about "the sunbeams, reflecting a thousand colours from the crystal snow": Beautiful, very nice, but I'm no poet. I found it extremely boring to see nothing but snow, week in, week out. Give me the tender green grass in the spring, or the waving golden grain in the fall: give me Living Nature instead of the Dead Winter landscape.

But I'd better not get too philosophical. Let me say first that I haven't worked since the 21st of February. Not because there was no work in the neighbourhood, but because I did more than I had expected to do; besides which, the end of a plank I cut off half of my right thumb. This proved to me that you have to be very careful with a circular saw.

Luckily we have accident insurance here in Ontario, although we are generally rather backwards as far as social legislation is concerned, quite backwards when compared to the Netherlands. But in any case we have accident insurance, so that each week I received $12.50 to keep my stomach busy and naturally the doctor's and hospital's costs were covered by the insurance.

My good life is now finished, the doctor told me the sad news that I was once again able to work, so I have to look for something else to earn my board. A number of people had already asked me to work for them, but I've had too many bad experiences. Quite often you have to wait a long time before you get paid your honestly earned wage: the average farmer here is not blessed with an exceptionally generous business capital, especially after the three past summers, which brought all the farmers partial or complete failure. No wonder that many are fairly discouraged.

Last summer it was the rain, practically day in day out. And rain is probably the greatest enemy of the farms in the neighbourhood as drainage has been too little utilized. What could the Friesian farmer do if he didn't have his ditches and canals.

In any case, I'll take a chance. Not on a grand scale, however. I've rented a small farm, seven acres is small, especially in Canada. But it's enough for a poor bachelor such as myself. And if the weather isn't too miserable this coming summer I should be able to get enough potatoes, carrots and beets, etc. off it to pay the rent and save a few pennies. Nothing ventured, nothing gained! About the rent: $30 a year is not too much for seven acres of good land, a house (very simple and small) and a barn.

This will be my third summer on this side of the ocean; I wish myself a lot of luck.

De Nieuwe Rotterdamsche Courant,
29 September, 1929 to 1 June, 1930

TORONTO THE BEAUTIFUL

29 September, 1929

My lady friends have often asked me: "How is one of those American (Canadian) households run without servants?" Right now, I want to spend some time writing about it because the servant problem, which presents such a difficult question for Dutch households, has been completely resolved here for years. But the solution has also brought with it a much freer, much simpler manner of living. What follows is a description of a household from the well-to-do middle class.

Here in Toronto every house in the newer neighbourhoods stands separately along the beautiful wide avenues with their shaded sidewalks. Every house has a front garden and most also have an area behind the house. The distance between two houses ought to be greater, as it's usually no more than a small paved sidewalk. Sometimes the space is wide enough to let a car through to the garage at the end of the little driveway. But most of the houses are too close together and this makes the rooms, whose windows face on the space, dark. The radio, the gramophone and other noisy instruments, most likely present a problem for the neighbours. One of the big shortcomings of most of the houses is the lack of closet space. In very old houses in Holland there are often too many closets but here there are too few.

Otherwise, all the houses are furnished with "all the modern conveniences." There's gas, electric light, running water and telephone. The central heating is fueled by coal and the huge furnace has to be lit by the householder himself. The newer houses are heated by oil which, just like gas, is delivered to the house by pipes. There's an automatic ignition in the cellar and a sort of thermometer also regulates the desired temperature. This heating is more expensive than coal heating but it's a lot easier and a lot friendlier. We have central heating using coal. If the furnace has been lit, we set the pointer of the "thermometer" on the desired number of degrees of heat and the temperature rises to that heat but not higher. The furnace has to be regularly stoked and sometimes cleaned out, which is a dirty and fairly heavy job. If desired, you can call in help which is usually paid $1.25 per hour. The cost of the coal is between $10 and $16 per ton. Telephone, gas and electric light is not expensive here. Everyone cooks on gas or has an electric stove. It's easy and clean. It goes without saying that electric irons, sewing machines and don't forget electric washing machines, mangles and vacuum cleaners are used. They make a quick and easy job of a lot of the formerly heavy work. All doors and windows have screens which keep the house free of flies and mosquitoes but which also means that the windows can remain safely open at night during the generally very warm summer months.

Keeping servants is only possible for the very rich. Finnish maids are very much in demand. People swear that they are healthy, strong, hard working and honest. They generally start with a wage of $35 to $40 a month and if, after a few years, they've learned the language, manners and customs and are naturally fully competent in their jobs, they can earn $75 to $80 sometimes even $120 a month with room and board in New York.

It's strange that Canadian families frown on servants and house-keepers from England. Scottish and Irish workers, however, are in demand. But the Canadians don't like English immigrants. They say that "there's too much unusable trash." As far as foreign workers are concerned, Hollanders and Germans have a good reputation. If Canadians want to say something very friendly and well mannered to me, they remember that one or other ancestral family member was also a Hollander. I don't know if it can be explained psychologically why most of the Greeks here open a hotel or restaurant and why they never have first class businesses because they're not clean enough. Practically all the fruit merchants are Italians. The better washing and ironing establishments are in the hands of the Chinese. Japanese and Chinese restaurants are famous. I like to eat there very much. They're nicely decorated, the food is exceptional and you're flawlessly served by the little yellow waiters, whose unmoving masklike faces make you wonder whether they're boys of 18 or men of 38! There aren't as many Negroes in Canada as in the United States. Many negresses go to work as household help and are very well paid by the hour or they work as domestic servants and have a very good reputation as such. Many Negroes are also housemen or porters in big businesses, in movie houses etc. The servants in the trains are always Negroes. In Harlem, a neighbourhood in New York, everyone is black, even the policemen.

I've been in a "nigger-church" in Toronto. The organist, my companion and I were the only whites. The preacher was extraordinarily black. He preached very nicely and spoke very clearly until he got wound up, this happens easily to Negroes, then he gibbered and jabbered confusingly and not at all understandably. The singing was also very nice. After the service was finished, a considerable number of them came to us, shook our hands and welcomed us. The minister did the same. I stood in the middle of a circle of brethren as black as anthracite and found that they all looked so much alike that I couldn't find the preacher again, even though I had listened attentively during the service and had therefore been sitting there looking at him.

But now to come back to the American (Canadian) household. A housewife here is always nicely dressed. Her clothing is, as long as she's busy homemaking, practical but always "tasteful." Pretty multicoloured washable short dresses or skirts, without sleeves or with half sleeves, so you don't see the charlady-like rolled up sleeves. A Canadian breakfast is "cozy" to fix and cozy to eat. The night before, the empty milk bottles are set out on the porch or the veranda along with a note indicating the number of bottles wanted. You buy a certain number of milk tickets from your milkman and as many tickets as you put in the empty bottles, that's how many full bottles he'll set down when he comes to your house in the early morning.

Americans and Canadians prefer coffee to tea with their breakfast. The coffee pots are practical. I have yet to see them in the Netherlands, but it wouldn't surprise me if they were already in use. It's an aluminum coffee pot in which you put as much water as you think you need. Inside is a coffee sieve held up by a narrow tube which extends to the bottom of the pot. You throw the ground coffee into the sieve, a teaspoon per cup. Then you put the top on: the pot is put on the gas stove and as soon as the water boils it rises through the tube and the boiling water drops fall on the coffee like a fountain. The coffee "sets by itself" and soon the rousing, stimulating smell circulates through the house while you're in your convenient kitchen further preparing the breakfast. You begin with fruit or a glass of fruit juice. The grapefruit is the most common fruit. Fruits are wonderful here and in good supply but not cheaper than in Holland. Fresh pineapples and also melons are exceedingly tasty and not expensive. The huge watermelons are a special treat for the Negroes.

The breakfast consists further of a bowl of oatmeal, mostly the ordinary oatmeal that you have to cook but in Holland they are also familiar with the kinds that are already prepared, the ones you mix with cold milk in your bowl. Then there's bread, usually (electrically) toasted with ham, bacon, fried eggs etc. The breakfast is eaten in the dining room but also in the kitchen if it's airy and roomy. Some houses have a small narrow room, a sort of addition to the kitchen which they call the "kitchenette" and which serves as a breakfast room. As most kitchens have hot and cold running water the washing up is easier. Instruments with long handles protect the fingers of the housewife when scouring pans. The peeling of potatoes and fruit, as well as other rough jobs which make the fingers and hands rough and grubby, can be done while wearing gutta percha (rubber) gloves.

You can order what you want by telephone at the butcher, baker and grocer, or you can go and choose it yourself. The store displays are very appetizing and the service is quick and mannerly. Sometimes a vegetable and fruit pedlar comes calling with his wagon but usually even this order is made by phone. Bread, milk, butter and groceries are excellent and no more expensive or cheap than in Holland. The meat is less expensive: the quality is very good, but the butchers cut it in such a strange way. You always find a bone where you don't expect one.

The vegetables are much more expensive and there's not as much choice as in Holland. Purslane, sorrel and edible pods are unknown here. In this great land, where everything is on a gigantic scale, even the heads of lettuce are very big; the potatoes are also huge and certainly not as tasty as the Dutch; the young carrots measure out as colossal stewing carrots; the fresh peas are the size of marbles. The asparagus are all colours of the rainbow. Tomatoes, cauliflower, onions, celery are excellent. A favorite vegetable here are the young corn cobs, "greencorn." The cobs have to be very young. They are peeled out of their green husks and cooked in boiling water for fifteen minutes and eaten with salt and butter. Those who have a unique rich imagination will think of young peas; more prosaic people will mumble "chickenfeed."

A housewife here has no problems with the incessant bell ringing of tradesmen. Besides the tradesmen who look after the ordered goods there are salesmen who wish to display or recommend this or that new household article. It's sometimes painful to turn away an older man or woman who looks so tired. Sometimes they are young students who try to make their vacations somewhat productive by selling door to door.

The drive to earn money is in the blood of both young and old here. "Shall I cut your grass for a dime?" is what two nice boys asked me recently as they went from house to house with a lawnmower. They did a neat job and came back the next day to weed the garden behind the house. They continued working until everything was ship shape. They were in their bathing suits and after they had finished they ran down to the lake on their bare feet and returned to get their hard earned wages.

Many boys of 14 to 16 go to work for the farmer in their vacations to earn some money picking strawberries and berries. Girls also do this; they're called "farmerettes."

One shouldn't think that these boys and "farmerettes" are poor children. Sometimes, if there are a lot of flies, caterpillars, or harmful beetles, the municipal government pays a fixed price for a kilo of the insects and then it turns into a contest between the boys and the girls as to who can catch the most.

But I've wandered away from the household again. Every house has one or more bathrooms with built-in sinks. The bedrooms don't have built in sinks. A lot of work is expended on the bedrooms. The floors in all the rooms are almost always waxed "hardwood" over which are laid beautiful carpets. It makes it warm and comfortable. The curtains and the colour of the walls are coordinated with the carpet and the fabric on the furniture. Americans and Canadians have good taste as far as that's concerned. The paintings and engravings are not very tasteful. In the bedroom, the bed is covered by a nice spread, usually silk and in the colour of the curtains. The English and the Americans do not remove the bedclothes as is the custom in Holland. You don't need a lot of blankets here, with the warm summers and central heating in the winter. The blankets and the sheets are turned back, left like that for a little while; the pillows are shaken up and then the sheets, blankets and spread are neatly put back. A dressing table with decorative toilet articles and many mirrors, a lot of electric lights and pretty lamp shades make the bedroom very comfortable and quickly give it a "luxurious" appearance. Our huge cavernous bedrooms, in those old big Dutch houses which were never heated in the winter, where you usually first had to melt the wash water on those cold winter mornings and then dry yourself with numbed fingers and a hard frozen towel, were shiveringly "character building."

The mealtimes, besides breakfast, are luncheon and supper. The master of the house seldom comes home before supper and he spends his "noon hour" either in his office or in a lunchroom. Whoever's home lunches on sandwiches, fruit, tea or coffee. Supper, we would call it dinner, consists of meat, vegetables and potatoes, always with a salad (cucumber or fruit salad) and dessert, usually a pie with fruit. Nothing further will then be eaten. Hospitality is great here and they have a very easy manner of making you welcome.

If you have guests for supper (around 6 p.m.), then the ladies are taken to one of the bedrooms where they can quietly fix up their hair, cheeks and lips. In the dining room, the table is cozily and beautifully covered, sometimes with a pretty, big tablecloth but usually with all kinds of embroidered or lace cloths which belong with each other and which harmonize with the little serviettes or napkins. On every plate stands a glass of fruit on ice. Soup is not served. The meat (as in England) is carved by the master of the house. The plates of the guests are placed in front of him; he puts some meat on every one; the woman of the house sees to it that every plate has potatoes, vegetables and gravy. Not eating your plate clean is regarded as a sign of good table manners.

Because there are no servants, the host and hostess have to serve. This has led to the simplifying of the dinner. There aren't many dishes. The dessert is a cake or pie with ice cream. This is followed by cheese and coffee and tea. One of the female guests helps the lady of the house clean up the table.

I'm describing a dinner at home here. At official dinners, usually given outside the home, the menus are as extensive as in the "old country." In such a domestic circle, wine is not served, but the conversation is no less animated. In the beginning, I used to laugh to myself when I heard those well-off Canadian gentlemen propose a toast with a glass of ginger beer or orange juice in their hands.

After dinner is finished, a pleasant chat in the living room, or the veranda or porch. Naturally everyone has a radio and the preference is to listen to that hideous jazz music. One lady told me straight out: "Oh, I don't like the music at all, but I think the noise is wonderful." Lots of bridge is played here and the radio drones, crackles or sings throughout it all, and leads my thoughts desperately away from the game. Sometimes you're sitting there having a pleasant chat and all at once the radio booms right through it. However, if it gets too drastic for me, I just calmly turn it off even if I'm a guest. I don't understand how people can stand to hear that continuous unmusical music.

After the guests have left, then comes the housewife's less pretty task of having to do the dishes. But all the family members, women and men, help out. No gentleman here is ashamed to peel the potatoes or shell the peas or pick the beans or scrub the floor.

Life is somewhat simpler here, maybe a little "bohemian", but it's very natural. You're always welcome in anybody's house but you have to take pot luck for supper and you have to be prepared to help out. Having guests and overnighters always means extra bother in Holland, not here; giving a little dinner in Holland always brings along a lot of trouble for the hostess: not here. One course and then the dessert is the general custom. If a bridge drive is organized one evening, for let's say 12 people, then the hostess can be sure that the guests will bring their share of sandwiches or cake. (This is also an English custom. – *Ed.*)

There are always boring little jobs in a household which are routine and can't be avoided: such things as scrubbing and scraping. Those who can afford it hire a scrub woman and those who lament the expense do it themselves. The household without servants brings with it a greater measure of freedom, that's for sure. It's made the American and Canadian housewife handy and spry. She's boss in her own home and husband and wife are true, brave friends, even in the carrying out of those less than pleasant household chores.

The children have to be taken along when mother and father go out. In a big department store here, there's a sort of children's playground on the top floor, with sand and all kinds of toys, where the little ones can play under the supervision of a young lady while the mother does her shopping. At the big annual exhibition that's held from the 23rd of August to the 7th of September there was a special building where lost children were looked after, but also a safe open air playground where the children amused themselves under supervision. For 10 cents an hour you could leave the little ones safely behind while you freely amused yourself at the Exhibition. (A similar organization existed at the Rotterdam Nenijto. – *Ed.*)

Life is not cheap here, but one lives freer and is therefore luckier in many ways than in the old country. Everyone is neatly dressed. The other day, a gentleman wandered through the busiest streets trying to demonstrate that men, just like women, could be dressed in a cool and comfortable fashion. He wore an immaculate, sky blue pair of pajamas, bare feet in snow white tennis shoes, a neat sky blue hanky in the pocket of his pajamas and he was bareheaded. He didn't scandalize anyone. Only the big hotels refused him entry to the lobby, the lounge and the dining room because of his costume.

The rental of a house, of a respectable house of about six rooms, is $60 to $70 a month. Many young people take a pair of furnished rooms and pay about $35 a month for a kitchen–living room and a bedroom with shared use of the bathroom and central heating. I have seen apartments (we would call them flats) which consisted of a little living room, very small kitchen, tiny bedroom and bathroom, central heating and electric light for $35 per month. The house was just finished when I saw it and the apartments were all empty. How even one person could move around in such a little bedroom when there was a bed, a chair and a chest in it, seems like an insoluble puzzle to me. None of the ordinary houses have great high rooms and hallways like those beautiful old Dutch houses. The rooms are smaller and lower. A housewife here, who looks after her household well, has to be industrious and practical but all kinds of ingenious appliances come to her aid and the result is: more freedom and more enjoyment of life.

5 December, 1929

The streets of Toronto are generally very neat, except where they're ripping up and rebuilding, a hobby which every municipal government seems to indulge in, preferably at the busiest intersections.

A tough, but good, law here is that all stray dogs are rounded up. The dog catchers travel throughout the city from 9:00 a.m. to 4:00 p.m. with their wagons and catch (with their nets) all those dogs which are found on the street without their masters or mistresses. In the evenings, the newspaper describes the kind of dogs which have been captured. The owner can retrieve his dog from the dog pound after paying a fee of $2. The dogs are kept there for four or five days and receive food and drink. If they haven't been released by then, they're given to the Humane Society which tries to find them a good home; it that's not successful, they're quickly and painlessly put down.

Wooden bins with the exhortation, "Help to keep the street clean," are set on the corners. The intention is that used newspapers, blowing paper etc. will be deposited therein. I once saw a virtuous old gentleman do a variation on Peg-Leg-Pete as he ran after some fluttering papers with his pointy cane and industriously stuffed them into the bin.

In the beautiful, wide avenues of Toronto all the houses have front gardens which are not separated from the sidewalk by gates, chains etc. The flowers, plants and trim lawns in those little gardens are never vandalized. The type of guttersnipe that has to wreck or dirty everything isn't seen here. Youth has an abundance of play and sport grounds. Toronto is a fairly young city and the city council had, when it wanted to develop parks, all the hilly and forested terrain necessary at its command, so to speak. All the parks have an abundance of fields for play and sport grounds. When I see the boys and girls from the lower classes so cheerful, so full of fire, so freely participating in sports and I see, close by, the well kept garden beds and borders with beautiful flowers which haven't been ripped up or trampled, then my thoughts go to those men in our big cities who, with so much idealism attempt to give some direction to the adolescent street urchins. If I could only send them a couple of those great big roomy fields!

People here really like a bit of fun and my purpose in this letter is to talk about a number of these amusements. I begin with those amusements which are held on a fixed date. There is Empire Day on 24 May. This date is really the birthday of Queen Victoria who was festively remembered with vacations for the youth, parades and fireworks. However, the monarch became so old that when she died, the Canadians, had become accustomed to having a special holiday on the 24th of May, had to be permitted to continue their celebrations. They then named the day "Empire Day." It's become a sort of "Guy Fawkes" day, lots of fireworks by and for the youth. July 1 is Dominion Day. The lawns and the benches in the parks are full of cheerful picnicking people. Schools, offices and factories are closed or dismissed earlier than usual.

July 12 is the day for the "Orangemens'" parade. Orangemen's Day was instituted some thirty years ago by an Irishman in remembrance of the battle between the Protestant king-governor William Ill and his Catholic opponent. But in reality it's more directed at Catholicism which is the major religion in former French Canada. Orangemen's day is celebrated with an endlessly long parade. One sees many banners on which William is pictured at the battle of the Boyne.

All kinds of Protestant societies from different parts of Canada join the parade and in almost every group there's a man walking around with an open Bible as a symbol of Protestantism. There's also a man proudly sitting on a steed and dressed as William Ill. He's the principal figure in the parade. A considerable number of bands are involved in the parade, such as the Scots in their kilts with their flutes and their bagpipes.

In former French Canada, still full of old historical remembrances, the inhabitants speak a kind of patois that is neither French nor English but a surprising mixture of the two. The elite in Montreal still speaks good, beautiful French. A part of the Canadian public wants to ban anything in the schools of former French Canada that refers to the French past. "One country, one king, one language" is what they write on the banners which you can also see carried in the Orangemen's parade. The whole parade is, however, not against France nor aimed at the French language but against Catholicism. Orange is the chief colour in the long, long procession: orange banners, orange sashes, orange flowers. Generally, the parade runs quietly to its conclusion. I also saw Indians in war paint walking along in the procession. They also apparently sympathized with the importance of the religious question.

When I see all the advertisements on Saturday evening announcing the different Sunday religious services, I realize that the total number of varieties are puzzlingly large. I want to write a few words about a number of sects because I've never heard of them in Holland. First of all there's the Pentecostal sect. The Pentecostals in Toronto have their own halls. They don't have any designated ministers at their gatherings. If one of those present gets "the Spirit", he begins to speak and to call but Pentecostals appear to be very nervous and emotional and before long many others get the Spirit and an intense excitement develops. Arms and legs come into motion. Chairs are broken because of their convulsive movements but it doesn't end in fighting, it's only ecstasy. Sometimes the leader is catapulted out of the pulpit by his fiery oratory but even that ends without accident. As he says: he's led by the Spirit.

I suggest that anyone who's not a Pentecostal choose a seat close to the exit. The least fright or disturbance brings the Pentecostal into action. Someone told me that he was in a barber shop having a haircut while the gentlemen in the chair next to him was being shaved. The barber's helper accidentally dropped a pair of scissors or a brush and the unexpected noise was enough to make the lathered client jump up and begin to give a witness of the Spirit in a pouring out of excited, confusing language. Only after the Spirit had passed, could the barber finish off the man's face. It sometimes happens in the train as well that an unexpected sound will cause a traveler to jabber words without end or sense in an unknown language. The other passengers glance up from their reading material or over their big newspapers but they don't laugh. You hear them say: "Pentecostal" and the literature is replaced. Once the Spirit has finished raging in the Pentecostal, his eyes lose that staring, absent appearance and while still a little pale from so much ecstasy, he once again takes his place among the more phlegmatic travelers.

An even more excitable sect are the Hornerites. As far as I know they don't have any halls of their own in Toronto. Their seat is Kingston. The Hornerites also get the Spirit but their expression is more furious and fanatic. Men and women turn furiously in circles, throw themselves on the ground, strike their heads against the walls, the floor and against the treads of the pulpit stairs, under the influence of the cry: "Jesus, save me!" If they hold a religious service on the street, they first lay down piles of straw in order to protect the banging heads, the kicking legs and swinging arms. Someone who had seen it told me that it reminded him of the fanatical dances of the Dervishes. I've been in Kingston, but I found that beautiful little city in an extremely dull, peaceful state.

The Holy Rollers are a very strange sect. Windsor, Ontario is their seat. The Holy Rollers call upon a character out of the Old Testament but I don't know which one. The older men call themselves prophets. All the men wear long beards, which makes them appear somewhat Jewish, but they aren't Hebrews and they call themselves Christians. The young ladies of the sect regard it as a great honor, as something holy, to spend a night with one of the prophets. The English law finds that to be less than "Holy" and as a result this sect quite often finds itself in collision with a judge. Sometimes they're banned but they always turn up again. They have a famous band which is very popular. They're also outstanding baseball players, which in the eyes of Canada and the United States excuses a lot.

The Dukhobor sect also gives the police a lot of extra work. This is a Russian sect which can be found in Western Canada and the United States. The majority of them are farmers. They refuse to wear any clothing. All the strange religious sects which can flower here in America, are they the result of the mixing of all kinds of races and nationalities and from the fact that money, money, money is the foremost ambition, because most immigrants don't know what true refinement and culture is, while their souls, like all other human souls, also have religious longings?

I want to talk about another sect, also strange, but much, much more appealing and of higher standing than the former. It's the Mennonite sect. You have to look for them in and around the little cities of Kitchener and Waterloo. Kitchener was called Berlin before the war, but political hatred during the war gave it its new name. Kitchener and Waterloo are neat, prosperous places, founded by German immigrants. The Mennonites are a German sect. They're rigorously religious, dress themselves in black coats, jackets, hats, shawls, all according to an old design. They don't want anything to do with electric light, automobiles, any of the new inventions. These things are, in their eyes, works of the devil. The majority of the Mennonites are farmers. They are known for their great honesty and fidelity, for their great cleanliness and for their delicious sausage, which is never adulterated and which they deliver to the customers in their old fashioned horse and wagon. The main highways in Canada are wide and beautiful for cars but the rural roads are not at all ideal. If a driver sees a Mennonite with a horse and wagon driving ahead of him on one of the rural roads, he might as well be patient because he can toot, grumble and swear as much as he wants but the Mennonite won't move over for a devil's wagon!

But now I'm going to return to my amusements. Labor Day is

the first Monday in September. This day falls in the time of the great exhibition here. Labour Day means a day off for everyone and Labor Day falls at the same time as Civic Day (also a day off for everyone) in the bordering American states. As a result, the number of cars and the number of travelers who arrive by train or boat is overwhelming, and the beloved "Ex"(hibition) does a very good business.

During Exhibition time there aren't enough sleeping accommodations and so the tourists sometimes sleep in their cars or in tents that they've brought along. Those who organize their homes as tourist facilities make a pretty good profit and naturally that's the whole intention. As all the homes have one or more bathrooms and all have built in sinks with running water, there's not much to clean up after the departure of the guests, who have had to come to some mutually agreeable arrangement about the use of the washing facilities.

The cost per person, per night, is usually $1, at Exhibition time $1.50. The hostess provides a bed and towels but she doesn't have to provide any breakfast. I know families who can put up 20 tourists in their fairly small homes. Families of 4 or 5 persons sometimes sleep in one room. Life is just simpler here!

The tourists usually pay in advance and sometimes have already departed before the hostess gets up. Naturally, there's always the chance that you'll meet tourists with a peculiar understanding of good manners, honesty or cleanliness but you don't hear a lot of complaints about that.

The tourist season has now begun and huge numbers of cars are coming from the United States, primarily it is said, because Canada is less "dry." Those who want to drink wine or liquor here have to apply for a licence and then they can buy what they want in the government stores. By the bottle naturally and they can only enjoy the contents in the house, not on the veranda or the porch because that is "in public." Hotels and restaurants are not allowed to supply the desired potables. As soon as the tourist cars get near the city where they want to stay overnight, they look for the familiar signs, which are electrically illuminated at night and on which is written "Tourists-garage" or "Accommodation for Tourists." At the same time, the families who want to have guests either send their children out or they themselves stand at the side of the road. If they see a car coming, which they recognize by the colour of its license plate as not being from Toronto, they stick out a little sign which says "rooms" or "tourists." The avenue on which I live, runs out onto the main highway along the lake and as I live right near the corner, I often amuse myself watching the tourist hunt.

The innumerable cars form an unbroken stream but the number of people who want to provide accommodation for the tourists is also great. There's a lot of competition, generally honest and fair, which is not surprising considering the many refined families who make their houses available. It's a very common way of supplementing income here. There aren't many expenses attached to it, once you've got organized. Couches and makeshift beds are also serviceable. Sheets and towels surely don't have to be made of real linen. Usually, the housewife owns an electric washing machine and electric mangle, or otherwise there are laundries which do a good and fast job. Even so, just once, I'd love to see the face of a Dutch "man of the house" as he has to put up with using his bedroom and kitchen as dining and living rooms for a couple of weeks in the summer! But maybe his face would brighten up if, as a result, he could record a profit of $600 or $700. There are enough people here who also rent out their own bedrooms and sleep on the veranda or porch. As long as it brings in the money!

The tourists have breakfast in a tea-room or cafeteria. In a cafeteria you help yourself. At the entrance you take a tray from one of the piles and push it along the prepared and priced foods: sandwiches, cakes, eggs, fruit, fruit salad. You can also get hot dishes. You fill a glass with water or fruit juice or you take a small pot of tea or coffee along with a cup and saucer and in the cup is a little creamer. Then you grab the necessary forks, spoons, knives and paper serviettes, go past a young lady who quickly inspects your tray, adds up the cost of what you've taken and places the bill on your tray. Then you look for a place in the big room and start to eat. On the tables you'll find sugar, pepper, salt, pickles and vinegar. After you've finished, you leave your tray behind and exit from the room past a cashier, whom you pay. No tips. What you get there is good and cheap. There are many fewer employees necessary than in an ordinary tea room.

There are also groceterias in which you help yourself to the required groceries which are generally packed in various weights or are weighed up by a clerk. When you enter you have to surrender your bag in order to prevent theft. There are piles of big baskets. You take one, wander through the store and put what you want into the basket. When you're finished you go to the cashier and pay for what you've bought. In the groceterias the goods seem to be of as high a quality as in the ordinary stores but much cheaper. This is because they don't need as many clerks. The groceries are also not delivered to your house and the buyer has to carry them home by himself....

Hallowe'en is on October 31. It's the day on which witches whirl through the air on broomsticks; at night the spirits and ghosts of the dead who cannot find rest in their graves wander around. The young woman, who has the courage to venture out into the night all alone, with a mirror in her hand, will suddenly be gifted with second sight, and appearing in the glass will be the image of the man she will marry. In the last weeks before Hallowe'en the display windows of all the stores have witches and black cats. The youth have their Hallowe'en evening, they put on costumes, decorate themselves with feathers, paint and bells, then go to the houses in the neighbourhood, shrieking "Shell Out!" All the families have baskets of fruit and candy waiting in the hallway and they hand this out to the Hallowe'eners. As soon as the store owners hear "Shell Out", they open the doors and throw out a couple of handfuls of treats before the young people, who might do a lot of mischief that night, can enter.

In the countryside, the pranks are rougher and cruder: wrecking fences; hauling wagons and equipment out of the barns and taking them a far distance away; barricading bridges and roads, all kinds of those "practical jokes" about which even the victims can still laugh. But this is increasingly becoming discredited, in my eyes a sign of the progress of culture. Here in the city, practically all of the families have their own Hallowe'en parties. The fun is then kept at home. I heard about a large group of ladies, all between 40 and 60, who had dressed up that evening as little girls; they had to talk baby talk, play with a rattle and enthusiastically do those kinds of idiotic things.

I don't believe, that a household in Canada or the United States could exist anymore without a radio. The radio plays all day long: at breakfast, while the housework's being done, at lunch and during supper, while conversation's going on and while bridge is being played. I think that an American can't die if he doesn't hear the radio on his deathbed. There are a great many moments when I sincerely hate the radio, but recently I felt somewhat soft hearted towards it, this occurred when I heard a very delightful witty speech given by the English prime minister. What a pleasant, pliant, melodious voice he has! And then that evening of the big celebration which Ford gave for the genial "Al" (Thomas Alva Edison), when I was able to hear the speech. The words of professor Einstein, sadly enough, didn't come over very clearly for us because of the static. I believe that every Saturday evening in New York, they send a greeting to Commander Byrd.

Practically every family has a radio. The other ambition is to have an automobile. Every young girl's heart here is filled with dreams of a "boy" with a "car." The association between the two sexes is also very free here. The boy can make long trips with his "beloved" in his car. Love guarantees that the couple doesn't pay enough attention to the red and green lights and as a result a lot of accidents happen with cars which contain more conscientious people. Almost every day, you can read in the paper that the police magistrate has asked one of those reckless youths: "did you have your arm around the young lady when the accident occurred?" And that fact is not regarded as a mitigating circumstance.

In our country there are, and unfortunately rightly so, a lot of complaints about the decline in polite behavior but you can hear of some awful examples here as well. Recently, I heard about a hostess who gave a party to which some twenty young men had been invited. Every young man was asked whether he had rum or whiskey with him. Everyone had a full flask, and the hostess requested that they give the flasks to her until the party was over. She didn't want the young men and her young female guests to disappear for a while, with the car and the rum, during a break in the party. Only three of the twenty remained, the rest refused to stay, if that pleasure was to be denied to them.

Another example is as follows. At an evening party, the supper had been carefully set out in the dining room. Now, it's the custom here, to set a filled plate at each place with the small plates for fruit salad, and so forth, next to it. When the hostess indicated that supper was served, it turned out that the young ladies and their cavaliers had departed in their cars and had taken their suppers with them and the following day she did not get all her porcelain, silver, glass or napkins back. The danger, which is inherent in all those "nice" rides with the "boys" in their "cars", has caused someone to give the following advice: permit a greater amount of freedom under your own roof, then you can avoid the rides in the privacy of the dark park avenues. As a result, you now hear people talking about "petting parties" after a dance where the young ladies and their cavaliers are permitted and even given the opportunity to, let's say, flirt in a very close and intimate way in a secluded and half lit corner. But I have to add that such "innovations" rouse a lot of indignation and luckily not only with the "old-timer."

An elderly person recently told me: "I don't approve of these things, but let's honestly admit that everything's more in the open now and so just seems more brazen whereas the same thing used to occur on the sly in the past because people will be people. The result will be the same as with the ladies' short skirts. In the past, when a gust of wind blew the long dresses up and exposed perhaps a glimpse of leg just above the ankle, there was a lot of grinning, and witty remarks were made. But now that all the dresses are short and ladies' legs are a daily spectacle, nobody pays much attention to them. Curiosity is satisfied. The freedom which the younger generation now demands has been denied too long to former generations. And as far as poor manners are concerned, that's mostly the fault of the parents and less of the children. You have to learn good manners at home." And I was in total agreement with him on the last point.

The beautiful long summer is past and everyone is preparing himself for the winter. The houses are getting their storm windows: all the fathers of the houses are carefully plugging up the drafts; the central heating is on, but only at half strength. Canada is beautiful in the fall with its wonderful clear sky which is dark red at sunset; with its pretty warm harvest colours in the woods; with its shining "great" full moon, "harvest moon." And now in November, when the first snow is expected, it will only remain for a short time and then bring "Indian summer": warm, sunny days and frosty nights. But Indian summer, however nice, doesn't last long.

The leaves pile up in the park avenues. They're swept up but after a couple of hours there are new ones but the nice bare tree branches are once again full of little buds. Squirrels become tamer and come and eat the nuts out of your hand. A big parti-coloured woodpecker hammers on the tree trunks. Huge, wide, beautiful Lake Ontario is still blue and quiet. But after Indian summer, the mists rise up out of it: great grey cloud formations will sweep over it and usually around Christmas the first snowstorm will come to give this part of Canada its blinding white splendour.

I end this letter with a few couplets from that picturesque poem "Indian Summer" by Brant Hamerton:

> *Once in the year, when Autumn*
> *Has laid her hands on the trees,*
> *And the fragrance of her presence*
> *Sweetens every vagrant breeze*
> *When every hill with a glory*
> *Of crimson and gold is crowned,*
> *The souls of the Indian warriors*
> *Return to their native ground.*

Then he, who has eyes to see them
May watch by some pleasant stream,
While the light canoes come dancing
And the restless paddles gleam,
And he, who has ears that are quick to hear,
May note in the woodland pass
The furtive sound of the Redman's feet
Stirring the leaves and grass.

February 9, 1930

On Christmas day, one of our friends called us in the morning to remind us that a Christmas greeting would be sent from Eindhoven to America (via Long Island) between twelve o'clock and twelve thirty. It was snowing quite heavily outside and I was afraid that the atmospheric conditions would spoil the reception. But no, they announced that Philips, Eindhoven Holland would speak next and a second later a clear Christmas message to America arrived, first in Dutch and then in English. After that, we heard two Christmas carols from the beginning of the 17th century and after that a few closing words, also first in Dutch and then in English. How many Hollanders, in the United States and Canada, were listening at that moment to that greeting from far, old and faithful Holland, with the same warming emotion? "The love of native land, is innate to everyone."

I had to relate this first, before I begin on the actual subject that I want to deal with in this letter. This time, I want to deal with advertising and publicity, both of which America is famous for. A song is sung here that begins with the words: "I'm only a dreamer. Aren't we all?" Everybody likes to brag a little, one does it in a humorous or unashamedly impudent way, another does it with more consummate modesty but we're all braggarts and snobs, it's very much part of the times. Americans, and the Canadians as well, love to boast and sometimes there's something childlike in that boasting. The worth of something for them is measured by the number of dollars it costs. Recently, when Henry Ford gave that lovely party for Edison's jubilee and reconstructed on his estate (so to speak), the youth, the striving and the searching of the great inventor, most Americans failed to see Henry Ford's beautiful, warm, sympathetic meaning but they said with some pride: "and that must have cost Ford such and so many thousands of dollars!"

If they build a library, a museum, a bridge, a station, an opera house etc., the first thing that they'll tell you is the total number of dollars that something like that costs. And the national pride swells with every million dollars that can be mentioned. A peculiar contradiction: in his ordinary, private life you will never hear an American (Canadian) brag about his lovely house, his expensive car etc.

Whoever does business will meet competition and the question of success is connected to the question of how to browbeat and score off the competition. Naturally every businessman takes advantage of advertising in newspapers and magazines but it isn't always easy to create something new and arresting. When a manufacturer wants to introduce a new product in the market, let's say a new perfume or new shampoo, he sometimes offers a large prize, as much as $1,200, and pays it out to the individual who can think up the most suitable name or the most appropriate slogan. Thousands try to win the prize and so the new product is known everywhere, even before it's introduced to the market.

There are two gigantic department stores in Toronto. One is Eaton's and the other Simpson's. Everyday, there are pages full of advertisements from these companies in all the newspapers. The advertising alone must cost a fortune annually. Every year, about four weeks before Christmas, Eaton's sponsors the Santa Claus parade in Toronto. The only thing Santa Claus has in common with our Saint Nicholas is the name. Santa Claus is a sort of lovable winter king, clad in purple velvet set off with white trimmings. A long white beard streams from his chin and he wears a purple beret on his head which is trimmed with fur. He lives in the neighbourhood of the North Pole and usually makes his entrance in a sleigh pulled by reindeer. This year, however, he was sitting on a giant silver "polar fish" which lay on a high wagon. Numerous coloured balloons whirled about the fins and the tail of this beautiful fairy tale fish. The parade was beautiful and charming. It always takes place on a Saturday because the schools are closed then. The trains were full of children who were going to see the arrival of Santa Claus. I stood near the Parliament Buildings. The streets and the lanes, along which the parade was to pass, were kept clear by mounted police. It was a pretty sight to see all those hundreds of children arrive: white children of all classes, the rich ones stepping out of beautiful cars, the less well to do coming by tram or on foot: little Negroes, yellow Chinese, all of Toronto's youth was on foot to see the arrival of Santa Claus on that cold but sunny Saturday morning. And finally, there came the parade. There were three bands.

There were all kinds of familiar persons from the fairy tale world. Cinderella rode in her golden coach; and on a giant goose sat Mother Goose; on another wagon you could see Jack and Jill; old Mother Hubbard; little Miss Muffet and the other important characters from the nursery rhymes. And at the end of the long, varied, fairy-tale-like parade, came the huge wagon with the marvelous silver North Pole fish and high up on the fish sat Santa Claus with his fiery red cheeks and his snow white beard. Then the cheers burst loose and the children yelled: "Santa! Santa!" And Santa laughed and waved to all sides. During the following days, he could be found at the Eaton's store at certain designated hours. The young people could bring him their wish lists there.

"Toyland" was the name of the departments at Eaton's and Simpson's where the toys were displayed. And what toys! You almost felt like a kid again when you wandered through that world of fantasy and reality.

Eaton's takes pride in the fact that it holds itself strictly to its advertised prices. The company once advertised fur coats for $198, but a period was put after the 1 in the advertisement. When a customer asked for one of the advertised fur coats, picked one out and presented two dollars as payment, the clerk began to laugh and said that the coat cost $198. But the customer took the advertisement out of her purse. That's what it said: $1.98. The clerk went to the manager but true to its principles—the company absorbed the loss. The customer got the beautiful coat for less than $2 but it was made clear to any other interested parties that those coats had been sold out.

In all those big department stores, with their extensive staff of clerks, consummate perfection rules. The service is quick and polite; you can bring back or exchange whatever you buy, it's all nicely organized. In the last days before Christmas, the crush was scary and I don't understand how there could be sufficient supervision over everything then.

Not too long ago, someone told me about an interesting Ford advertisement. The great manufacturer went for a ride with a friend in his car, which was not a Ford. They got stuck in the mud on a side road and the expensive car couldn't move forward or backwards. So they called in the help of a farmer who freed the car from its distressing position with a couple of horses. But the farmer grumbled; "That's what you get with such an expensive car. Why don't you get a Ford? They're smaller and handier." "Do you have a Ford?", Ford asked the farmer, who hadn't the least idea to whom he was speaking. "Naturally", said the farmer, "And I wouldn't want any other kind. I've had it for a while and it's not new anymore but it does its duty faithfully." A number of days later, the farmer received a brand new Ford and the automobile king of Detroit must be convinced that this farmer will, unasked, make the most wonderful publicity for him.

A great big department store in Chicago, as an introduction, once advertised that, at a certain hour, 25 men's overcoats of excellent quality would be thrown out of the second story. At the appointed hour, it was black with people in front of the store. And exactly on the announced hour, the 25 overcoats flew down but few people got any enjoyment from it. The majority grabbed and pulled so fiercely in order to get one that all 25 coats were torn to pieces. But the company didn't pay any attention to that; the publicity had been successful.

For the last while, Chicago has not had the reputation for being a safe city. But it's been notorious for that once before. I don't think that too many readers will remember the History of Jesse James.[3] Twenty-five years ago Jesse James was the leader of an infamous gang in Chicago. Everyone knew and feared the big, robust bandit who calmly appeared everywhere with, I don't know how many revolvers in his pockets. If he thought it was a good idea to leave the city for a while, then he knew he would get a good reception at every farmer's because nobody dared to deny him hospitality or turn him over to the police because of fear of the relentless vengeance of his gang. The police also didn't know how to apprehend him and so Jesse James, who had I don't know how many murders and thefts on his conscience, walked with his head held high through the streets of the city, always with one hand in his pocket holding a loaded revolver. He was a terrifying hero to the youth of Chicago and a sort of romantic bandit to many women. A large reward was offered, I think $15,000, to whoever could capture Jesse James, dead or alive. And finally one of his friends was prepared to play the Judas role. One day when Jesse James was having lunch with this friend, the man's wife called the tall bandit to help her hang up a pair of curtains. Jesse James did as he was asked and stood unaware in the desired position with his back to his betrayer and with his hands up in the air.

His friend then shot him dead. Jesse James' brother then provided the police with all the necessary information to capture the whole gang and as a reward was set free. They call that giving "states-evidence" in the United States and "King's evidence" here in Canada. The same department store that threw down the 25 overcoats actually hired the

---

3. The author of the letters was apparently not too familiar with the History. Jesse James was assassinated by Bob Ford on April 3, 1882 in St. Josephs, Missouri and was not a Chicago gangster.

brother as a publicity stunt and the inhabitants of Chicago gathered in droves to take a look at the brother of the notorious bandit. The brother sat on a sort of stage and next to him lay the pistols, knives etc. of the once greatly feared, mighty Jesse James.

Nowadays, the radio is also used to advertise. Sometimes you listen to a beautiful concert with great pleasure and after every number you're informed that this and that manufacturer of sausage, chewing gum, toothpaste or cod liver oil has the pleasure to bring you this concert and this is followed by a recital of all the blessings which the product of this manufacturer brings to humanity. That kind of disturbance is worse than applause.

For the last couple of weeks, there's been a silly advertisement on the radio, every Thursday evening, for Martha Washington candies. The Laura Secord candy stores are quite famous in Canada. Laura Secord was a Canadian heroine in some war. The Martha Washington candies are the most famous in the United States, named after Washington's daughter. The Martha Washington advertisement is as follows: everyone can send in the first line of a song to a designated address, it can be an old song or new one; a made up line, it doesn't matter. On the radio you hear a man's voice read one of these lines and a pianist and a singer have to be able to sing that line immediately. That is to say that they have to have some kind of melody instantly. They try to find a familiar tune to which they can sing the line of verse.

If they can't do it, and they're not given a lot of time, the sender is given a two pound box of bonbons from the Martha Washington stores. Everybody in the United States and Canada can take part. The beautiful concert only lasts a mere half hour and is very entertaining, particularly when the singer and the pianist laugh heartily and infectiously about the often impossible and, at the same time, truly laughable content of many of the entries.

In the fall, a lady approached us and invited us, on behalf of a real estate company, to come to look at some land. We hesitated at first, but the agent impressed on us that it was publicity for the company which, though I naturally understood that not everyone was going to buy land, wanted its aspirations and its objectives (business here is invariably conducted for exclusively noble reasons) to be known in wider circles. We were picked up with a car. First a nice, long ride through and outside the city and finally we arrived at a large empty construction ground, very nice and picturesque, which had been divided into lots of various sizes. Every lot had a picket with a number. There was a great big tent and a number of smaller tents. In the big tent, we met the other invited guests, probably about two hundred people. We received a hot lunch and after that a very nice, fascinating and rousing speech about Toronto and its apparently shining future, and the conclusion was, naturally, that you couldn't make a better investment than purchase of land in the immediate neighbourhood of Toronto and especially of the land on which we happened to find ourselves. Those who immediately wanted to buy land could find an agent in the smaller tents. And truly, four or five lots were sold that afternoon and this was announced through some kind of megaphone.

The ladies who invite the people receive a dollar for each couple that they bring to the land and a pretty good percentage of the sale price if the invited decide to buy. It all sounds a lot better for the agents, who get no other remuneration, than it really is. The agents have to invite the people personally and be careful about the neighbourhoods in which they deliver their invitations. And the odds that a sale will be completed are not very high. And yet, the company employs some thirty female agents who voluntarily carry out this work as a way to earn some additional income in their free time. Every church here has a Ladies' Committee which assumes responsibility for Sunday school, Christmas celebrations, the girls' and ladies' clubs and so forth. A big laundry and clothing dye-works gives $25 to the Committee for every 100 visitors that it brings to the factory on visitor's day. That was how I came to visit the factory and I found it very, very, interesting.

I have not yet become reconciled to the Canadian newspapers. In the first place, I find the format extremely boring. Then there's the irritating habit of breaking off an article on say page 1, sometimes in the middle of a sentence, and resuming it on page 4. All the news reports are mixed together, all with bold "headlines." It makes reading tiring and you get the feeling that your eyes are going to start blinking from all that back and forth. Every trivial piece of news is blown out of proportion and you have to search for interesting reports about foreign politics. Pictures of all kinds of unknown bigwigs are printed helter-skelter throughout the paper. The number of people reaching their hundredth birthday or celebrating their golden wedding anniversary is difficult to estimate. Lots of room is given over to the sports heroes. Recently, when England's prime minister was here, there was even a picture of a Toronto woman in the paper because she had lived in the town where Prime Minister MacDonald had been born and her mother had seen him go by once in a while. If a child falls into boiling water or if it's run over by a car, the picture of the child, its parents and grandparents all appear in the newspaper. Naturally, lots of room is given over to all the details of a criminal offense, if possible with the requisite pictures. A young lady here in Toronto, is the proud guardian of a little bottle containing the scorched finger of a Negro. She received this little gift from her fiancée who lived in one of the southern states where a lynch party took place. It satisfies the curiosity of a young country still in the process of civilizing and is as well an example of the uncongenial hunt for sensation, so common in our times.

The movie houses in Toronto are beautiful and comfortable but nothing like the Roxy or Paramount in New York. The price of admission is not high here. You get an outstanding seat for 35 cents. The "movies" are always packed and on Saturday afternoons you can see long lines queuing up on the sidewalk to get a seat.

The public seems to have been drilled, from childhood on, to enter theaters, boats or trains in an orderly manner. But to come back to the movies, here as in Europe, the required advertisements are displayed, sometimes in a glittering form. The program alternates film and variety numbers; there's usually a very good orchestra.

On Saturday afternoons, the movies are particularly filled with young girls who work in offices and department stores the rest of the week. They're elegant, sprightly little persons, slim, well-dressed, powdered and painted, who totally enjoy the romantic world which they see displayed on the silver screen, who laugh joyously or cry broken-heartedly at the dramatic parts and who must have a very strange picture of life forming in their pretty but empty heads. For them, life is bustling to the tram which takes them to the department store or the office, a hurried lunch in a cafeteria at noon, followed by office or store, after that home to supper and, if there's a chance, off to, a movie or dancing, or both if possible, with a boy in the evening.

A curious expression here for an effeminate young man is "sissy." The word has absolutely no bad connotation; it's simply the nickname for an overdone fop, who shapes his eyebrows, reddens up his lips so that his pearl teeth appear brighter, who, if necessary, gives his pale cheeks a little brown-red tone in order to look sportsmanlike and in all things tries his best to imitate a hero from the film dramas. He's also called a "matinee-sissy" because he wants to resemble the hero of the dreams of the "office-girls", who are the most faithful attenders of the matinees.

Toronto is a very large city and naturally big and small crimes occur daily. But I want to end this letter by relating a curious example of honesty. There are boys on the corners of some streets who sell newspapers. They have an open box or tray next to them, into which the money is thrown. Sometimes a customer some distance away, calls them over and they run to him with a pile of papers as fast as a rabbit, but they very confidently leave their change trays behind. Nothing is ever stolen from them. Old Stastok would say, "America is a strange land, even if I say so myself."

March 27, 1930

The 2nd of February is Candlemas. That's when the groundhogs come out of their dens and look around to see if they can spot their shadows. If they can see their shadows, then the sun is shining, but then it's also a very cold winter day and the groundhogs crawl back into their dens knowing that they can proceed with their winter hibernation for another number of weeks. But if it's a drizzling, somber day, then they know that the thaw and the rain are coming and that spring is near. The 2nd of February was a drizzly, somber day this time and for several days it seemed as if the old legend was true and that an early spring would soon arrive but the snowstorms soon came back and "Jack Frost" gave us evidence of his presence.

I want to mention another legend here which deals with the coming of spring. In earlier times, so goes the tale, the Indians sacrificed a young maiden to the Spirit of Niagara Falls in the last week of February. The girl would be tied up in a canoe and the boat shoved into the middle of the stream above the Horseshoe Falls (this is the name of one of the beautiful falls which is horseshoe-shaped; it's on the Canadian side). It would be carried along faster and faster, to fall with the sacrifice into the boiling and foaming mass of water where the Spirit would take them, as nothing was ever retrieved of the boat or the girl.

Human sacrifices are no longer made there but the Spirit of Niagara Falls now exacts a couple of wild swans every year. On the 23rd and 24th of February, people keep watch to see if the wild grey swans pass over Niagara Falls. It they're observed, it's regarded as a sign that the birds know that the worst cold is past and that spring is near. On their flight, the birds land on Lake Erie and let themselves be carried on the current but not all of them are able to bring themselves to safety before the water carries them, with ever greater speed, to the falls. The wild grey swans have been seen there again, but not exactly on the 23rd or 24th of February; it was a couple of days later.

In and around Toronto, the snow has melted away; the days

lengthen wonderfully; the air is so clear and the lake has such beautiful green-blue colours, that we're really beginning to think about spring. Yesterday, an old gentleman who had discovered the first Canadian robin in his garden and who was overjoyed to once again see that migratory bird, donned his straw hat and appeared as an aged messenger of spring to the amazed eyes of the citizens of Toronto. The Canadian robin is about the size of our blackbird; it's somewhat leaner; the feathers are shiny brown-black and the breast is blood-red. It's a beautiful bird, not at all shy. It's classified with the songbirds, but its song doesn't amount to much. Real songbirds like our blackbirds, thrushes and nightingales are not found here.

It's been a hard winter, which began quite early in November. I received letters from Holland in February informing me that snowdrops, crocuses and herbs were already flowering in sunny spots in the garden. That almost makes me homesick! There's not a hint of green or flowers here. Grass isn't even thinking about becoming green. Spring is bleak here and the true spring probably won't arrive until the end of May. There's an anecdote about an immigrant who asks a countryman who's been in Canada for a while: "Is the summer very warm here?" and the answer is: "I don't know, I've only been here for eleven months."

But even if the winter is hard, it's beautiful. In the parks and in the rural areas, the snow is blindingly white with its blue shadows of trees and bushes. A walk, when the wind is utterly calm, with a deep blue sky above you, in the stimulating cold, while the snow sings under your feet, is refreshing and healthy, at least if you're well-fed and dressed warmly. A walk, in a snowstorm through one of the parks where you know the way, is beautiful and glorious but it makes you shiver when you think what it must be like to be lost in such a snowstorm in the endless, lonely forests of northern Canada. Naturally, there's lots of participation in snow and ice sports here. You can see skiing here in High Park but that sport does demand greater heights than Toronto has to offer.

You could undertake a study of fur on the trains, which are well heated incidentally, because you can see so many different fur coats and jackets made from all kinds of fur-bearing animals. The "cops" (ordinary police officers) and the "Mounties" (mounted policemen) appear quite "Balkan" with their heavy overcoats and high Astrakhan hats. It's been an awful winter for the unemployed, among whom were many immigrants. A great amount of snow fell, which had to be cleaned up, and a lot of the unemployed earned a fair wage, but this was of course only temporary.

The question of the unemployed is as difficult to solve here as anywhere else in the new or old world. And here in Canada it's part and parcel of the immigrant question. One of the grievances that Canadians have against the English is that England sends out so many people to fill important and not so important appointments which could be performed, at least as well, by Canadians. The latter know the country and the customs, don't they, and are a lot more useful than the newly arrived English who frequently forget that Canada is no longer a colony but a Dominion. Many of these English look down on the Canadians, they regard the language here as incorrect English and fancy themselves as being superior in refinement. Canada has its high schools and universities. Why shouldn't they be able to deliver enough suitable people to replace the greenhorns they send over here.

Many good, educated, useful Canadian workmen lose the chance to get ahead here because of that, and it's a fact that a great number of useful Canadians annually depart for the United States where they have a faster chance of succeeding. The climate, the money, the language, and many of the customs and ways of doing things are the same for them there as here. The United States, so they claim here, has a more progressive view of business and the state of affairs than the English Canadian government.

Another complaint is that England rids itself of many of its unemployed in Canada and among those unemployed are many totally useless individuals who come here to be burdens on the tax paying Canadians. Although a lot of jokes are made about the miserliness of the Scotch and the cheerful simplicity of the Irish, they're welcome as immigrants and workmen but a great dislike exists for English immigrants. One often reads in advertisements for workmen this addendum: "Englishmen need not apply."

One should not, however, see an "independence from England" movement in this. Perhaps each Dominion will want to become completely independent in the future and perhaps Canada will eventually join the United States so that, together, they may form the sovereign states of North America, but that is still far distant music of the future! Besides the Scotch and Irish, Hollanders, Germans (the war hatred has calmed and Canadians once again recognize the good that they offer), Swedes and Finns are welcome as immigrants. Our Netherlands language is frequently called "Holland-Dutch", while they mean German when they refer to "Pennsylvania-Dutch."

But to come back to the immigrants once again. This great Canada with gigantic lakes, beautiful rivers, with extensive territory that still has to be pioneered but will provide good arable land for grain and fruit while other districts give up a treasure of minerals, this Canada can still use thousands of immigrants but you cannot be cautioned enough not to come to Canada as an immigrant if you're not thoroughly grounded in a trade or a profession which you hope to practice here; if you don't have enough capital to be able to hold out for a while; if you're not absolutely healthy and strong; if you don't possess a large measure of courage, willpower and persistence.

I don't believe that there's another city in Canada where so many big gatherings of all kinds of companies are held as in Toronto. The "Convention" of the Canadian Jewelers was held here in February. I was sent an invitation to the "Fashion Revue and Jewel Exposition" which was part of the festivities. The show took place in the glittering Royal York Hotel. A fantastic and tastefully decorated stage was set up; the room was enveloped in partial darkness and a searchlight followed the models who had been beautifully dressed by first class salons and who were overloaded with sparkling and glittering jewels and precious stones. It struck me that most of the brooches were being worn on the back, which is quite impractical. I have never seen so many valuable chains, buckles, bracelets, rings, earrings and pendants in all kinds of colours and hues, and everything was real. It looked like an Oriental fairy tale. But to be honest, nothing bores me faster than a fashion show. There was a cheery bit of variety, because male models displayed the most beautiful shirt studs and cuff links, watches and watch chains, tie pins, pencils and so forth. There was one watch that had been dropped from the 22nd floor to the street, and after that test was picked up still intact and ticking along in a lively fashion. But I've forgotten the name of that wonder watch.

Around 50 conventions are going to be held in Toronto this year but the most gigantic and spectacular convention will be here from 9–14 June. It's the Holy Shriner convention. The Holy Shriners are a kind of Masonic order; actually I believe that it's a designated order in the larger Masonic fraternity in the United States. Most of them seem to be very rich and they seem to do a lot of good with their wealth. They're coming to Toronto, from all over the United States and Canada, to erect a peace monument. Toronto has about 700,000 inhabitants and about 350,000 Shriners are expected, some of whom will also bring along their wives. At the same time, of course, hundreds of ordinary strangers will come to the city in order to see the gigantic Shriner's parade. They'll bring along elephants, Arabian horses and perhaps other animals. The Holy Shriners will be enveloped in Oriental robes. They wear a fez which is decorated with oriental symbols. The potentate of Al Malaikah

Temple, Mystic Shriners of Los Angeles, was here with his secretary in order to reach agreement on the housing of 450 "nobles." But the biggest problem for the reception committee in Toronto is: "what are we going to do with all of them?"

The Royal York Hotel is adding 1,600 rooms to its already colossal and beautiful size. 300 Pullman sleeping cars will be required but in spite of that all the other hotels, and that includes some good sized buildings, will not be able to accommodate the overwhelming mob of visitors. A call went out to private homes, and the reception committee now has to go and inspect the accommodations which have been offered.

I hope to write more about it in June, after the convention has been held. Something happened here the other day, which disturbed people of conscience. In general, there are fewer Negroes in Canada than in the United States, maybe it has something to do with the climate. Among the Negroes in Toronto are doctors, lawyers, and preachers, and English law guarantees them the same rights as the whites enjoy. But, even though the Canadians say: "I don't dislike Negroes", in their hearts they look down on the coloured races, and a white girl who might want to get married to a Negro, even if he's educated, would no longer be received by her friends and relatives. She'd probably have the same experience if she got engaged to an Indian, a Chinese or a Japanese. That's the case for every coloured race. Now there was a young white girl in the little town of Oakville, who wanted to get married to a Negro and the young couple were already living together before they got a marriage license. The mother of the girl called in the help of the police but the police couldn't separate the couple because the girl was older than 18 and if she chose a Negro as her husband, then that was her business. The mother then went to the Salvation Army but that wasn't successful either. The girl remained faithful to her black lover.

Then the mother called in the help of the knights of the Canadian Ku Klux Klan, or as they prefer it, "The Invisible Empire Knights of the Ku Klux Klan of Canada." Their motto is: "Non sibi sed alteris." They're Protestant and they claim to have nothing against Negroes if they profess to be faithful subjects of the British empire etc., but they help those who ask them for aid, in this case the mother of the girl. They claim to have nothing in common with the American Ku Klux Klan but they do wear the same ghostly masquerade outfit if they think it necessary. A number of members of the Canadian K.K.K. went to the Negro's home in a car. He came outside and confirmed that the girl was with him, whereupon the girl also came outside and on the advice of the K.K.K. went along with them in the car which took her to the Salvation Army.

It was probably the smartest and the safest thing for the young couple to give in. As soon as they get a license they'll get married anyway. Afterwards it was discovered that "the Negro" didn't have a drop of Negro blood in his veins but he did have some Indian blood and the pictures of the parents, the grandparents and the great grandparents of "the Negro" appeared in the newspapers to prove how free he was of Negro blood. Even though there wasn't a shred of evidence that the K.K.K. had used force, not even disturbing the domestic peace because the couple came outside willingly and the girl came along willingly, yet the fact is that the K.K.K. meddled in other people's affairs which were none of their business, and roused the indignation of the Negro population of Toronto in particular, which called a meeting under the leadership of well known Negroes. This was also well attended by whites and by prominent Israelites.

The issue isn't what the K.K.K. did, because the business turned out all right, but it's about the fact that the K.K.K. dared in Canada, the land of free British subjects, to threaten the personal freedom of those subjects and perhaps commit to deeds against Negroes for which the American K.K.K. has made itself so notorious. A judicial action was demanded against the K.K.K., which did take place but which all ended rather meekly. One of the participants got a fine. They hadn't done much that was criminal in this incident but it mustn't become a habit for the K.K.K. to nobly play the judge. They say that most of the members of the K.K.K. are rich and in the land of the dollars there must be truth in the old Dutch rhyme:

> 't Geld, dat stom is,
> Maakt recht, wat krom is.
> (Money, which is silent,
> Straightens that which is crooked.)

1 June, 1930
Corporal punishment still exists in Canada, as it does in England itself. The punishments are hanging and flogging. Women and girls are not flogged but women are hanged. Capital punishment is never applied to minors. A belt is used to flog the boys and a kind of knout for the men. They are tied to a post, are undressed to their waist, and a doctor is

present to check the pulse of the flogged person. In some places in the United States, the flogging is done by an electrically powered lash to assure that the blows are regular, and land with the same intensity. This doesn't exist in Canada, as far as I know. A severe flogging is applied to those men and boys who have been guilty of mistreating women, children and animals.

There's a female police magistrate in Toronto who punishes such offenses very severely. A husband who has abused his wife goes to jail for a couple of months and gets a good flogging besides that. An adult man can seldom tolerate more than 10 blows without falling unconscious, as a result, the flogging is split up into installments. A few days before he's released, he gets his last bit of flogging, so that he returns home with a very sore back which will remind him for days what awaits him if he acts like a brute again. The other day a man was sentenced to seven years imprisonment plus thirty strokes. The flogging was divided into three installments during the first 15 months of his imprisonment.

In a city not far from here, a couple of overgrown 17 year old louts were guilty of aggravated assault. The punishment, which is quickly adjudged and applied here, consisted of a fine, a severe flogging and besides that, the boys also had to pay the flogger. Canadian boys of that age generally earn something on their own even if their parents are well to do, as a result, the full punishment is borne by the guilty here. In our country, the parents would end up paying the fine. Men and boys have respect for flogging and while they remain outwardly unmoved by a judgement of a term in jail, they can never hide their emotions when it's followed by: "and so many blows with the rod."

I hope that capital punishment will never be reintroduced in our country but perhaps a good beating with a strap or the rod would have a salutary effect on those who are found guilty of mistreating people and animals, hooliganism, insulting strangers, vandalizing plants and benches in parks etc. But the punishment has to be applied as quickly as possible after the offense.

The death penalty is abhorrent, and along with that goes the fact that a jury decides "guilty" or "not guilty." A number of months ago, a butcher here in Toronto was murdered by a certain Stewart, who didn't have a single grievance against the victim. The murderer admitted his guilt and because he had been in the war other veterans of the great war tried to get a mitigation of the judgement but their petition didn't help: the judgement was "hanging." The *Mail and Empire* of 23 March contained the following description of the execution:

Edward Stewart, war veteran, 33 years old, was hung yesterday not far from the place where the crime was committed. While thousands of workers in Toronto rushed to their work at the sound of the factory whistles that chilly grey morning, Stewart had to go a distance of 33 steps, one step for every year of his life and climb the scaffold where death awaited him. The door of his cell was opened at one minute before eight and with wide staring eyes he saw a sheriff and the hangman enter. Stewart looked intently at the sheriff, smiled painfully and then said softly: "I want to thank everyone in this jail who's been so kind to me." He stood up fast, turned himself around quickly and brought his hands to his back. The hangman cuffed his wrists with a leather belt. After that, Stewart quickly walked out of his cell and into the "death hall" from where he had to walk another 33 steps. The electric light still burned in the hallway and through the open door came the daylight and the mingled light made his hair shine blond and white. His face was flushed red and for a moment he gave a startled look to the small group of men who were standing by the entrance to the room where the scaffold awaited him. After he had mounted the scaffold, he looked down for a moment to the trap door on which he stood, then up at the new noose above his head. He clicked his heels together, which were then tied by the hangman. The hangman then pulled the black satin hood over his eyes, placed the noose around his neck, brought a lever into motion which opened the trap door under the feet of the condemned. There was a short sigh made by the moving air, the cracking and the crunching of the new hemp noose and eleven pairs of eyes staring at the opening in the floor of the scaffold. The hangman stepped calmly ahead, looked down and then said to the director of the jail, "He's dead, Sir." The director relaxed his tightly clenched jaw muscles, slowly turned around and departed, followed by the others. Nine seconds had passed between the time that Stewart had stepped on the scaffold and the instant that he disappeared into the deep. Seven minutes later, the jail doctor declared that life was no longer present in the condemned.

And a number of minutes later, the hangman and the reporter for the *Mail and Empire* were on the street and passing the house where the murder had been committed. The hangman quietly lit his pipe. "The younger generation," he said, shaking his head, "won't listen to advice." Such extensive reports of executions, murders, of the family circumstances of the victim and the murdered, preferably with pictures, are very popular articles in the newspapers here and certainly not just in what is called the yellow press. Yellow in this case means "eager for sensation."

Yellow can also mean "cowardly." When the war broke out in 1914, the young girls yelled, "you're yellow!" at those young men who had not yet volunteered for the army, or they gave them a feather which had the same insulting meaning.

The craving for sensation, which is so strongly cultivated by the newspapers and the films produces, I believe, that strange mixture of sentimentality and hardness in the American character. Before I leave the somber subject of capital punishment, a few oddities about the hangman. Every condemned person is hung in a new noose and the used noose becomes the property of the hangman, who sometimes makes quite a little windfall out of it. He sells the noose piece by piece. If it's a very notorious murderer, then each inch of the noose will sometimes bring a couple of dollars! There's also a society here in Canada which is committed to getting rid of the death penalty and not long ago the society sent a poem to the hangman, who's a civil servant, inviting the official hangman to join with those who want to abolish capital punishment. The poem stated that the death penalty belonged to the barbaric middle ages and that the hangman was one of the monsters out of this grey past. The Canadian government hangman, who has hanged more than 500 criminals (I don't know if the hanging of the five hundredth was celebrated as a jubilee) naturally felt insulted by the poem, sent it back to the sender, and wrote a short, sharp answer on the back that ended with the words: "if a jury ever declares you guilty and a judge sentences you to death, then I'll come and hang you with pleasure."

As I'm discussing a somewhat somber subject, I also want to say something as about the funeral customs here, customs which are repugnant to me. Whereas with us a beloved deceased is handled with great respect, here everything is driven by a lugubrious inclination for "show", again a sort of search for sensation. As soon as the doctor has ascertained that death has taken place, the funeral director is summoned. He takes the corpse along to his place, his "laboratory" I would almost call it, takes along with him for the deceased, if it's a woman or a girl, her nicest dress or if it's a man, his best suit. The corpse is embalmed; the hair is dressed; the cheeks and lips are painted; if the face has sunk, then the cheeks are filled; the wrinkles are worked away; the nails are polished etc. and then the deceased is dressed as nicely as possible and brought home again in a casket. A casket is shaped like a coffin but is often covered on the outside with plush or velvet, sometimes with what appears to be beautiful wood; on the inside the casket is stuffed with soft coloured silk. The deceased lies there like a made up wax doll; the floral pieces are arranged around it; a lamp with a soft rose shade casts a rose tinted light on the unnaturally yellow face.

I endured the funerals of an older married woman and a very young girl. At both, a sort of service for the dead was held before the actual burial. The service for the older lady was held in her own house. The chapel which belonged to the funeral director's business was engaged for the young girl. There was an organ in the chapel and the service was sober and solemn, but the idea that you just let strangers haul away your beloved deceased and then got them home again actually unrecognizable, shocked me so much then that I was overcome for a moment. After the service was over, the casket was driven to the cemetery where the actual vault stood in the grave. The pallbearers, mostly friends of the family of the deceased, carry the casket from the hearse to the grave and the remainder of the ceremony is completed quite quickly then.

I just want to tell about a partly sad and partly comic experience of my own here. I spoke with one of the funeral directors and told him that funerals were conducted quite differently in Holland. Perhaps he found us quite backward in this respect. He took me along to his "showroom" and proudly displayed his newest installation: he pushed on a button and a door swung open and there stood 12 beautiful caskets for adults. If it hadn't been for their shapes you would have thought they were huge jewelry boxes, padded with silk and satin in the softest shades. Then he pushed on another button, and again a door opened and 12 childrens' caskets, all very luxurious, moved forward. I began to find it all very strangely nightmare-like but I had not yet come to the end of my adventure. The proud mortician took me to another room where he stored the bottles of embalming fluid. They were also the newest thing on the market. Most of those chemicals were made in Germany. He opened a couple of bottles, smelled them and asked if I didn't think the fluid had a lovely fragrance. It smelled bracing, a little bit like turpentine but the whole thing made me slightly ill. Afterwards I had to meet his wife who offered me tea and lovely sandwiches but my appetite was quite small and everything seemed to taste like turpentine. A brisk walk along the lake, after all that, was a reviving remedy.

Recently, I was at the market. They hold the market every day here but Saturday's is the busiest, so I went on a Saturday morning. The market is held in big halls, not as big as those in Paris, but a lot fresher and cleaner. The Mennonite farm women, in their old fashioned clothes and caps, were selling their sausage, headcheese, eggs, chickens, jam and fruit. Everything looked very clean and tasty. There was also a fish section. I saw, among other things, the giant sturgeon and also the big shrimp which one is so often served in Norway. But I was most attracted to the flowers which are not at all as abundant here as in Holland and which are so expensive even though they claim that you can get them for a song in Toronto compared to the prices which are asked in Montreal.

Spring has now arrived here, all at once. Last year at this time it was very much colder. At the moment we've had a couple of days of 82 degrees Fahrenheit. The trees and bushes are budding like mad and the fruit trees are in full bloom in the Niagara area, Canada's fruit orchard. Lake Ontario once again has its wonderfully beautiful blue green colours; the air is clear, the sun is so warm; the stars are huge and sparkling and the Northern Lights play and flicker across the night sky. Now comes the return of the wonderful "open-air" life of Canada. All the husbands are painting the gables of their houses, in their overalls. Chairs and tables are put out on the porch or verandas again. The veranda and garden rocking chairs are put out and filled with particoloured cushions. The canoes are gliding on the lake again and the motorboats are rushing on. And in the big department stores, they've put out spring shoes and summer garments and also garden implements, plants, flower seeds and a lot of rose bushes "guaranteed genuine from Holland!"

Quite a few plants froze in our garden. The winter is too harsh. Chrysanthemums are grown here in conservatories and greenhouses but not in the garden. Holly, which is so hardy at home, can't be grown in our garden. The harsh cold damages a lot of plants and this, combined with the dry climate, makes the growing of flowers very expensive.

The travel season is coming up and a lot of publicity is being made in the papers for Europe: the Belgian festivals and Oberammergau's Passion Play serve as lures. Many Americans and Canadians aspire to see Europe, especially Paris and the Mediterranean. They know that Paris is in France, naturally, but where exactly France is, is less clear to them. It's "somewhere in Europe," in any case. Friends of mine here in Toronto, the best, excellent people, very rich, took their first trip to Europe a couple of months ago, on a French ship. The trip began in New York. The Canary Islands were the first port of call. Other places visited were Algiers, Gibraltar, a couple of Spanish ports, Nice and in Italy, among others, Naples. The ship followed a pretty route; the service on board was outstanding; among other things there was free wine, genuine good French wine at table! And that's important to "dry" Americans and half dry Canadians!

In every harbour, guides and cars stood ready to show the

travelers interesting novelties which had been newly prepared for them. They also paused in Nice for a couple of days but the party had only enjoyed the fashionable cafés and the hotels; they had seen nothing of the beautiful scenery or the picturesque spots filled with historical significance, and since they know nothing about history, that didn't matter either. They hadn't gone to Paris, but they had "seen it in the distance, when they were going along the French coast!!" Naples had been very nice and Vesuvius, which was violently smoking, was "very cute." But Pompeii had made an impression, although the remarks which they made about it were more odd than striking.

The souvenirs, which they bought along the way were also peculiar and the stores in Europe, no doubt, know the tastes of their American customers. One of the treasures brought back was a small electric lamp, whose pedestal is carried by a pair of fauns, a pair of beautiful roguish figures, no doubt borrowed from a classical sculpture. But they didn't know what a faun was, they didn't even know the word. They had bought it because they thought it was "funny," these two little kids with their goat's feet.

Americans and Canadians (I generalize, naturally) are, in my eyes, in many ways big children. In general knowledge they're not as advanced as we are. We Europeans are unquestionably their betters in the intellectual area, and in refined manners and behaviour. But they're ahead of us in the practical area. They're more open-minded and therefore more spontaneous in their opinions about anything that has an effect on them. They don't brood over psychological problems but they can make accurate and sensitive remarks about what strikes them in people or business. American (Canadian) humour is quite different from the humour of various European countries, even very different than that of the European. They're more sturdily set in the practical life, and the heavy struggle which they have to undergo before success comes (success in America means piles of dollars) makes them hard and tough with their youth who have just begun that struggle and from whom they demand the same will power and persistence that they have proved they possess. But they do understand that knowledge and education are necessary to make a nation great and strong, and the sums of money which are contributed by individuals for the establishment of universities, laboratories, hospitals, schools etc., are therefore enormous.

The elder Rockefeller, who gave fortunes to all kinds of foundations and institutions, always walks around with his pockets full of new American quarters (sic: dimes). If someone asks him for money, then that person gets one of those new quarters. Not too long ago, when he went up in an airplane for the first time and flew a little distance above an airfield and then landed safely, he gave a handful of new "dimes" (American ten cent pieces) to the pilot; and the pilot, who knew about the eccentricity of his passenger, laughed as heartily as the parchment like, mummified multi-millionaire himself.

Toronto is preparing itself to welcome the Shriner's convention about which I spoke in my previous letter. Kilometres of bleachers have been built along the big highway which borders the lake. I don't know how many millions of feet of lumber have been used. The festivities will last from 9 to 14 June and the parade of the Shriners in their oriental robes, with elephants, Arabian horses etc. will be the biggest and most wonderful one ever held in North America!! And there are a lot more interesting things on the summer program of "Toronto, the beautiful!"

A SELECT BIBLIOGRAPHY OF THE DUTCH IN CANADA

Breems, Bradley Gene. *'I Tell Them We Are a Blessed People': An Analysis by Way of a Dutch-Calvinist Community."* Doctoral dissertation, Department of Sociology and Anthropology, University of British Columbia,

Ganzevoort, Herman. *A Bittersweet Land. The Dutch Experience in Canada, 1890-1980.* Toronto: McClelland and Stewart, 1988.

_____ and Mark Boekelman. *Dutch Immigration to North America.* Toronto: The Multicultural History Society of Ontario, 1983.

Graumans, Joe. *The Role of Ethno-Religious Organizations in the Assimilation Process of the Dutch Christian Reformed and Catholic Immigrants in Southwestern Ontario.* M.A. thesis, University of Windsor, 1973.

Hartland, J.A. *De Geschiedenis van de Nederlandse Emigratie tot de Tweede Wereld Oorlog.* The Hague: Ministerie van Sociale Zaken en Volksgezondheid, 1959.

Krijff, J. Th. *100 Years Ago. Dutch Immigration to Manitoba in 1893.* Windsor: Electa Press, 1993.

Lowensteyn, J.H. *A Social History of the Dutch in Quebec.* M.A. thesis, Department of Sociology and Anthropology, Concordia University, 1986.

Lucas, Henry S. *Netherlanders in America. Dutch Immigration to the United States and Canada, 1789-1950.* Grand Rapids: W. B. Eerdmans Publishing Co., 1955.

Petersen, William. *Planned Migration. The Social Determinants of the Dutch-Canadian Movement.* Berkeley: University of California Press, 1955.

Schryer, Frans J. *The Netherlandic Presence in Ontario. Pillars, Class and Dutch Ethnicity.* Waterloo: Wilfrid Laurier University Press, 1997.

INDEX